When Does Gender Matter?

WHEN DOES GENDER MATTER?

Women Candidates and Gender Stereotypes in American Elections

Kathleen Dolan

OXFORD
UNIVERSITY PRESS

OXFORD
UNIVERSITY PRESS

Oxford University Press is a department of the University of Oxford.
It furthers the University's objective of excellence in research, scholarship,
and education by publishing worldwide.

Oxford   New York
Auckland   Cape Town   Dar es Salaam   Hong Kong   Karachi
Kuala Lumpur   Madrid   Melbourne   Mexico City   Nairobi
New Delhi   Shanghai   Taipei   Toronto

With offices in
Argentina   Austria   Brazil   Chile   Czech Republic   France   Greece
Guatemala   Hungary   Italy   Japan   Poland   Portugal   Singapore
South Korea   Switzerland   Thailand   Turkey   Ukraine   Vietnam

Oxford is a registered trademark of Oxford University Press
in the UK and certain other countries.

Published in the United States of America by
Oxford University Press
198 Madison Avenue, New York, NY 10016

CIP data is on file at the Library of Congress.

ISBN: 978-0-19-996827-5 (hbk.); 978-0-19-996828-2 (pbk)

To Tom, Olivia, and Clayton,
For everything

CONTENTS

List of Figures and Tables   ix
Acknowledgments   xiii

1. Candidate Sex and Gender Stereotypes in American Elections   *1*

2. Studying Gender Stereotypes and Women Candidates   *18*

3. Attitudes, Stereotypes, and Support for Women Candidates   *49*

4. Do Stereotypes Shape Evaluations of Candidates?   *91*

5. The Role of Stereotypes in Vote Choice Decisions   *123*

6. Gender Stereotypes in Other Places? Candidate Quality
   and Issue Campaigns   *143*

7. The Landscape for Women Candidates   *186*

Appendix A: Candidate Lists   *199*
Appendix B: Variable Construction   *201*
Appendix C: Campaign Ads and Websites   *205*
Appendix D: Survey Instrument   *208*
Appendix E: Additional Vote Choice Analysis   *222*
Notes   *225*
Bibliography   *227*
Index   *239*

LIST OF FIGURES AND TABLES

Figures

2.1   Number of Women Candidates for the U.S. House 1970–2010   26

2.2   Number of Women Candidates for the U.S. Senate 1970–2010   26

2.3   Number of Women Candidates for Governor 1970–2010   27

3.1   Vote for a Woman President   51

3.2   Men Better Suited Emotionally for Politics   51

3.3   Governed Better or Worse if More Women in Office   52

Tables

3.1   Attitudes about Women in Politics   55

3.2   Traditional and Gendered Political Knowledge   60

3.3   Emotional Suitability   62

3.4   Abstract Policy Stereotypes, All Respondents   63

3.5   Abstract Trait Stereotypes, All Respondents   64

3.6   Abstract Policy Stereotypes by Respondent Sex   65

3.7   Abstract Trait Stereotypes by Respondent Sex   66

3.8   Ideology of Typical Congresswoman by Respondent Sex   68

3.9   Ideology of Typical Congressman by Respondent Sex   68

3.10   Demographic Predictors of Abstract Attitudes   69

3.11   Demographic Predictors of Abstract Female Policy Stereotypes   70

3.12   Demographic Predictors of Abstract Male Policy Stereotypes   71

3.13   Demographic   Predictors   of   Abstract   Female   Trait
        Stereotypes   72

3.14   Demographic   Predictors   of   Abstract   Male   Trait
        Stereotypes   72

3.15   Predictors of Abstract Gender Attitudes   78

3.16   Impact of Abstract Stereotypes on House Vote Choice   80

3.17   Baseline Gender Preference and House Vote Choice   83

3.18   Number of Women in Office and House Vote Choice   85

3.19   Gender Parity in Government and House Vote Choice   86

3.20   Emotional Suitability and House Vote Choice   87

3.21   Same-Sex Representation and House Vote Choice   88

4.1   Distribution of Abstract Stereotypes   95

4.2   Distribution of Specific Evaluations of House Candidates   96

4.3   Distribution of Specific Evaluations of Senate Candidates   97

4.4   Distribution   of   Specific   Evaluations   of   Governor
        Candidates   98

4.5   Policy and Trait Evaluations of Democratic Women in Mixed-Sex
        House Races   102

4.6   Policy and Trait Evaluations of Republican Women in Mixed-Sex
        House Races   104

4.7   Policy and Trait Evaluations of Democratic Women in Mixed-Sex
        Senate Races   106

4.8   Policy and Trait Evaluations of Republican Women in Mixed-Sex
        Senate Races   108

4.9   Policy and Trait Evaluations of Democratic Women in Mixed-Sex
        Governor Races   112

4.10   Policy and Trait Evaluations of Republican Women in Mixed-Sex
        Governor Races   113

4.11   Policy and Trait Evaluations of the Democratic Candidate in
        Male-Only House Races   117

4.12   Policy and Trait Evaluations of the Democratic Candidate in
        Male-Only Senate Races   118

4.13   Policy and Trait Evaluations of the Democratic Candidate in
        Male-Only Governor Races   120

5.1   House Vote Choice in Mixed-Sex Races   *129*

5.2   Senate Vote Choice, Democratic Women versus Republican Men   *132*

5.3   Governor Vote Choice, Republican Women versus Democratic Men   *135*

5.4   Vote Choice in Male-Only House Races   *137*

5.5   Vote Choice in Male-Only Senate Races   *139*

5.6   Vote Choice in Male-Only Governor Races   *140*

6.1   Candidate Education by Sex   *145*

6.2   Candidate Experience by Sex   *147*

6.3   Median Candidate Spending by Sex   *148*

6.4   House Race Outcomes   *149*

6.5   Senate Race Outcomes   *150*

6.6   Governor Race Outcomes   *150*

6.7   House Ads by Candidate Sex   *156*

6.8   House Ads, Mixed-Sex Races   *158*

6.9   House Ads, Women Candidates   *162*

6.10   Senate Ads by Candidate Sex   *163*

6.11   Senate Ads, Mixed-Sex Races   *166*

6.12   Senate Ads, Women Candidates   *167*

6.13   Governor Ads by Candidate Sex   *168*

6.14   Governor Ads, Mixed-Sex Races   *170*

6.15   Governor Ads, Women Candidates   *171*

6.16   House Ads, Male-Only Races   *172*

6.17   Senate Ads, Male-Only Races   *173*

6.18   Governor Ads, Male-Only Races   *174*

6.19   House Websites by Candidate Sex   *177*

6.20   House Websites, Mixed-Sex Races   *178*

6.21   House Websites, Women Candidates   *179*

6.22   Senate Websites by Candidate Sex   *180*

6.23   Governor Websites by Candidate Sex   *181*

6.24   House Websites, Male-Only Races   *182*

6.25   Senate Websites, Male-Only Races   *183*

6.26   Governor Websites, Male-Only Races   *184*

E.1   Senate Vote Choice, Republican Women versus Democratic Men   *222*

E.2   Governor Vote Choice, Democratic Women versus Republican Men   *223*

ACKNOWLEDGMENTS

For many years now, my research has focused on understanding how voters evaluate women candidates. In doing this work, I have been fortunate enough to get to know many people whose contributions have helped shape my thinking. In ways big and small, this project has benefited enormously from those interactions.

First and foremost, I need to thank those whose financial support made the project possible. I am grateful to Brian Humes and Carol Mershon of the National Science Foundation for their faith in the project and for the grant that supported its execution. I also want to thank several people at the University of Wisconsin–Milwaukee for their generous support: Dean Rodney Swain and Associate Dean Jim Moyer of the College of Letters and Science and Nigel Rothfels of the Office of Undergraduate Research.

I also need to thank several people who provided feedback on various aspects of the project in its early phases. The survey instrument benefited from the advice of Richard Fox, Kim Fridkin, Jennifer Lawless, Zoe Oxley, and Kira Sanbonmatsu. Cheri Maestas, Barbara Norrander, and Brian Schaffner provided helpful comments and suggestions on early versions of the project as panel discussants. Angela Chnapko, my editor at Oxford University Press, has been very supportive of the project from the beginning and has provided terrific support and advice during this process. I also thank Augustine Leo, Elisabeth Graves, and the reviewers for their comments and support.

Over the years, I have been fortunate to be a part of a community of scholars who have provided intellectual stimulation, support, and friendship. The women and men who study women/gender politics have created a community of people who care about their research and also care about each other. It is a joy to work with people who have been colleagues, mentors, and friends: Kira Sanbonmatsu, Jennifer Lawless, Richard Fox, Kim Fridkin, Peggy Conway, Sue Carroll, Lee Ann Banaszak, Karen Beckwith,

Lisa Baldez, Christina Wolbrecht, Laurel Weldon, Zoe Oxley, Michele Swers, Sue Thomas, Cindy Simon Rosenthal, Beth Reingold, Leonie Huddy, Barbara Burrell, Sue Tolleson Rinehart, Monica Schneider, Angie Bos, Heather Ondercin, Mary-Kate Lizotte, and Erin Cassese.

I also couldn't have accomplished this work without the excellent research assistance of a terrific group of students at the University of Wisconsin–Milwaukee. Katie Zettl, Mike Bugalski, and Ryan Lynch did an enormous amount of work coding the media data. Tim Lynch's contributions as my research assistant for the last three and a half years cannot be adequately acknowledged. He has been involved in every aspect of the project from beginning to end and has gone above and beyond in everything he has done. His general excellence is reflected in the finished project, which is better for his involvement. And when we were not talking about the project, we were talking about baseball, which is another of his strong suits. Except for the whole being a Yankees fan thing.

Finally, I couldn't have done this work without the support of my family and friends. It has been almost 30 years since Lynne Ford and I met in graduate school, and she is still my best friend. My husband, Tom Holbrook, has been endlessly supportive, both at home and at work. People often ask how we can spend as much time together as we do, working together all day and then being home together at night. I can't imagine anything else. After more than 20 years together, he is still my favorite person. Except for my other favorite people, of course: our children, Olivia and Clayton. The last time I dedicated a book to them, they were six and three years old. Today they are 15 and 12 and have grown into amazing, interesting, wonderful people. They continue to bring great love and joy to my life, so, again, I dedicate this to them.

When Does Gender Matter?

CHAPTER 1

Candidate Sex and Gender Stereotypes in American Elections

I do think that being a woman has a positive upside in the campaign, probably offset by more sexism.... I myself find that I get a tremendous upside from being a woman and I don't spend a lot of time worrying about sexist remarks that people make.

Nancy Pelosi, Speaker of the U.S. House of Representatives (D-CA)

When Speaker of the House Nancy Pelosi was asked in June 2008 whether sexism had played a significant role in Hillary Clinton's loss of the Democratic presidential nomination to Barack Obama, she seemed to suggest that a woman candidate's sex could be both a positive and a negative. Indeed, the presidential election of 2008 was thought to be a breakthrough moment for women candidates in the United States. Senator Hillary Clinton, the first woman candidate with a real chance of winning a major party's nomination for president, won 18 million votes before losing the nomination to then-Senator Barack Obama. Governor Sarah Palin became the first woman on a Republican Party ticket when Senator John McCain chose her as his vice-presidential running mate. Each woman campaigned around the country as a highly visible symbol of how far American women have come in political life. And yet, at the same time, each woman served as a symbol of the somewhat unsettled nature of public thinking about the role of women in politics. Whether it was a heckler calling on Clinton to "Iron my shirt" or a public debate about whether a mother of young children had the time to be vice president, the 2008 campaign was marked by both positive and negative debates about the ability of women to serve in high-level office. Any excitement generated by these historic candidacies was tempered by discussions of whether Clinton was too abrasive and not sufficiently warm to be president and whether Palin was smart enough, too pretty, or too encumbered by motherhood to be one heartbeat away.

While highlighting the travails of Hillary Clinton and Sarah Palin as examples of the challenges women candidates face in combating stereotypes may seem obvious because of their high profile and visibility, subsequent elections have continued to offer evidence that women candidates are often viewed through the lens of gender stereotypes. In 2010, Kelly Ayotte, the attorney general of New Hampshire and a candidate for an open U.S. Senate seat, had to respond to concerns that being elected to the Senate would leave her with little time to be a good mother to her two young children. In running for governor of her state that same year, Oklahoma Lt. Governor Jari Askins was asked whether, as a single, childless woman, she had enough life experience to understand the concerns of the average Oklahoma family. In 2011, as U.S. Representative Michele Bachmann sought the Republican Party's nomination for president, *Time* magazine put a somewhat unflattering picture of her on its cover, over a headline that called her "The Queen of Rage." In 2012, Illinois Attorney General Lisa Madigan, who was considering a run for governor, was asked at a public forum whether she thought it was possible to be both a good governor and a good mother to her children.

Clearly, much of the debate about the characteristics and qualifications of these women candidates and officeholders was rooted in reactions to their sex and in gender stereotypes about the appropriate role for women in public life. Indeed, one of the major pillars in the story of the status of women candidates for elected office in the United States is that voters rely on gender stereotypes to evaluate these women and their suitability for office. As political scientists have examined several aspects of the realities of women's underrepresentation in political life, findings on the presence and direction of gender stereotypes have been a reliable starting point for understanding the context in which women are perceived. A long line of research has documented that the American public often relies on stereotyped thinking about women and men in political life (Alexander and Andersen 1993; Burrell 2008; Huddy and Terkildsen 1993b; Kahn 1996; Koch 1997; Rosenwasser and Dean 1989). This work suggests that public reliance on stereotyped attitudes will hurt women candidates at the polls as voters draw on negative assumptions about women's traits and abilities. These findings, combined with episodic attention to sexist treatment of women candidates, feed concerns about public attitudes toward women candidates and raise questions about whether gender stereotypes can derail women's potential success.

Yet, at the same time, while individual candidates may experience questionable treatment from the media or public, there is little evidence that these examples of sexism are fatal to their candidacies. It is clear that the historic nature of the 2008 elections continues to shape our thinking about the experiences of women candidates. Since they lost, it is easy to think that gender stereotypes and sexism contributed to the fate of Hillary Clinton and Sarah Palin, and campaign observers have spent a significant amount of time rehashing the gendered dynamics of their races. Yet neither lost because of her sex. When we engage in this sort of discussion, however, we often end up neglecting to explain how sexism fails to derail the candidacies of many other women. Kelly Ayotte is now a U.S. Senator from New Hampshire. The sexist attitudes that caused some voters to worry about her ability to be a good mother did not doom her candidacy. Lisa Madigan has been elected attorney general of Illinois three times while, we assume, being a good mother. Kirsten Gillibrand, Stephanie Herseth Sandlin, and Cathy McMorris Rodgers, among others, have been successful at convincing voters that mothers of young children can also be effective members of Congress. We can probably safely assume that all of these women experienced stereotyping or sexism at some point in their candidacies. These attitudes may have been present, but they were not determinative. If we are quick to point to the assumed impact of stereotyping in the campaigns of women candidates who lose, we must also acknowledge that these attitudes are not necessarily responsible for the fate of women candidates. Indeed, analysis of voting returns demonstrates that women who run for office win at the same rate as similarly situated men, which would suggest that women's levels of representation are not necessarily the result of public antipathy toward their candidacies (Seltzer, Newman, and Leighton 1997).

This conflicting reality leaves us with questions about how to make sense of the political world facing women candidates. Do women who run for office face a sometimes uphill battle against entrenched sexism, or is their sex less an obstacle than some observers would suggest? Do voters evaluate women candidates as women first, punishing them at the polls if they do not fit traditional gendered expectations, or are voters able to see these candidates as more than just women? These questions persist from election to election, supported or refuted with anecdotal candidate experiences that may or may not represent a broad-based reality. And so we are left with a puzzle. On one hand, we can document the existence of voter gender stereotypes, while on the other, we can examine election results that point to women's success. Solving the puzzle, then, involves bridging the gap between these two realities, determining how much stereotyping of women candidates the public actually engages in and illustrating how voters who hold stereotypes end up evaluating and choosing (or failing to choose) women candidates—specifically, how, when, and even whether they employ gender stereotypes in their voting decisions when faced with women candidates. It is easy to see blatant stereotyping when it occurs in high-visibility campaigns and assume that these attitudes shape a woman's fate. It is more difficult to move away from anecdotes to consider the experiences of larger numbers of women candidates in different circumstances and investigate whether their sex and gendered attitudes influence their success. Systematically examining whether gender stereotypes handicap women candidates when they run for office allows us to rise above a reliance on anecdotes and examine the landscape facing women.

In exploring the impact of candidate sex on election dynamics in the United States, this book considers the relationship between voters and women candidates, examining the influence of political gender stereotypes on the candidate evaluations and vote choice decisions people make in elections involving women candidates. The argument made here is that current research and conventional wisdom may overestimate the centrality of gendered attitudes and political gender stereotypes in the success or failure of women candidates. In examining these issues, I employ survey and campaign data from the 2010 elections to consider the impact of gender stereotypes and evaluate their influence alongside a host of other important political factors. While the analysis suggests that stereotypes are not completely irrelevant in elections, there is considerable evidence that women candidates are not routinely hampered or harmed by them.

WHY CANDIDATE SEX MATTERS IN AMERICAN POLITICS

The focus on candidate sex in U.S. elections on the part of scholars, campaign operatives, and media analysts flows, naturally, from the stark reality of women's underrepresentation in elected office in the United States. While women now hold more offices than at any time in our nation's history, they are still very far from parity with men. After the elections of 2012, women hold 18 percent (98 of 535) of the seats in Congress, five of 50 governorships, 23 percent of statewide elected offices such as attorney general and lieutenant governor, and 24 percent of state legislative seats (Center for American Women and Politics [CAWP] 2013). While there is no magic "right" number of women in office, observers usually point to the disparity between women's presence in the population (approximately 51 percent) and their presence in elected office to signal concern.

Women's underrepresentation receives as much attention as it does in our system for several important reasons. At its most basic, a democratic system like ours should be open to all who seek representation in government. If there are biases in the system, either formal or informal, or structural roadblocks that exclude particular groups or individuals, we need to know that. Women candidates have traveled a path that was long shaped by formal exclusion and informal norms that hampered their integration into political life. But the contemporary period is as free as any in our history. While some informal obstacles may still exist (Sanbonmatsu 2006), recent research convincingly demonstrates that the primary reason for women's underrepresentation is not that they are poor-quality candidates or are routinely unsuccessful when they run but, instead, that they do not run nearly as often as do men (Lawless and Fox 2010).

Women's representation in elected office also has important consequences for the governmental system. Jane Mansbridge (1999) suggests that women's presence in office signals their capacity for self-governance, or what she calls "ability to rule." Given the history of women's exclusion from political life, this is an important demonstration of women's capacity. Mansbridge also argues that having more women in office increases the overall legitimacy of the democratic system and strengthens the attachments between women and the system. Other scholars demonstrate that women officeholders can serve an important function as role models for other women, both youth and adult (Atkeson and Carrillo 2007; Campbell and Wolbrecht 2006).

Finally, women's underrepresentation also raises concerns about women's ability to advocate for their own unique needs. Countless studies of women officeholders have documented the substantive and stylistic ways in which women behave differently from men. Whether it is in their pursuit of issues that differentially affect women (abortion, sexual harassment, pregnancy) or policies on which women place greater emphasis than men (education, welfare, health care), women's presence has been shown to make a difference in the way government works and the outputs government provides (Burrell 1994; Dodson 2006; Pearson and Dancey 2011; Swers 2013). For all of these reasons, women's representation is vital to our system, which makes understanding the reasons for their underrepresentation equally so.

Women candidates run for office, and they win or they lose. In seeking to explain their victories or losses, academics, campaign strategists, and media pundits try to determine what role their sex and gender-related issues played in the outcome. It is an almost irresistible urge, since most observers assume that the fate of women candidates must be tied, at least in part, to their sex. This is particularly true when a woman candidate loses an election, and it is true even when there is significant evidence that other factors were at play. Christine Quinn, speaker of the New York City Council, lost her bid for the Democratic nomination for mayor in September 2013. The day after the primary, a *New York Times* article entitled "In Quinn's Loss, Questions about the Role of Gender and Sexuality" offered a campaign postmortem and tried to determine how Ms. Quinn had gone from early front runner to a third-place finish:

> Exit polls showed no gender gap in the results and indicated that Ms. Quinn lost for a number of reasons—her close association with the plutocratic incumbent mayor, her rivals' ability to outmaneuver her on the issue of stop-and-frisk policing, and her inability to be a change candidate in an election in which voters sought new direction.
>
> Still, her supporters wonder: Why has New York, home of tough, talented women like Eleanor Roosevelt and Anna Wintour, proven resistant to female candidates? (Kantor and Taylor, September 12, 2013, p. A23.)

Despite evidence that Quinn lost for clear political and policy reasons, the reporters could not resist wondering how much of her loss could be attributed to her sex. They go on to say that no one "blamed her loss wholly, or even mostly, on her gender," which leaves the implicit sense that it must have had some role, even if only in intangible, unknowable ways. This is because it is ingrained in most political observers, and even a good number of scholars, that a woman candidate is a woman first and this reality shapes her being a candidate. This belief, while not without some basis in evidence, reflects how important candidate sex and gender-related issues are thought to be to women candidates.

Candidate sex and gendered considerations are as central as they are because they shape so many aspects of the experiences of women who run for office. Political scientists and other scholars have examined the ways in which women candidates experience the political world differently than do men, offering insights into how, when, and why their sex and gendered issues are relevant. While these experiences touch on different phases and elements of the election process, their commonality is that gender stereotypes about women, whether held by voters, political elites, or women themselves, are at the heart of most of them.

Women Considering Candidacies

While voter antipathy toward women candidates was long considered a primary reason for women's underrepresentation in government, recent evidence of women's success at the ballot box has shifted attention away from the end of the election process to the beginning. While an obvious reality for much of our nation's history, the small number of women candidates for office did not receive a significant amount of attention until fairly recently. Given that women made up approximately 20 percent of the nominees who ran for Congress in 2012, it is not surprising that women make up 18 percent of the House and 20 percent of the Senate (CAWP 2013). The important question is why the number of women candidates is as low as it is. Here we see a clear role for gender. In an exhaustive examination of more than 3,500 women and men who possess the education and occupational skills to be credible candidates for elected office, Jennifer Lawless and Richard Fox (2010) find that women are much less likely to consider running for office for a host of reasons relating to socialization and family experiences and what they call the "gendered psyche." They find that women are less likely to have been exposed to politics or encouraged to think about running for office in their childhood and adult homes. Women are more likely to be encumbered by family and childrearing responsibilities than are men. And perhaps most importantly, women devalue their own skills and abilities more than do men and are much less likely to see themselves as viable candidates than men. This tendency to undervalue their own credentials is true even when Lawless and Fox compare women and men with similar backgrounds and expertise. Their data clearly show that women's political and nonpolitical life experiences make it much less likely that they will pursue a career in politics than will men.

The conclusions reached by Lawless and Fox are supported by other scholars who examine differences between women and men who do run for office (Dodson 1998; Sanbonmatsu 2002a). What is evident here is the lasting impact of the life experiences and attitudes of women. For example, Sarah Fulton (2012) finds evidence that women are often stronger candidates than are men. This is because many women anticipate that they will experience gender bias in running and, as a result, delay their candidacies until they pass what Fulton calls the "quality threshold." Consistent with the findings of Lawless and Fox (2010), this threshold for credibility tends to be higher in the minds of women than in men. Kathryn Pearson and Eric McGhee (2013) find that women who run for the U.S. House are more likely than men to have held elected office before seeking a House seat. They also find that Democratic women candidates raise and spend more money than Democratic men, although Republican women have no financial advantage. The results of these studies confirm that the process of becoming a candidate is influenced by gendered considerations that are experienced differently by women and men.

Women's Opportunities to Run

Women's political lives can clearly be shaped by their personal decisions about whether to run for office, but these choices can also be influenced by external forces. Indeed, there is a good deal of evidence that suggests that women's opportunities are controlled, at least in part, by the attitudes and actions of elites in our system. Primary among these are political party leaders. In the United States, party leaders still do a lot to recruit candidates for office. However, there is significant evidence that women are not recruited to run as often as are men. Kira Sanbonmatsu (2006) finds that, despite evidence of women's success at the polls, party leaders in many states still believe that women have a harder time being elected than do men. Many of the party leaders Sanbonmatsu interviewed believed that there were districts in their own states where women would not fare well. Relying on these sorts of beliefs, whether accurate or not, results in parties in some states making fewer efforts to recruit women candidates. This is consonant with David Niven's (1998) finding that 64 percent of women elected to local office in four states (Ohio, New Jersey, Tennessee, and California) believed that party leaders discouraged women from running for office. As further evidence of this connection, Sanbonmatsu finds that states with the strongest party organizations tend to have fewer women candidates than states with weaker parties and more candidate-centered politics. Her data suggests that this effect is twofold: Party leaders make fewer formal attempts to recruit women, and the informal networks of political elites remain largely male, which denies women opportunities to participate in the candidate recruitment process. Niven (1998) also finds a role for diversity in recruitment networks, identifying women leaders as more likely to identify potential women candidates than male leaders. This lesser likelihood of parties recruiting women to run for office is also problematic in light of Lawless and Fox's (2010) finding that being recruited by a party official is much more important to women candidates than it is to men. In this example, structural forces combine with individual-level psychological predispositions to dampen women's chances of emerging as candidates for office.

Beyond the role of political parties, other aspects of our system of elections can shape women's opportunities. Jennifer Lawless and Kathryn Pearson (2008) find that women candidates, even incumbents, tend to draw more primary opponents than do men, making their path to nominations potentially more challenging. Richard Fox and Zoe Oxley (2003) find evidence that women are less likely to run for statewide executive offices that require policy expertise in stereotypically male policy domains, such as law enforcement, crime, economics, business, and agriculture. Given that more statewide executive offices correspond to masculine policy areas than to feminine ones (such as education), this pattern can limit women's opportunities to run. Two other political realities also have a differential impact on women as candidates. In the United States, incumbent candidates have an enormous advantage in seeking reelection. Since incumbents at every level of office are overwhelmingly male, these men generally hold on to their seats, limiting opportunities for new office-seekers to break in to office. Women, who are less likely to be incumbents, have fewer seats to hold and fewer opportunities to gain new seats. Finally, opportunities for women are not evenly dispersed across political parties. Contemporary figures indicate that 65–70 percent of women who run for office in the United States do so as Democrats. This party imbalance creates uneven opportunities for women and particular challenges for women Republicans (Lawless and Pearson 2008; Ondercin and Welch 2009).

Women Candidates and the Campaign/Media Environment

Another way in which candidate sex can shape elections is through the campaign environment. Here we would include both decisions that candidates make about their campaigns and the coverage those campaigns receive in the media. Women running for office are bombarded with information about how to position themselves in campaigns to maximize positive reaction and minimize the impact of negative stereotypes (Bystrom et al. 2004; Lansing 1991; Witt, Paget, and Matthews 1994). Women candidates have less leeway here than do men, having to think about their physical appearance, dress, and presentation style in ways that most men running for office do not (Kantor and Taylor 2013). Women are counseled to avoid emotional tones, both positive and negative, in their campaign advertisements, in favor of a more neutral approach that appears to be favored by voters (Hitchon, Chang, and Harris 1997). Campaign strategists often advise women candidates to avoid negative advertising and attack ads, since a negative approach is inconsistent with public stereotypes of women as "nicer" than men (Lansing 1991; Trent and Friedenberg 1995). However, since negative ads have become an increasing part of a candidate's campaign strategy, doing so can put women at a political disadvantage (Kahn 1996; Williams 1998). More recent research presents evidence that women candidates can safely employ attack ads and may even benefit from using them to neutralize gender stereotypes (Gordon, Shafie, and Crigler 2003).

Besides tone and style, women candidates must also make decisions about the content of their campaigns, with regard to both the issues on which they will campaign and whether they will run "as women." This is a place where women candidates can receive conflicting advice, with some observers suggesting that women play to the strengths that voters expect, while others warn of women being harmed by a narrow focus on female issues and priorities. Recent work demonstrates that women can benefit from a focus on issues and personality traits that voters associate with women candidates (Fridkin and Kenney 2009; Herrnson, Lay, and Stokes 2003; Iyengar et al. 1997). At the same time, it is clear that while women candidates may place some emphasis on their sex and on gendered issues, most strive to present campaigns that balance attention to issues that will appeal to a range of voters (Dolan 2005; Sapiro et al. 2011).

Once candidates make campaign decisions and present themselves to voters, media reaction to these campaigns becomes relevant. And for quite a while in history these reactions were clearly gendered. Women candidates for office generally received less media attention to their campaigns than did men, and the coverage they received was more likely to raise questions about their electoral viability (Kahn 1996). Reporters also tended to focus more on their personal life and family and less on issues when covering women candidates (Devitt 1999; Kahn 1996). These differences were evident across different types of office (Bystrom, Robertson, and Banwart 2001; Fowler and Lawless 2009; Heldman, Carroll, and Olson 2005). However, as the number of women candidates increases over time, other research finds changes in the tone and amount of coverage women receive. Kevin Smith (1997) finds much smaller differences in coverage of women and men running for Senate and governor in the 1990s than in earlier decades. Dianne Bystrom and her coauthors (2004) find evidence to support parity in coverage for women running for statewide office, and Lonna Rae Atkeson and Timothy Krebs (2008) echo that finding in their examination of mayoral candidates. Indeed, they find that the presence of women candidates for mayor actually expands the range of issues covered in campaigns to include more attention to issues on which women candidates are favored. Finally, in an examination of press coverage of 350 House races in 2010, Jennifer Lawless and Danny Hayes (2013) find no evidence of bias in newspaper reporting on women versus men, concluding that reporters' portrayal of candidates is shaped more by their party identification and incumbency status than anything else. They argue that traditional expectations of gender bias in media coverage are not warranted in the contemporary world.

Women Candidates and Voters

Women who run for office need many things to be successful. They need to believe in their own potential and throw their hats into the ring; they need to be able to raise money and convince political elites of their viability; they need to craft campaign themes and issue positions and spend countless hours interacting with the public, the press, and opponents. But at the end of the day, what women candidates need more than anything else is enough people who will vote for them. The relationship between candidates and voters is the key to the whole enterprise and, building on all of those earlier decisions and actions, is what makes or breaks a candidacy. This is no different for women candidates than it is for men. However, for women candidates, who have emerged in contemporary times from a political and social history that was at times antagonistic to their presence in politics, this relationship is particularly important.

From a time when women did not have the legal right to run for office in the United States to a world in which the top five elected statewide and congressional officeholders in New Hampshire—the governor, both U.S. Senators, and both U.S. Representatives—are women, our society has clearly experienced an evolution in its thinking about women candidates for office.[1] And yet, even in 2014, women candidates can experience a somewhat conflicted relationship with voters. As the anecdotes that opened this book suggest, this is because we still often think about women in gender-stereotyped ways. We assume that women have a particular set of personal skills and policy interests, and we evaluate their fitness for office through that lens. But this lens of gender stereotypes can be inconsistent. Each election cycle offers examples of sexist or dated thinking that signals potential roadblocks for women—Lisa Madigan being asked whether she could be both a good governor and a good mother, for example. Yet, at the same time, we can sometimes lionize women and their stereotyped strengths. The very positive coverage of several women U.S. Senators and their role in jump-starting the negotiations that led to the end of the government shutdown in 2013 typifies this. Several media articles were full of unquestioning discussions about women officeholders being much more willing to compromise, roll up their sleeves, and get to work than are men. Susan Collins (R-ME), Kelly Ayotte (R-NH), and Lisa Murkowski (R-AK) may indeed be hardworking women who grew frustrated by the grandstanding of their colleagues, leading them to seek a solution to the stalemate. But the coverage did not ascribe these superior abilities to their individual abilities and experiences as successful legislators but, instead, to their being women. So while it is clear that stereotypes can color our impressions of women candidates, it is less clear whether this coloring is more positive or negative.

It is also clear that we know quite a bit about the presence of gender stereotypes in our political world, but we know less about whether these attitudes are important to how voters actually choose candidates for office. It may well be the case that many voters in New York City found Christine Quinn's voice to be "grating," but did that really determine whether they voted for her or not? Did voters really factor U.S. Representative Kristi Noem's three children into their calculation about whether she would be a better representative than her opponent Matt Varilek, who has two young children of his own? Are voters concerned that a woman candidate may not have military experience, and are they equally concerned about a man in the same situation? Are the high-visibility anecdotes from women's campaigns representative of a broader set of attitudes toward women candidates or simply idiosyncratic situations? The short answer to these questions is that we really do not know. For as much information as scholars and political pundits have about candidates and elections and voters, we do not have a lot of appropriate information about how voters evaluate women candidates and whether these evaluations rely heavily, or at all, on gender stereotypes. In this book, I seek to correct that information deficiency.

A NEW LOOK AT THE POLITICAL IMPACT OF GENDER STEREOTYPES

This attempt will require new thinking about the ways in which we examine whether and how voter gender stereotypes influence women candidates. While scholars have accumulated considerable knowledge on these questions, this work has been conducted in fairly consistent ways. Here

I argue for a new approach. First, instead of focusing on whether the United States is ready to elect a woman president, we need to expand our consideration to other important offices. The presidency is an office for which no woman major-party candidate has ever run, and yet an enormous amount of time and effort is spent in measuring public reactions to that possibility. At the same time, all around us, women candidates are running for every other office at the local, state, and national levels. If we are interested in whether gender stereotypes matter to women's election, we need to study the women who could actually be affected by them—women who are running below the level of the presidency. In this project, I examine women running for Congress and governorships, two different offices that are both important to advancing women's interests. Another way that we can take a fresh approach to studying the impact of stereotypes on women candidates is to broaden our pool of candidates for study. The several books written on the 2008 candidacies of Clinton and Palin provide excellent descriptions and analyses of the dynamics of these races. But their highly unique nature limits our ability to apply any of the lessons from those campaigns to the situations of other women. I seek to offer more generalizable information about the utility of stereotypes in elections with women candidates by examining the dynamics of races involving almost 650 candidates. A third improvement offered by this project is a focus on the people whose attitudes and behaviors are most relevant to an examination of gender stereotypes—actual voters who are taking part in elections in which women candidates are running. Journalistic accounts of gender and stereotypes in campaigns will offer a quote from a voter or an anecdote from a day on the campaign trail. Scholarly work on stereotypes is often conducted with small groups of unrepresentative subjects in experimental settings. Here, I analyze the attitudes and behaviors of a nationally representative sample of 3,150 U.S. adults who experienced either single-sex (man versus man) or mixed-sex (woman versus man) races for Congress and governor. Finally, this project reminds us that when we consider the fate of women candidates, we have to seek explanations that go beyond the influence of their sex. Why is it that we seem to assume that elections with women candidates are different somehow? Why are traditional campaign dynamics assumed to be altered when one candidate is a woman? Why do we cite clear and reasonable explanations for a woman's success or failure (à la Christine Quinn) and then turn to trying to figure out how and why her sex was important? I do not mean to argue that a woman's sex never shapes the context of a campaign. But I do suggest that in thinking about the impact of candidate sex, we often forget that the traditional influences on elections—political party, incumbency, campaign spending—are in operation regardless of the sex of candidates (Dolan 2004). In this analysis, I attempt to consider the potential impact of gender stereotypes on women candidates alongside other traditional political variables. In doing so, I am able to place candidate sex in context and consider its relative influence on election outcomes.

CHAPTER OVERVIEW

The primary goal of this book is to contribute to our understanding of the impact of gender stereotypes on the relationship between voters and women candidates. To accurately assess this relationship, we must reevaluate the influence of political gender stereotypes *in the real world*, as they influence specific voter attitudes and behaviors and as they operate alongside more central political and contextual variables such as political party, incumbency, and candidate experience. Indeed, the primary hypothesis advanced is that gender stereotypes are less likely to influence electoral outcomes than traditional political variables and do so less often than the existing literature and conventional wisdom suggest. Each substantive chapter addresses a particular aspect of this broad hypothesis.

Chapter 2 begins the examination by laying out the framework of the argument. Important here is a discussion of stereotypes, their utility in political decision making, and the state of our current understanding of their impact on the fortunes of women candidates. Stereotypes are generally understood to be a time-saving device that people employ in cognitive tasks when they have relatively little information about an object or a situation. However, during elections, there is often a considerable amount of information available to voters, which can limit the need to rely on stereotypes. Another important element of this discussion is an evaluation of the methodological issues surrounding the study of gender stereotypes. Because of the relatively small number of women candidates and the challenges of surveying voters in real elections, much of the existing work on voter gender stereotypes has been conducted in experimental situations and with hypothetical candidates. While this research has provided a strong foundation, this consistent methodological approach has had consequences for our ability to evaluate the experiences of women candidates in the real world. Since real candidates do not exist in a vacuum, we must acknowledge all of the elements of elections that might work to limit the impact of stereotypes. I outline several of these considerations in hypothesizing that the role stereotypes play in political decision making is less significant than previously thought.

Chapter 3 begins by examining the assumption that the success of women candidates depends, in part, on voters holding positive attitudes about their presence in political life. The first step here is an analysis of a set of attitudes related to people's support for a political role for women. Relevant attitudes include gender preferences in candidates, ideas about the contribution women make in office, and thoughts on levels of women's representation in the United States. Gender stereotypes are introduced here, with a focus on measuring the abstract gender stereotypes that voters hold about the policy interests and character traits of women and men who run for office. A second step examines whether these attitudes about women in politics are related to political decisions voters make, specifically whether people vote in ways that are consistent with these attitudes. This chapter provides evidence that earlier work on gender stereotypes inflates their importance by comparing an analysis of the impact of stereotypes on hypothetical election circumstances with an analysis of their impact on vote choice in races with real women candidates. The conclusion here is that the disparity in findings between hypothetical electoral situations and real-world elections suggests that a reliance on hypotheticals paints an inaccurate picture of the impact of gender stereotypes in elections involving women candidates.

Chapter 4 takes a more detailed look at the impact of voter gender stereotypes by exploring their relationship to a concrete political action—evaluating candidate pairs in an election. Candidate evaluations are an important attitudinal precursor to vote choice, so understanding whether and how voters use abstract gender stereotypes to evaluate specific women and men is an important starting point. The analysis in this chapter allows for more complexity of understanding with regard to stereotypes by considering how stereotypes influence evaluations relative to a host of relevant, real-world political variables. Beyond this, I consider whether and how the political party of the woman candidate and the office for which she runs work to shape the impact of gender stereotypes. Finally, to more fully understand how gender stereotypes relate to candidate evaluations, I compare races in which women candidates run against men with those races in which men run against other men. While the literature on stereotypes focuses almost exclusively on their relationship to women candidates, examining male-only races helps us gauge whether stereotypes are activated in all elections or only those in which women run. Here I find that stereotypes have no clear or consistent impact on voter evaluations of candidates and that the party of the woman candidate shapes stereotyped reactions. This finding, in concert with the finding that gender stereotypes can be significant in male-only races, requires us to recognize that partisan stereotypes can interact with gender stereotypes in races with and without women candidates. Finally, the analysis demonstrates that the impact of stereotypes depends on the office women seek.

In chapter 5 I turn to the central element of the relationship between voters and candidates—vote choice. In doing so, I provide a test of one of the primary assumptions in the existing literature, which is that gender stereotypes about women and men can push voters toward or away from particular candidates. The analysis here examines the relationship between stereotypes and voting for women candidates in a similar fashion to that in chapter 4 by examining the impact of stereotypes relative to the traditional influences on vote choice while also considering the party of the woman candidate, the office she seeks, and the dynamics between gender stereotypes and vote choice in male-only races. Here I find very little support for the notion that the gender stereotypes voters hold have any real impact on their selection of candidates. Instead, elections in which women run look very similar to those in which they do not, with traditional forces of political party and incumbency shaping voting for women in the same way that they shape voting for men.

Chapter 6 moves beyond the relationship between voters and candidates to consider the impact of candidate sex at other points in the election process. As I summarized earlier, candidate sex and gender issues can shape the decisions women make about becoming candidates and, once they do, how they will campaign. Past research suggests that when women emerge as candidates, they have a stronger set of credentials and experiences relative to men. To examine whether this is the case for the candidates in this data set, I draw on background data that measures candidate education, previous office-holding experience, and campaign fundraising. I also examine race results for all candidates in the data set to determine whether similarly situated women and men win their elections at the same rate. The second examination involves looking at the campaign decisions candidates make. One important question about whether voters evaluate women candidates through the lens of gender stereotypes involves asking whether candidates stimulate stereotyped evaluations through the campaigns they run. Utilizing campaign advertising data and campaign websites for the candidates in the data set allows me to examine whether women contribute to the stereotypes people hold as a result of the ways they present themselves in their campaigns. In all, this analysis finds that the women candidates represented in this project are of equal quality to or higher quality than the men candidates. At the same time, I find that women and men make very similar decisions on how to portray their policy priorities in their campaigns, behaving like savvy partisan politicians and not playing to gender stereotypes.

Chapter 7 concludes the book by reviewing the major findings of the analysis and discussing the conclusions that we can draw. Here, I identify ways in which our current understanding of the impact of gender stereotypes on elections may be lacking and discuss how these findings fit with other recent works that question conventional wisdom about the challenges facing women candidates. In doing so, I encourage scholars to continue to move the examination of gender stereotypes into the realm of real elections. As the number of women candidates increases, I argue that we need to develop ways to systematically examine real-world elections to increase our leverage over these important questions. Finally, I take stock of future directions for research as we continue to unravel the puzzle of the role that candidate sex and gender stereotypes play in American elections.

CHAPTER 2

Studying Gender Stereotypes and Women Candidates

One legislator in particular told me I was just a mom in tennis shoes and I had no chance of changing things.

Patty Murray, U.S. Senator (D-WA)

That's right. I am Elizabeth Warren and I am running for the U.S. Senate because that's what girls do.

Elizabeth Warren, U.S. Senator (D-MA)

Anecdotes about visible women candidates in recent elections, such as those introduced in the previous chapter, highlight the intuitive sense we have that being a woman candidate in American politics can be fraught with complication. These episodes of sexist, or at least gendered, treatment of women garner attention and raise concerns about the public's attitudes toward women in political life. As we move away from a political history in which women were virtually excluded from public life into a contemporary time in which the number of women serving in elected office has steadily increased, such a focus on a candidate's sex can seem unnecessary. The evolution in societal attitudes toward women candidates, as illustrated by Patty Murray's experience in 1980 and Elizabeth Warren's confidence in 2012, seems clear. Yet, as we continue this evolution of women's integration into American political life, it is important that we address head-on questions about the role that candidate sex can play in shaping women's opportunities and outcomes.

While it is clear that the sex of a candidate can influence several different aspects of elections, the primary focus here is on the impact it has on voters. Public attitudes about whether politics is an appropriate pursuit for women have been at the heart of women's opportunities since the founding of our nation. While laws forbidding their candidacy certainly played a role, social attitudes have long created clear barriers to women's political ambitions. For much of our history, women were excluded from political life because of widespread beliefs that they did not possess the requisite skills and abilities to be successful in politics. At the same time, politics was seen as corrosive and antithetical to women's nature. Even in relatively contemporary times, Duverger (1955) suggested that public hostility toward women and beliefs about their abilities were primary contributors to women's underrepresentation in elected office. While social and cultural attitudes have continued to become more accepting of a political role for women, we still need to give attention to the relationship between women candidates and voters so that we can determine whether these types of attitudes still limit women's success. Doing so requires us to consider gender stereotypes. Indeed, the long history of antagonism toward women's political life involved dominant social and cultural assumptions about women's nature and women's capabilities—in a word, stereotypes. These judgments were not simply about specific women who sought elected office but, in fact, assumptions about all women, what they were capable of and what they were not. As such, the attitudes being used to evaluate women were not much different from what we think of as stereotypes today.

If stereotyped thinking has had a primary place in the way people approach women candidates, it should not surprise us that the examination of gender stereotypes has had a prominent place in the research on the political success of these women. Political science has produced an impressive body of research that confirms that voters look at women candidates and women officeholders from a gendered perspective, ascribing certain stereotyped issue position competencies and personality characteristics to them. These stereotypes involve thinking about a range of traits, skills, and abilities that we assume are relevant to political candidates and officeholders. In terms of gender-linked personality traits, women candidates and officeholders are generally viewed as more compassionate and honest than men, warmer and more expressive, and better able to deal with constituents such as citizens groups than are men. Men, on the other hand, are viewed as more competent, decisive, stronger leaders, and possessing a greater ability to handle a crisis (Alexander and Andersen 1993; Burrell 2008; Huddy and Terkildsen 1993b; Kahn 1996; King and Matland 2003; Lawless 2004; Leeper 1991; Paul and Smith 2008; Sapiro 1981/1982). Trait stereotypes are relevant to political candidates since several studies have found that people evaluate the stereotyped masculine traits (experience, leadership) as more important in politics than the feminine traits (honesty, compassion), particularly as the level of elected office being considered rises from the local to the national level (Huddy and Terkildsen 1993a; Lawless 2004; Rosenwasser and Dean 1989).

Evaluations of women candidates and officeholders generally conform to stereotyped thinking about issue competencies as well. Women are assumed to be more interested in, and more effective in dealing with, issues such as child care, poverty, education, health care, women's issues, and the environment than are men, while men are thought to be more competent at dealing with economic development, the military, trade, taxes, and agriculture (Alexander and Andersen 1993; Brown, Heighberger, and Shocket 1993; Dolan 2010; Huddy and Terkildsen 1993b; Koch 1997; Rosenwasser and Dean 1989). In terms of political ideology, numerous studies find that women are perceived as more liberal than men and that they are often perceived as more liberal than they actually are, based on objective measures of ideology (Koch 2000, 2002; McDermott 1997).

Perhaps the most important aspect of stereotyped evaluations of women candidates is that ideas about the abilities and competencies of female and male candidates may serve as a basis for voters to choose or reject a particular candidate. A role for gender stereotypes in vote choice is suggested by Sanbonmatsu's (2002a) work on what she calls a "baseline gender preference." She suggests that many people have an underlying preference to be represented by a woman or a man and that this predisposition is determined, in part, by gender stereotypes. This preference can combine with issue position preferences to move voters toward or away from a woman or man candidate. Cindy Simon Rosenthal's (1995) findings support the notion that people often favor candidates of one sex or the other based on their assumptions about what those candidates are like or what they will do in office. Stereotypes can also interact with elements of the context of an election to shape voting. For example, Monika McDermott (1998) finds that, in low-information elections, people rely on ideological and issue stereotypes about women candidates in determining whether they will vote for them. Other work demonstrates that the issue environment of an election can trigger stereotypes that can help or hinder women. The stereotyped belief that women are more honest and concerned with ethical government than men has been shown to help women candidates increase their support among voters who value these issues (Dolan 2004; McDermott 1998). At the same time, Lawless (2004) suggests that stereotypes about women's inferiority on terrorism and military issues since September 11th create challenges for women candidates, who may face more scrutiny from voters whose primary issue concerns involve terrorism and military issues.

Taking current research into account would suggest that voters have clear and fairly consistent gender-stereotyped ideas about the skills and abilities of women who run for office. Many scholars and campaign professionals believe that this voter reliance on gender stereotypes is a negative for women candidates. Yet, at the same time, it is somewhat difficult to find empirical evidence of a negative impact for gender stereotypes in the real world (Huddy and Capelos 2002). Since the 1980s, election returns have told us that "when women run, women win" (Burrell 1994; Fox 2006; Newman 1994). In comparing women and men candidates who are in similar electoral circumstances, we see that women win election at comparable rates to men, and sometimes even higher. In looking at trends, we see that women's representation at every level of office has increased steadily over the same time period. In fact, recent work suggests that the primary reason for women's underrepresentation in elected office is not that women do not win but that women do not choose to run or that institutional forces still inhibit their ability to do so (Lawless and Fox 2010; Sanbonmatsu 2006). This work suggests that there are clear social and cultural dynamics that limit women's political role, but there is little evidence that public antipathy is an important part of that dynamic.

What these conflicting messages in the literature do suggest is a need to examine more fully the impact of gender stereotypes on the circumstances and fortunes of women candidates, with a particular focus on determining whether and when voters employ stereotypes in making important political decisions. Currently, we know a good bit about two aspects of the experiences of women candidates: We know that voters hold political gender stereotypes, and we know that women win elections. What we know much less about is what happens between these two realities: specifically, what use is made of the stereotypes voters hold, how they are employed, and whether they matter in a real way to the outcome of elections. Consequently, this gap in our knowledge raises several questions. If voters hold gender stereotypes about candidates, do they necessarily use them in shaping their candidate evaluations and vote choice decisions? If stereotypes do matter, do they matter in the same way in all circumstances? Do they matter in elections for different kinds of offices? Do stereotypes matter in the same way for women and men? Do they interact with other stereotypes, such as party stereotypes? How do stereotypes stack up against other influences on voter decision making? There is clearly a host of unanswered questions, and we have a clear need for research that engages gender stereotypes and examines what happens when voters are faced with women candidates so that we can identify whether these gendered attitudes influence women's success at the ballot box.

According to social psychological theory, stereotyping is the process by which people, through either direct experience or other exposure, develop beliefs about the characteristics of social groups (Macrae, Stangor, and Hewstone 1996). In encountering an individual who is a member of a group, people assume that this individual shares the characteristics of the group (Fiske and Neuberg 1990). Social psychologists suggest that gender stereotypes are among the most pervasive and persistent stereotypes people hold, in part, because a person's sex is one of the first things we encounter about him or her. Gender stereotypes are also as prevalent as they are because gender is a socially relevant category that shapes almost every facet of human life. The centrality of gender to so many aspects of life is thought to give these group-based beliefs about women and men particular power. Stereotyping is as pervasive as it is because it provides individuals with a way of sorting through an information-dense world to develop evaluation shortcuts and to simplify their interactions with the world. While stereotypes are a useful tool in navigating many aspects of life, they are particularly useful in areas in which people are minimally engaged, such as politics (Conover and Feldman 1989; Popkin 1993; Rahn 1993). For example, we know that people rely heavily on shortcuts and stereotypes such as political party identification to provide them with information about political candidates or issues that they may not have the time or inclination to gather on their own. These heuristics are also used to incorporate new information, so that when a person encounters an unfamiliar situation, she or he can apply existing beliefs to develop an evaluation as needed (Fiske and Taylor 1991). In the context of analyzing political candidates, research suggests that candidate characteristics, such as race, sex, age, or religion, can offer cues that allow voters to extend prior beliefs about group members to individuals (McDermott 1998, 2009; Philpot and Walton 2007). These group-based stereotypes can provide a starting point or a set of expectations for what an individual candidate will be like.

Gender stereotyping, then, involves ideas and beliefs about what women and men are like, what abilities they possess, and what behaviors and activities are appropriate for each. Social psychologists suggest that gender stereotypes about women and men are based on a number of different elements of the ways women and men exist in the world. Alice Eagly (1987) advances the notion that the division of labor between women and men, and the resulting social roles of woman as homemaker and man as worker in a paid occupation, forms the basis for stereotypes about the traits and abilities of the sexes. Other work points to the status differences that flow from the different roles of women and men, which lead to women consistently being assigned lower levels of social status than men (Wood and Karten 1986). Finally, power differentials also serve as a basis for gender stereotypes. As a concept, power differs from social status, in that status relates more to *perceptions* of the abilities of members of a group, while power generally refers to the *actual* control individuals have over resources and outcomes (Deaux and LaFrance 1998). As with social roles and status explanations, power relations generally find that women are in less powerful positions than are men, whether in social, economic, or familial relationships. Women's different, and often inferior, position in the world compared with men's translates into a set of beliefs about the competence and traits of each sex.

It is easy to see that the belief structures that shape stereotypes in the world at large—gendered division of labor, status differences, and power difference—mirror the realities of women and men in the world of politics. Women were formally excluded from politics for so long because the gendered division of labor in society kept them out of the public sphere. Once "inside," women often focused on "female" issues that fit with expectations about their interests and abilities. Women, who were long thought to lack the requisite rationality and intelligence for politics, entered political life with perceived lower status and less actual power than their male colleagues. Clearly, over time, women have become integrated into political life and leadership, but they have often been viewed through a lens of traditional gender attitudes in ways that may or may not match reality. This application of general gender stereotypes to the political world can become problematic for women candidates since evidence suggests that these stereotypes can be at odds with the expectations that voters have for political candidates and leaders (Dolan 1997; Huddy and Terkildsen 1993a; Lawless 2004).

LIMITATIONS ON THE INFLUENCE OF STEREOTYPES

As demonstrated earlier, political scientists have produced a significant body of work that addresses and examines political gender stereotypes. Much of this work begins by identifying the stereotypes people hold and examining their impact. As Nichole Bauer suggests, implicit in much of this work is the assumption that the presence of stereotypes means that these stereotypes are "always and unavoidably" related to evaluations of women candidates (2013, 23). This, coupled with the assumption that stereotypes generally lead to *negative* evaluations of women candidates, creates an impression that women candidates face potential problems in elections. However, this perspective is somewhat more simplistic than work on stereotypes in social psychology would suggest. According to Ziva Kunda and Steven Spencer (2003), group stereotypes are not automatically applied to individuals, and researchers err in assuming that stereotype presence (activation) necessarily leads to their application in any given situation. Indeed, social psychologists paint a more complex picture of stereotypes in ways that have bearing on understanding how they may or may not be relevant to politics. First, there is evidence of significant variation in stereotype-holding across individuals, which suggests that they might not be as universally automatic or as deeply embedded as many believe (Bargh 1994). In a political context, this could lead to the impact of stereotypes being neutralized as the actions of those who hold stereotypes are balanced out by the actions of those who hold more egalitarian views. Second, while stereotypes do indeed allow people to make judgments about individuals in the absence of information, stereotypes can also dissipate quickly in the face of contact with, or information about, an individual (Kunda and Spencer 2003; Locksley et al. 1980). Since political campaigns are almost exclusively about presenting information to voters, we might expect stereotyped views of candidates to be fairly short-lived once voters learn about candidates. Third, stereotype application depends, in large part, on characteristics of the environment and on the motivation of individuals, who often employ stereotypes to support their desired impression of an individual (Blair 2002; Kunda and Sinclair 1999). Given that every candidate, and every electoral situation, is unique, we should not expect one uniform voter reaction to elections in which women candidates run. Finally, stereotypes do not necessarily exist in a vacuum, with evidence suggesting that different stereotypes can interact and complicate the ability of any particular stereotype to shape evaluations (Deaux and Lewis 1984; Kunda and Spencer 2003). While there are several variables that could interact with candidate sex, the most obvious political possibilities are stereotypes based on the political party and race of a candidate (Hayes 2011; McDermott 1998).

This social psychological approach suggests that scholars should reconsider how and when gender stereotypes are relevant to political settings in general and to the fate of women candidates in particular. If gender stereotypes are not automatically applied in the presence of women, we should not take the presence of stereotypes as evidence of their impact without more closely examining how stereotypes might be linked to voter attitudes and behaviors. If there is variation in stereotype-holding and application across individuals, we need to acknowledge that voters may not approach women candidates from one clear perspective and that stereotypes may not have one particular direction of influence. If contact and information can ameliorate the impact of stereotypes, we should consider whether and how stereotypes function in real-world elections, since elections provide voters with considerable amounts of information. Finally, if stereotypes can interact and affect one another, we need to consider how gender stereotypes operate in "competition" with other sorts of political influences, most important of which would be political party. In attempting to answer these sorts of questions, we can get a clearer picture of the role gender stereotypes play, or fail to play, in the fortunes of women candidates.

SHOULD STEREOTYPES REALLY MATTER IN POLITICS?

The conventional wisdom, built on an extensive body of work, suggests that political gender stereotypes should matter to evaluations and vote choice in elections with women candidates. But there are also several reasons to believe that their impact may be less dramatic than imagined, particularly in the contemporary period. These explanations fall into three broad categories—aspects of women candidates and campaign environments, limitations of stereotypes, and political and electoral context variables. Each of these sets of explanations asks us to consider different elements of contemporary elections and update our expectations about whether and how gender stereotypes might influence interactions between voters and women candidates. As we will see, there is much about the present-day world that might work to limit the impact that stereotypes can have.

Women Candidates and Campaigns

One aspect of women's candidacies that may have the effect of limiting the power of gender stereotypes is simply that there are more and more of these candidates over time. For most of the 20th century, the number of women candidates was small, but we see a steady increase beginning around 1990 and continuing today. Figures 2.1–2.3 present data on the number of women candidates for Congress and governor in the contemporary period. This increase has taken place at the national, state, and local levels and across the country, although with some variability depending on region (CAWP 2012b). One obvious result of this increase in the number of women candidates is the concomitant increase in the number of voters who have had the opportunity to participate in, or at least observe, an election involving a woman candidate. It may be the case that the increasing

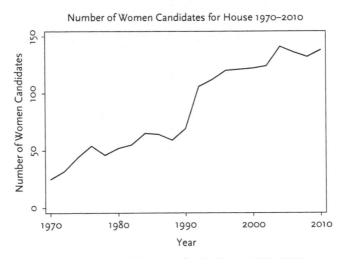

Figure 2.1: Number of Women Candidates for the U.S. House 1970–2010

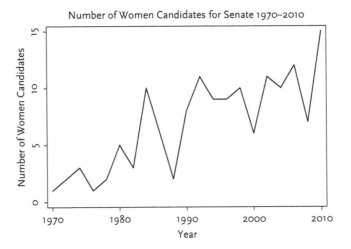

Figure 2.2: Number of Women Candidates for the U.S. Senate 1970–2010

number of women candidates has made them less of a novelty in elections and may have resulted in normalizing the experience of evaluating women candidates for more and more voters. This argument makes sense when we think about the time period in which much of the early research on the political impact of gender stereotypes was conducted, beginning in the 1970s and 1980s, before the number of women candidates was particularly high. The social psychology literature on stereotypes would suggest that, as women candidates become a more routine part of the electoral experience of a greater number of voters, and as an increasingly diverse group of women run for office, voters should be able to develop evaluations based

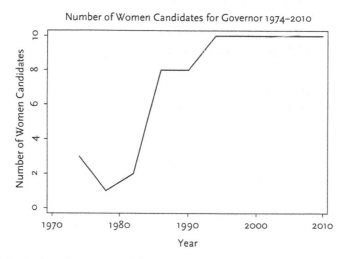

Figure 2.3: Number of Women Candidates for Governor 1970–2010

more on these experiences with individuals and less on stereotypes. Even voters who have not taken part in a race with a woman candidate should be more familiar with their presence in the political landscape.

Another aspect of women's candidacies that may limit the power of gender stereotypes involves changes in women candidates themselves. Since women are still underrepresented as candidates and elected officials, some scholars have advanced the notion that women winning at equal rates to men probably means that the women candidates who do emerge are superior to their male counterparts. This is a version of the belief that women need to be able to do things "backwards and in high heels" to compete with men (Fulton 2012). If women candidates are, on average, stronger candidates than men, it may be the case that their credentials and experiences are sufficiently accomplished to defuse the negative impact of gender stereotypes. There is clear evidence that the "quality" of women candidates has increased in the contemporary period, with more women coming from educational and occupational backgrounds that are similar to those of male candidates (Ford and Dolan 1997). Recent work on candidate emergence indicates that women candidates tend to hold off on candidacies until they consider themselves well qualified, which often results in their being better-quality candidates than men running for the same office (Burrell 1988, 1994; Fulton 2012; Fulton et al. 2006; Lawless and Fox 2010; Pearson and McGhee 2013). What has been dubbed the "Jackie and Jill Robinson effect" leads to women officeholders who may defy stereotyping because of their strong skills and experiences (Anzia and Berry 2011).

Because of the history of sexism in American elections, women candidates are often counseled to take steps to create images and qualifications that will produce positive associations in the minds of voters. The conscious decisions women candidates make about how to present themselves to the public can be attempts to dispel negative gender stereotypes or take advantage of more positive ones. In running for mayor of New York City in 2013, Christine Quinn, speaker of the New York City Council, was advised to change her dress, hair, and voice to appear more feminine to voters, some of whom found her to be somewhat masculine and inattentive to her appearance (Kantor and Taylor 2013). Hillary Clinton's request in 2000 to serve on the Senate Armed Services Committee was a clear attempt to burnish her foreign affairs and military credentials in a way that might make her less vulnerable to the common stereotype that women are less qualified to handle military issues. During her run for governor of California in 1990, Diane Feinstein's evocation of her experiences as president of the San Francisco Board of Supervisors in the wake of the assassinations of Mayor George Moscone and Supervisor Harvey Milk allowed her to demonstrate her leadership and strength in a chaotic time (Decker 2011). Two years later, in running for the U.S. Senate, she talked about her experiences as a grandmother to assure voters that she possessed the expected female qualities of warmth and caring (Pringle 2006).

There is significant work demonstrating that women candidates often do make strategic choices about their campaigns in their efforts to highlight or neutralize their sex and gender considerations. In examining women candidates for U.S. Senate and governor in the 1980s and 1990s, Kim Kahn (1996) found that women appeared in their own campaign ads more often than men, dressed professionally, emphasized their positions on policies, and worked to present themselves as possessing competence and leadership in order to dispel negative gender stereotypes. Bystrom and her coauthors (2004) also find that women candidates emphasize masculine traits in their campaigns to counteract any expectation that they are weaker than their male opponents. At the same time, women candidates can work to make gender salient when it might advantage them, such as by campaigning directly to women voters or focusing on women's issues when those issues are of concern to voters (Herrnson et al. 2003; Iyengar et al. 1997).

If candidates are successful in managing voter gender stereotypes as a result of these conscious attempts to "fill in the blanks" in voter thinking, we would expect that voters would rely less heavily on stereotypes (Bystrom et al. 2004). This suggestion is supported by work in political science and social psychology that demonstrates it is relatively easy to reverse stereotyped evaluations by describing someone in a nonstereotypic way (Gordon et al. 2003; Huddy and Capelos 2002; Huddy and Terkildsen 1993b). For example, Anne Locksley and her coauthors (1980) find that women described as assertive were perceived that way by others, despite the traditional stereotype of women's passivity. The same is true for men described in nonstereotypic terms. The authors conclude that information about a trait or behavior of an individual is often sufficient to decrease people's reliance on gender stereotypes as a source of evaluation. Ann Gordon and her coauthors (2003) find that women can increase their credibility on a stereotypical male policy issue by attacking their opponent on that same issue, suggesting a way for women candidates to neutralize stereotyped concerns that they are weak on issues such as defense and the economy. These works indicate that affirmative attempts by women candidates to blunt the power of stereotypes through their campaign strategies may well be successful.

Finally, an important element of how voters experience the campaigns of women candidates may be changing as well. It is the case, of course, that the vast majority of voters never experience candidates firsthand by attending a speech, rally, or community event. Instead, voters largely consume campaigns through candidate advertising and through media reporting. In earlier times, there was clear evidence of media bias in the coverage of women candidates, with women receiving less coverage, and less positive coverage, than men. A number of scholars demonstrated that the media focused more on questions of the viability of women candidates and on their personal lives and attributes (what is referred to as "hair, hemlines, and husbands") and less on their political experiences and policy positions than they did for male candidates (Devitt 1999; Heldman et al. 2005; Kahn 1994, 1996; Kahn and Goldenberg 1992). If voters were consuming media coverage that minimized the credentials of women candidates or presented them in traditionally gender-stereotyped ways, then we might have expected voters to view these women skeptically. However, it would appear that the increase in the number of women candidates and the campaign decisions they make may be having an impact on the way reporters present women candidates to the public. More recent work indicates that the patterns of gender difference in the coverage of candidates seen in the 1980s and 1990s are changing and becoming more equitable (Smith 1997). Looking across a range of offices, it is clear that women are generally receiving as much total coverage as men and as much coverage on policy and political positions, although some work still finds that women's "novelty" as candidates is a continuing frame (Atkeson and Krebs 2008; Bystrom et al. 2004; Fowler and Lawless 2009; Hayes 2011; Meeks 2012). If we have moved to a time in which press coverage of women is not significantly different from or worse than the coverage of men, this too could contribute to a lessening of the impact of gender stereotypes on the fortunes of women candidates.

Limits of Stereotypes

Much of the existing work on the impact of stereotypes on women candidates takes as an implicit assumption the idea that voter stereotypes have a negative impact on these candidates. Numerous projects have demonstrated that people see women and men in gender-stereotyped ways, that they value "male" traits and characteristics more than "female" ones, and that the decision to support or oppose women candidates is influenced by these stereotyped beliefs (Alexander and Andersen 1993; Huddy and Terkildsen 1993b; Sanbonmatsu 2002a). However, this line of thinking neglects two realities: that stereotyped beliefs about women candidates are not always negative and that the way scholars have applied stereotypes to the study of political leaders may have important limitations.

While much of the literature on voter stereotypes of women candidates does find evidence that voters subscribe to traditional gender role stereotypes, whether those beliefs are a positive or negative for women is less clear. One concern is that voters often devalue "female" traits in evaluating political candidates and leaders, particularly as the level of office they are considering moves from local to national (Dolan 1997; Huddy and Terkildsen 1993a; Rosenwasser and Dean 1989). Other authors have suggested that women's perceived strengths do not always align with the policy concerns of voters, which could hurt the support they receive at the ballot box (Fox and Smith 1998; Lawless 2004; Leeper 1991; Smith, Paul, and Paul 2007). And yet, one thing this perspective fails to recognize is that traditional stereotypes about traits or policy expertise can work to the benefit of women candidates in some circumstances. Indeed, the classic example of this is the congressional elections of 1992, the so-called Year of the Woman. In that election, events conspired to create an environment in which women candidates were quite successful. After the Persian Gulf War ended in 1991, many Americans sought a return of attention to domestic issues. As a result of what became known as the "House Bank" scandal, a situation in which some members of the House were found to have been overdrawing their checking accounts at the House bank without penalty, voters appeared to want candidates who were free of the taint of corruption. President Bush's first veto of the Family and Medical Leave Act in 1991, his nomination of Clarence Thomas to the Supreme Court, and the subsequent Senate hearings on Anita Hill's charges that Thomas sexually harassed her highlighted gender issues in the United States and, in particular, women's underrepresentation in Congress. For some voters in 1992, candidates who were assumed to be more honest, competent on domestic issues, and "outsiders" to politics had special appeal.

While these circumstances do not fully explain the success of women candidates in 1992, they were a part of the story. The point here is that, for every concern that is raised about stereotypes being a disadvantage for women, there may be a time and place when women's presumed strengths are valued by voters. For instance, voters concerned about honesty and ethics in government have been more likely to vote for women candidates (Dolan 2004; McDermott 1998). Other work has demonstrated that, even when voters do use stereotypes to distinguish between women and men candidates, they can employ positive stereotypes about women (Kahn 1994). In a recent study of Senate candidates, Kim Fridkin and Pat Kenney (2009) found that voters held positive stereotypes about women candidates, believing that they were more honest, caring, and competent to deal with health care issues than were men, but held none of the expected positive stereotypes about men, such as that they might be better at economic issues or able to provide strong leadership. These findings suggest, at the very least, that we should not assume that all stereotyping of women candidates leads to negative evaluations or voter rejection and that we should be open to the ways in which women could be perceived as superior to male candidates on dimensions that voters value.

Beyond thinking about whether gender stereotypes of women are a negative or positive influence, we also have to consider the evidence that stereotypes may be diminishing. Beginning in the 1970s, most research demonstrated that large numbers of people held attitudes toward women and men in politics that conformed to traditional gender stereotypes. However, it would probably be somewhat simplistic to think that levels of stereotyping would stay constant over time, particularly when we take stock of the dramatic social, economic, and political changes that have taken place for women in the intervening years. In 2012, women made up 48 percent of the total U.S. labor force, 58 percent of U.S. college students, and 15 percent of active-duty military (Bureau of Labor Statistics 2013; Pew Research Center 2011). As women have moved out of the private sphere and into the public and political worlds, academic work suggests an easing of gender stereotypes and an increase in egalitarian attitudes toward women candidates (Burrell 2008; Dolan 2010; Eagly and Carli 2007; Fridkin and Kenney 2009). A recent study by the Pew Research Center (2008) demonstrated that the public evaluates women as being superior or equal to men on several trait dimensions associated with leadership—honesty, intelligence, ambition, and being hard working—and supports the idea that women and men are equally capable of being good leaders. In both experimental and survey-based research, the public appears to see women and men as more alike than different on several trait and policy dimensions. Deborah Jordan Brooks (2013) finds that experimental subjects evaluate women and men equally with regard to honesty, compassion, leadership, and their ability to handle a range of policy areas. Lawless and Hayes (2013) find that survey respondents in 2010 saw no significant differences between women and men candidates on competence, integrity, trustworthiness, or leadership. Fridkin and Kenney (2009) examine voter evaluations of incumbent U.S. senators and find that respondents evaluated women senators higher than men on every one of the traits and policy issues they consider. While some readers might suggest that people are often providing socially desirable answers to questions about women's and men's character traits in an effort to appear egalitarian, one can counter with the suggestion that stereotype diminution may be real. Voters today have lived in a world in which the roles and opportunities for women are less in line with traditional gender stereotypes than ever before. The attitudes they hold and express may be reflecting that reality.

One final way to think about the limitation of stereotypes for understanding how people react to women candidates is to consider whether we are examining the correct stereotypes. Indeed, several recent works raise concerns that general stereotypes about women are not necessarily applicable to women candidates and officeholders, or even more elite women, regardless of field. First, Alice Eagly and Wendy Wood (1982) demonstrate that people have diminished stereotyped expectations of higher-status women, as opposed to lower-status women. In evaluating others, people are much less likely to employ gender stereotypes as the status of the person they are evaluating rises. Too, Leonie Huddy and Nayda Terkildsen (1993b) find that hypothetical women and men candidates are perceived in accordance with how they are described, whether in stereotypic or nonstereotypic terms. Candidates described as being tough and providing strong leadership were perceived that way, regardless of their being women or men. Other work finds that stereotypes of women politicians are distinct from stereotypes of women in general and that we err when we conflate the two. In examining the stereotypes people hold about women politicians, Monica Schneider and Angela Bos (2014) conclude that "woman" is not the stereotype image that people employ when they evaluate women candidates. Instead, they argue, people see women candidates as a subset of the group "politician," not as a subset of "women." It is not an unreasonable stretch to assume that people may well see women candidates as relatively high-status individuals and may not apply general stereotypes of women to this particular group of women. If this is the case, we might do better by focusing on stereotypes about leadership or about politicians to understand voter reaction to women candidates, as opposed to gender stereotypes about women and men.

Political and Electoral Influences

As the preceding discussion demonstrates, gender stereotypes may have limited utility in shaping evaluations of women candidates in contemporary politics because of changes among women candidates and limitations of the stereotypes scholars employ. But, more than any of those things, we should not necessarily expect gender stereotypes to play a significant role in candidate evaluation and vote choice because of the primacy of other more central political and electoral influences, such as political party, incumbency, campaign spending, or electoral competitiveness. In the context of elections, voters know more about candidates than simply their sex, and a voluminous body of research points out the importance of party and incumbency in shaping candidate evaluation and vote choice (Conover and Feldman 1989; Downs 1957; Lau and Redlawsk 2001; Popkin 1993; Rahn 1993). The primacy of political party as an influence on voter attitudes and behavior is well documented, and party, in itself, provides voters with significant information about a candidate's ideas and beliefs. Expecting abstract gender stereotypes to be as useful in shaping voter behaviors is probably not realistic. Indeed, in the push and pull among these forces and voters' attitudes toward candidate characteristics, recent work suggests that party and incumbency continue to exert a stronger influence than do gender cues (Dolan 2010; Hayes 2005, 2011; Huddy and Capelos 2002; Philpot and Walton 2007).

Political party can also exert an influence on candidate evaluations and vote choice through partisan stereotypes. As Wendy Rahn (1993) suggests, partisan stereotypes exert considerable influence on the way that people process information about candidates and can have a considerable impact on decision making. While partisan stereotypes were initially thought to primarily structure the way people think about policy areas, more recent work suggests that candidate traits are also subject to evaluation through the lens of party (Hayes 2005; Petrocik 1996). In examining the ways in which people think about women and men candidates, we need to consider whether party stereotypes have an impact. This is particularly important in light of the work that demonstrates how the political parties in the United States have become increasingly gendered. In the past 30 years or so, parties in the United States have become increasingly polarized around most issues, but particularly around a set of gender-related issues, such as abortion, the Equal Rights Amendment, and women's work and family roles (Sanbonmatsu 2002b; Wolbrecht 2000). The Democratic Party has positioned itself to favor greater equality on these women's issues, while Republicans have tended to hold more traditional gender role positions. This gendering on policy issues has extended to traits, with people perceiving Democrats to have more traditionally feminine traits and Republicans to hold more masculine traits (Hayes 2011; Winter 2010). As a result, voter ideas about masculinity and femininity have become tied up with evaluations of the two parties and their candidates. If this is the case, we might see candidate evaluations depend not only on the sex of the candidate but on the party. Work on this possibility has been somewhat mixed. Most scholars find that party stereotypes overwhelm gender stereotypes, but other work demonstrates that gender stereotypes can still shape reactions to partisans (Hayes 2011; Huddy and Capelos 2002; King and Matland 2003; Sanbonmatsu and Dolan 2009).

One of the limitations in the study of the impact of gender stereotypes is that scholars do not often consider their effect relative to any of the factors that we know to be key in elections, leaving us with an incomplete sense of where gender stereotypes fit into the decision calculus voters make. Given that stereotypes are used primarily when people have little information to draw upon, we know less about whether and how stereotypes are employed when voters do know other things about candidates. Indeed, if we assume that people employ stereotypes in the absence of information, we need to acknowledge that campaigns provide exactly the kind of information about candidates that voters can use in place of stereotypes. Campaign activities, speeches, press coverage, advertisements, and the like allow candidates to differentiate themselves and present themselves as individuals, not simply group members. Assuming a role for stereotypes also suggests that they somehow disturb the usual dynamics of elections when women are present. Indeed, research that examines voting patterns in elections that involve women candidates finds that political party and incumbency are the primary influences on vote choice, just as they are in elections without women candidates (Dolan 2004). In the contemporary era of increased party polarization in politics at both the elite and mass levels, there is little reason to expect that the importance of party in an election would be dependent on the sex of the candidates (Bartels 2000; Fiorina, Abrams, and Pope 2006; Murakami 2008). In a political system in which incumbent candidates have significant resources and electoral advantages, we should expect that these advantages accrue to women and men candidates (Jacobson 2012). Given that there is very little research that compares the impact of gender stereotypes with the impact of more traditional political influences, we should limit our conclusions about the importance of stereotypes until we know more.

METHODOLOGICAL AND DATA LIMITATIONS

The preceding discussion identifies several reasons that suggest the political impact of gender stereotypes might be limited. Currently, much of the work on stereotypes takes the position that stereotypes are likely to matter to the political fortunes of women candidates. However, I argue that these conclusions result, in part, because existing studies share common data limitations. Research on the relationship between gender stereotypes and women candidates tends to rely almost exclusively on hypothetical candidates and election situations. These works employ experiments or survey questions about fictional women candidates (Adams 1975; Brooks 2013; Brown et al. 1993; Eckstrand and Eckert 1981; Fox and Smith 1998; Fridkin, Kenney, and Woodall 2009; Huddy and Terkildsen 1993a, 1993b; King and Matland 2003; Lawless 2004; Leeper 1991; McDermott 1998; Rosenthal 1995; Rosenwasser and Dean 1989; Sanbonmatsu 2002a; Sapiro 1981/1982). Beginning in the 1970s, one of the most common ways of determining the impact of political gender stereotypes has been to conduct experiments in which subjects read information about fictitious political candidates (speeches, campaign brochures, biographies, news stories, campaign ads) and answered questions about their reactions to the candidates (Brooks 2013; Ditonto, Hamilton, and Redlawsk 2013; Fox and Smith 1998; Fridkin et al. 2009; Gordon et al. 2003; Huddy and Capelos 2002; Huddy and Terkildsen 1993a, 1993b; King and Matland 2003; Leeper 1991; Sapiro 1981/1982; Smith et al. 2007). Another common approach, survey-based research, usually questions respondents about their attitudes toward candidates in hypothetical election situations, such as "in elections in which a woman runs against a man" (Brown et al. 1993; Dolan 1997, 2010; Dolan and Sanbonmatsu 2009; Lawless 2004; Sanbonmatsu 2002a; Sanbonmatsu and Dolan 2009).

Experiments can be an important tool for isolating the impact of some variable, say, the sex of a candidate, and determining the influence of that variable on political attitudes and behaviors. At the same time, our inability to generalize experimental findings to the broader world of voter behavior in which information about candidate sex competes with volumes of campaign-generated information is a significant limitation. Surveys about hypothetical candidates and election scenarios were useful as a way of allowing researchers to gather information about something that was a relative novelty—an election involving a woman candidate. However, both of these research designs rely on hypothetical candidates and artificial decision-making scenarios in which subjects have very little information on which to base their reactions. Most experimental examinations of the impact of gender stereotypes vary the sex of the candidate but do not provide any other information that might cue voter decisions (King and Matland 2003). While candidates in experiments can be made equivalent except for their sex, this is not true in the real world, where candidates are the sum total of many different factors—their political party, their incumbency status, their prior experience, the office they seek. And non-experimental studies, usually mass-based surveys, rarely focus on actual elections, instead relying on hypothetical candidates and generic election matchups, leaving us to infer from these findings about how attitudes toward hypothetical candidates might work to shape attitudes about specific candidates. As a result, these approaches do not allow us to examine whether and how stereotypes matter to candidate evaluations and vote choice in the real world, alongside multiple streams of information that might be available to voters. For this reason, they are limited in what they can tell us about the true impact of stereotypes on election outcomes.

In the absence of other information, candidate sex can appear to be an important influence on voters. But in the real world, candidate sex is unlikely to be the only information available to voters. When we examine research on the impact of additional information, we see that candidate sex becomes less important. For example, a meta-analysis of experimental work on gender stereotypes found that providing more information about candidates beyond their sex in hypotheticals drove down the impact of sex on the evaluations subjects made (Banducci, Everitt, and Gidengil 2002). In examining support for black women candidates, Tasha Philpot and Hanes Walton (2007) conducted experiments and found that black women voters are the most likely to support these candidates. However, when they conducted analysis of voting patterns in actual U.S. House elections in which black women candidates ran, they found no relationship between respondent sex and race and support for black women candidates. In the experiment, respondents only had the sex and race of hypothetical candidates to guide their decision making. In real elections for the House, voters had substantially more information about the candidates in their races, leading to a different set of relationships between voters and candidates.

While the literature on candidate sex and voter stereotypes has provided us a rich sense of how voters might evaluate women candidates, we have to acknowledge that these studies are incomplete for helping us understand the dynamics involved in voting for women candidates in real-world elections. In earlier times, the number of women candidates was small enough to require reliance on experimental designs and hypothetical survey situations. However, the steady increase in the number of women running has provided us with large numbers of voters who have taken part in elections with women candidates. These voters have made their evaluations and vote choice decisions, choosing between real candidates in real election situations. Before we can conclude that gender stereotypes are an important influence on evaluating and voting for (or against) women candidates, we need to examine these situations. We need data that allow us to observe the gendered attitudes that people hold, their attitudes and behaviors toward candidates in real elections, and additional information about candidates and electoral situations beyond the sex of the candidates.

NEW DATA

In reviewing the state of our knowledge on the role of stereotypes and their impact on women candidates, two things are clear—it may be the case that gender stereotypes are less relevant to voter evaluations of women candidates than we believe and that data limitations hamper our ability to examine whether and how voters employ gender stereotypes to shape their attitudes and behaviors toward women candidates. In an effort to improve the sources of data and shift the examination to the relationships between real voters and candidates, I conducted a two-wave panel study of a nationally representative sample of U.S. adults during the 2010 elections. The sample of 3,150 respondents was drawn from 29 states and stratified to include voters who experienced either single-sex or mixed-sex races for U.S. House, U.S. Senate, and governor. The survey was funded by the National Science Foundation and conducted in an online environment by Knowledge Networks through its KnowledgePanel. Relying on a sampling frame that includes the entire U.S. telephone population, Knowledge Networks uses random-digit dialing and probability sampling techniques to draw samples that are representative of the U.S. population. It provides, at no charge, laptops and free monthly Internet service to all sample respondents who do not already have these services, thereby overcoming the potential problem of samples biased against individuals without access to the Internet. As a result of this design, I have been able to examine real voters faced with real candidates in a way that includes a diversity of offices, candidates, and election contexts.

The primary goals of the survey were to examine the gender stereotypes that voters hold and determine whether these stereotypes could be linked to the candidate evaluation and vote choice decisions voters made in the elections in which they took part. This required gathering data on two different sets of items: gender stereotypes, which are largely abstract attitudes, and candidate evaluations and vote choice, which are specific attitudes and behaviors focused on actual candidates. To accomplish this, the first wave of the panel survey was carried out in September 2010 and was designed to probe respondents' general attitudes about the place of women in American politics, their abstract political gender stereotypes, their opinions on general political issues and actors, and information about their political participation. The second wave of the survey, conducted in October and November, shifted the focus from the abstract to the specific by gathering respondent reactions and behaviors toward the specific candidates they experienced in their elections. Asking questions about abstract stereotypes in the first wave and the specific candidate evaluations in the second allows me to insulate these two important sets of measures from each other. In all, the 3,150 respondents experienced more than 650 candidates for races for U.S. House (in 29 states), U.S. Senate (in 22 states), and governor (in 21 states). Full information on the candidates and races represented in the data set is provided in appendix A.

The panel study is one of the strengths of this project and offers a significant improvement over the designs usually employed to study stereotypes. As indicated earlier, the majority of scholarly examinations of gender stereotypes involve the use of experimental treatments in which subjects are offered information about a hypothetical woman or man candidate and asked to evaluate that candidate. Any differences between evaluations of the woman and man are assumed to be a function of candidate sex. Very often, the amount of information provided about a candidate is limited and does not mimic the complexity of real-world election environments, meaning that researchers cannot control for influences beyond candidate sex. Experimental examinations of stereotypes also commonly rely on non-representative samples of subjects, often college students or other easily attainable groups (Ditonto et al. 2013; Fox and Smith 1998; Huddy and Terkildsen 1993a, 1993b; Leeper 1991; Sapiro 1981/1982; Schneider and Bos 2013). And despite the fact that experimental results are not directly generalizable to the real world, many experimental studies conclude by talking about the consequences of their findings for real candidates and voters. These features of experiments combine to provide insight into people's abstract responses to hypothetical candidates and situations but not into how people evaluate real candidates in actual elections.

The other primary source of data typically used to study these questions about women candidates comes from public opinion polls or cross-sectional surveys such as the American National Election Studies or the Cooperative Congressional Election Study. Cross-sectional designs gather a snapshot of respondent views at one point in time but fail to allow for any examination of over-time attitudes and behaviors. And perhaps most centrally, while most public opinion polls and cross-sectional election surveys draw upon representative samples, they are not often concerned with examining gender stereotypes and so do not include appropriate measures of these attitudes. As a result of this intentional panel design, I have data from a nationally representative sample and survey responses from the same respondents at two different points in the campaign cycle, fully two months apart, on a wide range of gendered attitudes and stereotypes. This allows me to measure the abstract gender stereotypes respondents may hold separately from the candidate evaluations they make, thereby greatly reducing the possibility that responses to the abstract stereotype questions colored candidate evaluations. It also allows me to examine a range of influences on attitudes and behaviors and to control for those things known to affect evaluations and voting. The two months between waves also allowed people time to experience the full campaign without being long enough to fatigue respondents between surveys.

THE 2010 ELECTIONS

One of the important reasons to adopt the strategy of examining voters who experienced elections with women candidates is that we can—there are now enough women candidates running regularly to allow for this sort of examination. In each election year since 1992, there have been at least 100 women candidates for the House of Representatives and an average of 10 women candidates for U.S. Senate and six for governor across the country. As a result, political scientists have had increased opportunities to examine issues facing women candidates in the context of real elections, particularly over the last couple of election cycles, by surveying voters who have experienced elections with women candidates or who are represented by women elected officials (Dolan 2004; Fridkin and Kenney 2009; Hayes 2011; Lawless and Hayes 2013). The elections of 2010 provided a particularly good opportunity to investigate the impact of gender stereotypes on the fortunes of women candidates for several reasons. First, there was no presidential election to overwhelm voters and compete for their attention. Second, 2010 offers researchers the first election cycle in which to examine gender stereotypes after the historic candidacies of Hillary Clinton and Sarah Palin. Beyond this, the midterm elections that year also were more competitive than many in recent memory, particularly for Congress (Cook 2010). Too, the number and variety of women candidates in that year allowed for more partisan diversity among women candidates than is often the case in U.S. elections, with approximately 40 percent of the women candidates for Congress and governor running as Republicans.

Whether a result of the historic candidacies of Hillary Clinton and Sarah Palin or the speakership of Nancy Pelosi, or spurred on by the populist themes of the Tea Party and a general anti-incumbent mood, 2010 saw a historically high number of women candidates run for Congress and governorships around the country. A record-setting 262 women ran in primaries for the U.S. House. While there was significant, and surprising, parity in the political parties of these candidates—134 women Democrats and 128 women Republicans—Republican women were less successful in winning their primaries than were Democratic women. While 68 percent of the Democratic women (91 candidates) survived to run in the general election, only 37 percent of the Republican women (47 candidates) did. This resulted in a return to a more typical pattern of partisanship among women candidates in the United States, where about 65 percent of women who run for office do so as Democrats (CAWP 2010).

Record numbers of women ran for the U.S. Senate. Because of a confluence of circumstances, many of these women candidates gained a good level of national visibility and contributed to a remarkably diverse pool of candidates. Thirty-six women (19D, 17R) filed for U.S. Senate seats, with 15 (9D, 6R) winning their primaries. Among these 15 women were nine candidates running as challengers or for open seats. Two of the women Senate candidates were high-level corporate executives—Linda McMahon, president and CEO of World Wrestling Entertainment, who ran in Connecticut, and Carly Fiorina, former CEO of Hewlett-Packard, who ran against incumbent Barbara Boxer in California, creating a high-visibility Senate race between two women candidates. Other visible women candidates for the Senate included Tea Party–backed Christine O'Donnell (R), who defeated Congressman (and former governor) Mike Castle in the Republican primary in Delaware, and Sharron Angle (R), who took on Senate Majority Leader Harry Reid (D) in Nevada.

An equally impressive group of women sought to serve as governors in 2010. A total of 26 women (12D, 14R) ran in primaries, with a record-tying 10 (5D, 5R) winning to run in general elections. Among the 10 were two lieutenant governors (Jari Askins of Oklahoma and Diane Denish of New Mexico), a U.S. district attorney (Susana Martinez of New Mexico), a member of the U.S. House of Representatives (Mary Fallin of Oklahoma), and the chief financial officer of Florida (Alex Sink). Another corporate executive, eBay founder Meg Whitman, ran for governor of California. Two states had governor races contested by two women candidates. Susana Martinez (R) defeated Diane Denish (D) in New Mexico, while Mary Fallon (R) defeated Jari Askins (D) in Oklahoma. Martinez and Fallon became the first woman governors of their states. Martinez and Nikki Haley (R) of South Carolina became the first women of color to serve as governors in the United States.

LEVEL/TYPE OF OFFICE, PARTY, AND MEN

The data from the survey were collected to facilitate three different, but equally important, comparisons drawn from the literature on gender stereotypes and support for women candidates. First, surveying people who experienced races for the U.S. House, the U.S. Senate, and governor allows us to examine whether people use different considerations when evaluating and choosing candidates for different levels and types of office. Previous research on gender stereotypes and support for women candidates suggests that the level and type of office women seek may interact with stereotypes to shape women's opportunities, with voters' desire for male characteristics and competencies increasing as the level of office candidates seek increases from local to national (Huddy and Terkildsen 1993a). For example, stereotyped concerns about foreign policy can work against a woman seeking the presidency but may have no impact on a woman seeking election to county government (Burrell 2008; Dolan 1997; Huddy and Terkildsen 1993a). At the same time, past work suggests that people may have different policy and personality expectations for women who seek executive versus legislative office (Huddy and Terkildsen 1993a). Executive offices such as president, governor, and mayor are more clearly stereotyped with regard to their responsibilities (Fox and Oxley 2003) and clearly place officeholders in a position of single authority as compared with legislative office. Another important reason to examine different levels and types of office relates to the impact of electoral context on the information available to voters. The different levels and types of offices included here provide different information contexts in which we can examine the relative importance of information on the use of stereotypes in forming evaluations. Statewide races like governor or U.S. Senate provide more information and opportunities for voters to learn about candidates than more "local" elections like U.S. House. Also, races for Senate and governor allow us to control for constituency influences since they are statewide elections. On several dimensions, it is important to compare candidates for a range of offices, and considering races for House, Senate, and governor provides us with significant contextual diversity.

Another important comparison to make with these data is among women. Existing research on gender stereotypes provides fairly consistent evidence that the impact of stereotypes varies with the party of the woman candidate. For example, gender stereotypes tend to work to the advantage of Democratic women more often than Republican women (Sanbonmatsu and Dolan 2009), Republican women candidates tend to have a harder time winning party primaries (Lawless and Pearson 2008), and ideological stereotypes can hurt Republican women candidates with Republican voters but increase their appeal to Democrats and Independents (King and Matland 2003). At the same time, Jeffrey Koch (2002) finds that party and gender stereotypes lead people to evaluate Democratic women as more ideologically extreme than Republican women, which could result in fewer votes as people perceive Democratic women as too far from the mainstream. Regardless of whether there is a consistent benefit or price associated with these evaluations, it is clear that political party stereotypes interact with gender stereotypes to lead people to evaluate Republican and Democratic women candidates differently. This is most likely the result of a political reality in the United States in which stereotypes of women and stereotypes of Democrats overlap to a considerable degree. Both women and Democrats represent groups that people expect to exhibit a desire for consensus, compassion for the less fortunate, and a particular competence in dealing with policy areas such as education, health care, and welfare. Republican women, on the other hand, present voters with a contrast of gender and party stereotypes. Republicans are generally stereotyped as being tough and decisive and most effective on economic and international issues, none of which conform to traditional female stereotypes. The mixed message sent by the sex and party identities of Republican women can make the task of evaluating these women more difficult for voters. As a result, we need to understand more fully whether and how party stereotypes interact with candidate sex to shape reactions to women candidates.

Finally, to fully understand whether gender stereotypes are relevant to evaluations and vote choice in real-world elections, we have to compare the dynamics in races in which women ran against men and those in which two men ran. The literature on the impact of gender stereotypes on candidate success identifies the stereotypes people hold about men but does not generally consider whether they are related to voting for male candidates. By this I mean that most studies of political gender stereotypes examine their impact on women candidates when they are paired with male opponents, but there is no work on whether stereotypes are present or whether candidates are helped or hurt by these attitudes in races without women. Examining male-only races will allow us to see whether any impact for stereotypes is tied to the presence of women candidates or whether they influence male candidates too.

KEY PARTS OF THE PUZZLE

Overcoming existing data limitations means gathering data that connect two sets of measures that do not often exist together in current research—voter gender stereotypes and voter evaluations of and behaviors toward women candidates in real-world elections. Experimental research offers extensive measures of stereotypes but no information about real candidates or other important political variables beyond candidate sex. Survey-based research includes either stereotype measures and hypothetical candidates/ scenarios or questions about actual candidates that are devoid of measures of gender stereotypes. With few recent exceptions (Fridkin and Kenney 2009; Hayes 2011; Lawless and Hayes 2013), most work on stereotypes falls into one category or another. This project was specifically designed to overcome these limitations by including measures of gender stereotypes in the context of real elections.

Measuring gender stereotypes and reactions to women candidates can be a complex undertaking because of a concern that people will hide their true beliefs behind socially acceptable responses of egalitarianism. An often-cited example of this concern involves the 95 percent of Americans who report that they would vote for a woman candidate of their party for president (Jones 2012), which some observers feel is too high to reflect reality.[1] Indeed, research suggests that issues around gender can influence survey responses. Huddy and her colleagues (1997) find that people often report higher levels of support for women's issues in opinion surveys when they are interviewed by a woman. Recently, Matthew Streb and his colleagues (2007) employed a list experiment to raise concerns that high levels of support for a woman candidate for president might be exaggerated. At the same time, two recent studies of polling results from elections with actual women candidates find no evidence that polling overexaggerates support for women candidates for governor or U.S. Senate and that some surveys may actually underreport support for women (Hopkins 2009;

Stout and Kline 2011), particularly among those who live in areas of the country where traditional gender values are the norm. These works should suggest that there is no clear evidence that social pressure always works to overestimate support for women and women's issues.

Because of concerns about social desirability, there is debate in the literature about the best way to extract true reactions to gender issues and women candidates. Indeed, some scholars argue that experiments are a superior way to analyze stereotypes because they can be tapped more surreptitiously (Brooks 2013). However, given the way most experimental examinations of gender stereotypes and candidates are conducted, there is no clear reason to believe that subjects would be any more likely to be immune to pressure to hide biased reactions to a woman candidate than those responding to a survey. An experimental subject presented with the task of evaluating a speech or the qualifications of a woman candidate is engaging in the same general exercise as a survey respondent and may have the same sort of concerns that she or he will be judged by the experimenter. Since experiments are so limited in what they can tell us about real voters and their interactions with real candidates, we can successfully employ survey research and draw on current research on surveying sensitive topics such as drug use, marital infidelity, and sexual practices that demonstrates that offering more anonymity leads to more truthful responses from people (Schaeffer and Presser 2003; Tourangeau and Smith 1996). The data for this survey were collected in a Web TV environment, which allowed respondents the greatest level of anonymity by eliminating interaction with an interviewer. The respondent answered the questions alone in his or her own home. Recent research comparing Internet surveys with other methods of collecting survey data demonstrates clearly that there are lower levels of socially desirable answers from populations who are surveyed using this format (Dennis and Li 2007; Heerwegh 2009; Kreuter, Presser, and Tourangeau 2008).

Measures of Abstract Stereotypes and Specific Evaluations

If we are to examine whether and how stereotypes influence voter attitudes and behaviors toward women candidates, we need measures that tap the abstract gender stereotypes that have long been a part of the literature, as well as measures that get at more specific, real-world evaluations of individual candidates. Drawing on many of the trait and issue competence items used in the experimental literature on political gender stereotypes (Burrell 2008; Fridkin et al. 2009; Huddy and Terkildsen 1993b; Koch 1997; Lawless 2004; Sanbonmatsu 2002a), I created measures of what

I call *abstract gender stereotypes* and *specific candidate evaluations*. In the first wave of the survey, respondents were asked whether they thought *"women or men who run for political office"* were more likely to possess a particular trait or were better able to handle a particular policy area. The traits and issue areas included are those that have been identified by the literature as male or female in their stereotypic orientation (Fridkin et al. 2009; Gordon and Miller 2005; Sanbonmatsu and Dolan 2009). Male policy stereotypes measured here are crime, the economy, national security, immigration, and the deficit. Female policy stereotypes are education, child care, health care, and abortion. Stereotypical male trait measures include intelligence, decisiveness, leadership, and experience. Female trait questions tap beliefs about candidates' honesty, compassion, ability to build consensus, and ability to change government. Responses to these questions represent *abstract gender stereotypes* (see appendix D for all survey items).

The second wave of the survey was designed to elicit respondent evaluations of the traits and policy abilities of the individual candidates in the House, Senate, or governor's race in which they voted. Using the same trait and policy items described above, this set of questions asked respondents to say whether they thought that *one of the candidates in their race for House/Senate/governor* was more likely to possess a particular trait or was better able to deal with a particular policy area than the other candidate. The results of these questions stand as evaluations that voters made about the traits and abilities of the specific candidates they experienced in their races. I refer to these as *specific candidate evaluations*.

Gendered Attitudes

Beyond a focus on gender stereotypes, this project includes an examination of a series of attitudes that respondents have about women candidates and the appropriate place for women in our political and governmental system. As the number of women candidates increases and scholars attempt to understand how voters react to more women in the system, we have been hampered by a fairly piecemeal approach to these issues. To date, surveys that examine public opinion on these issues have generally included a very limited number of topics, focusing perhaps on attitudes toward having more women in office (Simmons 2001) or whether voters prefer women or men candidates (Sanbonmatsu 2003). But there are few studies that try to tap attitudes toward a range of issues surrounding women in politics. This project expands our understanding by asking respondents for their feelings and beliefs on a number of items. These attitudes address three different elements of reactions to women in the political system. The first set of questions examines general levels of support for the idea of women in office in the United States. One question asks respondents whether they think there *should be more or fewer women in office or if the current number is about right*. Another question allows respondents to be more specific in articulating support for women's presence in government by asking each to identify the *percentage of women and men in the best government the United States could have*. Here respondents could offer a number from zero to 100 for women and men, laying out what their ideal government looks like—majority-male, majority-female, or perhaps something close to parity between women and men. A second set of questions asks about attitudes toward representation. The first takes a cue from Sanbonmatsu's (2003) work on baseline gender preference for candidates by asking respondents *whether, in a race between equally qualified candidates, they would be more inclined to vote for a woman or a man*. Extending concerns about representation, I asked respondents whether they believe it is *important to be represented in office by someone of the same sex*. All of these questions are included to allow us to think more about whether and when people might take the sex of a candidate into account in making vote choice decisions. Depending on whether people think there should be more or fewer women in office or whether they want to be represented by a person who looks like them, they might make conscious choices to seek representatives of one sex or the other. The final set of gender questions in the survey attempt to tap how much people know about women in the contemporary political system. Wanting more or fewer women or having a sense of the appropriate level of women's representation may depend on how much respondents know about the present reality of women in office. To determine how much people know, I asked three questions: *How many women are on the U.S. Supreme Court? What percentage of the U.S. Congress is female?* and *Are women in Congress more likely to be Democrats or Republicans?*

Traditional Influences on Politics

One of the primary goals of this project is to examine the impact of gender stereotypes on the fortunes of women candidates relative to other, more primary, influences on candidate evaluation and vote choice. The measures included here focus on two broad sets of influences: respondent characteristics and campaign context variables. Here we consider the impact of respondent *sex, education, race, age, party identification*, and *political ideology*. Primary among the contextual influences are *the incumbency status of candidates, campaign spending levels*, and *the competitiveness of the election.* The inclusion of these variables will allow for a test of the relative strength of gendered attitudes and the more traditional influences on candidate evaluations and vote choice.

Candidate Quality and Campaigns

While the primary focus of this project is on voter gender stereotypes and their potential impact on the success of women candidates, we must acknowledge that gendered considerations can have an impact at other points in the process of a woman's candidacy. The data in this project allow me to examine two other places where candidate sex and gender stereotypes can influence elections. First, we can test whether the women and men candidates who took part in the elections in this sample are of similar professional and political quality. To this end, I collected information on the *education, political experience, campaign spending*, and *vote totals* of each candidate in the data set. The second consideration involves the potential impact of gender stereotypes in campaigns that result from decisions candidates make about how to present themselves to the public. Women candidates can make strategic choices about whether to campaign in line with stereotypes by focusing on "female" issues, or they can try to counter stereotypes by including more "male" issues in their presentations. To examine whether the candidates in this sample campaigned in stereotyped ways, I collected all of the *television advertisements* run by the candidates and all of their *campaign websites*.

HYPOTHESES

The primary hypothesis that motivates this study is that gender stereotypes will have less influence on attitudes and behaviors toward women candidates than existing research would suggest. Several specific hypotheses to be tested in subsequent chapters focus on various elements of the relationship between women candidates and voters:

H_1: Abstract gender stereotypes will be more likely to be related to abstract attitudes about women in politics than they will be related to vote choice.
H_2: Abstract gender stereotypes will be less likely to shape candidate evaluations and vote choice than will traditional political influences such as political party and incumbency.

H$_3$: Abstract gender stereotypes will be more likely to influence attitudes and behaviors toward Democratic women than Republican women.

H$_4$: Abstract gender stereotypes will be more likely to influence attitudes and behaviors in House races than in Senate or governor races.

H$_5$: Abstract gender stereotypes will be visible in attitudes and vote choice in male-only races, particularly for Democratic male candidates.

H$_6$: Women and men candidates in the sample will be more similar than different in their professional and political experiences and in the issues they present in their media campaigns.

CONCLUSION

Throughout our nation's history, ideas about appropriate roles for women have shaped the ways in which women participate as political candidates and officeholders. Even today, anecdotal evidence suggests that gender-stereotyped expectations about women operate in elections and in the minds of voters. However, important elements of political and social life may work to limit the impact that gender stereotypes have on the fortunes of women who seek political office. By learning more about how voters think about real women candidates and examining whether abstract attitudes translate into actual behavior in real elections, we can better understand how much of the reality of women candidates is shaped by reactions to their sex. We turn first to an analysis of gender stereotypes and attitudes toward women in politics and the impact these attitudes can have on support for women candidates.

CHAPTER 3

Attitudes, Stereotypes, and Support for Women Candidates

Let's get the job done. I am willing to negotiate. I am willing to compromise.
Barbara Mikulski, U.S. Senator (D-MD)

We work well together and we look for common ground.
Amy Klobuchar, U.S. Senator (D-MN)

One of the things we do a bit better is listen.
Heidi Heitkamp, U.S. Senator (D-ND)

We need to be pragmatic. This is a solution that is good for the country.
Lisa Murkowski, U.S. Senator (R-AK)

I am very proud that these women are stepping forward. Imagine what they could do if there were 50 of them.

John McCain, U.S. Senator (R-AZ)

In October 2013, the Republicans and Democrats in Congress failed to reach a deal to extend a spending bill that would have funded many of the activities of the federal government. As a result, large parts of the government were shut down for a 16-day period. Hundreds of thousands of employees were furloughed, parks and museums were closed, and most nonessential functions were suspended. After more than two weeks of impasse, movement toward a resolution began in the Senate, where Senator Susan Collins (R-ME) took to the Senate floor to call on her colleagues to rise above partisanship and work together to reopen the government. Several of the other women senators joined her effort and, over the course of a week, helped Collins pull together a bipartisan group that crafted a compromise bill to end the stalemate. In the immediate aftermath, the women of the Senate received significant media attention for their role in bringing the shutdown to an end. When asked how they were able to accomplish what others had failed to do, these women offered the perspectives in the quotes that open this chapter. They were willing to compromise; they wanted to put the good of the country before partisan victories; they listened. They described a way of doing business that has come to be thought of as a feminine style of leadership. Contrasted with the more traditionally male politics of confrontation and conflict, this more feminine way of doing business was clearly viewed by many as more effective and successful (Khimm and Taylor 2013; Newton-Small 2013; Weisman and Steinhauer 2013). In the immediate aftermath of the reopening of the government, several media outlets produced stories focusing on the women senators and their successful efforts to broker a bipartisan accord. They were consistently praised in these articles, and their differences from their male colleagues were highlighted. Indeed, as the headline of a story in the *National Journal* asked, "Do Women Make Better Senators than Men?" (Lawrence 2013). While this is, of course, a difficult question to answer, Senator John McCain gave voice to the thoughts of many when he wondered what could be achieved with more women in the chamber. Besides helping to reopen the government, Collins and her women colleagues had done enormous good for the reputation of women leaders, something that marks a significant shift in the historical public thinking about women in political office.

Indeed, for much of our political history, one of the major impediments to women's participation as candidates and officeholders was the lack of support for that participation among the general public. In thinking about the evolution of acceptance of a political role for women, we know that social and cultural attitudes about the appropriate spheres of life for women and men limited women's opportunities. Women were understood to be best suited for home and hearth, leaving the important work of political leadership to men. Beyond the barriers raised by political parties, electoral structures, and laws that limited their candidacies (Duverger 1955), women faced hostility to the notion that they could run and serve equally with men. While there have been examples of women running for and holding office in the United States at least since the post–Civil War era, it is only in the mid–20th century that we see the beginnings of a steady, if slow, integration of women into candidacy and office-holding. This period of change is marked by shifts in public attitudes about the possibility of political leadership for women, which occurred during a time of greater social, educational, and occupational opportunities for women. While public support for women candidates is not the sole, or even primary, explanation for the contemporary integration of women into elected office, it is an important one.

The current time period would suggest that the American public is more supportive of a role for women in political life today than it has ever been. Opinion polls show clear trends away from sexist attitudes toward women and toward more egalitarian positions about women's abilities and opportunities. Figures 3.1–3.3 highlight several of these positive trends. Since the 1930s, the Gallup Organization has asked people for their reaction to the idea of a woman candidate for president. As is not surprising, very

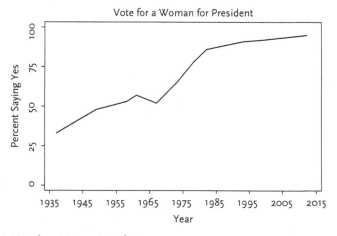

Figure 3.1: Vote for a Woman President

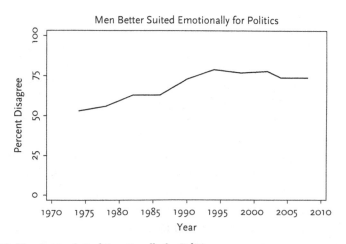

Figure 3.2: Men Better Suited Emotionally for Politics

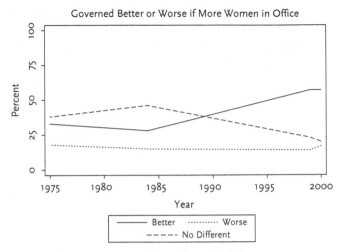

Figure 3.3: Governed Better or Worse if More Women in Office

few people in those early times were willing to entertain the idea of supporting a woman for president. Since then, however, the public has slowly and steadily become more comfortable with the idea, such that we now see overwhelming majorities of people say that they would support a woman candidate of their own party for president. This increase in support for a woman in the White House has mirrored the decline in support for the idea that women are not well suited emotionally for politics. Women's assumed greater emotionality was long thought to be one of the major factors disqualifying them from public life. However, upward of 75 percent of Americans disagree with the idea that women are less emotionally well suited for politics than men. Finally, over the past 40 years, we have evidence that people have come to value the skills and abilities that women can bring to the political system. When asking whether people think that our country would be "governed better" if there were more women in elected office, we see affirmative responses to this question rising from 33 percent in 1975 to almost 60 percent in 2000. In 2000, those who thought that more women would be a positive for government did so because they saw women as more honest, conscientious, reliable, and fiscally responsible than men (Simmons 2001).

We often assume that people must have positive attitudes toward women candidates to be able to support them at the ballot box, and we also assume that voting for women is a reflection of the presence of equalitarian views about women and men as political leaders. In fact, we have relatively little evidence that either of these is true, as we do not often have data that allow us to connect gender attitudes with vote choice in elections involving women candidates. In reality, voters may have a whole host of positive attitudes about women in politics, and these attitudes can be unrelated to their vote choice. Or people may have neutral, or even negative, attitudes about women in politics but vote for a woman candidate for other important reasons. Indeed, the concern about sexist attitudes in the public is motivated, in part, by a concern that people will vote in accordance with these attitudes, to the possible detriment of women candidates.

One of the goals of this project is to examine a range of public attitudes about women candidates to see whether those attitudes are (1) supportive or not and (2) related to voting for women. This investigation is important for two reasons. First, we need to continue to understand what people think about women's integration into political life so that we identify the evolution of this thinking over time. Second, we need to know more about the role that attitudes play in the political actions that people take. At an intuitive level, it would make sense that people's attitudes about the representation of women in government would be tied to their behaviors in mixed-sex races (Dolan and Sanbonmatsu 2009; Paolino 1995). Kira Sanbonmatsu (2003) suggests that people who desire greater gender balance in government may be motivated to give money to women candidates and turn out and vote for these women when given the opportunity. Phil Paolino (1995) finds evidence in the 1992 Senate elections that women voters who saw the underrepresentation of women in Congress as a problem were more likely to vote for women candidates for the Senate. However, beyond these few studies, we have relatively little research that connects attitudes with vote choice.

Although past research has not been able to connect voters' gender attitudes about women in politics to their behaviors in elections, the data presented here give us a first opportunity to examine whether this is the case. The survey conducted for this project asked respondents several questions aimed at understanding people's beliefs about women and their suitability for elected office. These questions measure concerns about the appropriate level of women's representation in office, whether the sex of a candidate or officeholder is an important consideration, and whether or not people hold stereotyped views of women and men candidates. The goals of this chapter are to demonstrate how voters feel about women in political life and determine whether these attitudes and stereotypes are relevant to the political decision voters make. This analysis unfolds in several stages. First I provide a look at the attitudes respondents hold toward women in the political world and determine whether these attitudes are supportive of women or not. In this context, I examine the kinds of voters who are most positive about a political role for women and those who are less so. The next step in the analysis offers a first look at the political impact of gender stereotypes. I argue that previous work sees an important impact for stereotypes, in part, because of the reliance in this work on abstract election scenarios with hypothetical candidates. In attempting to provide an alternative, I compare the impact of gender stereotypes on abstract attitudes about women in politics with an analysis of the influence of stereotypes on a concrete political decision—vote choice in elections in which women candidates run against men. Finally, I test the proposition that positive attitudes about women in politics are an important element of the success of women candidates. Here I examine the relationship between a series of gendered attitudes and people's willingness to vote for a woman candidate in real elections. Each of these analyses addresses a piece of the puzzle about the importance (or lack thereof) of the attitudes that people hold about women in political life.

PUBLIC ATTITUDES TOWARD WOMEN IN POLITICS

Support for Women in Office

The first set of attitudes to be examined involves getting a sense of how people feel about current and future levels of women officeholders (Table 3.1). Currently, women are dramatically underrepresented in elected office, making up 19 percent of the members of Congress, 23 percent of statewide elected officials, and 24 percent of state legislators (CAWP 2013). One question in the survey asks respondents whether they think there should be more women in "important political office such as governors and members of Congress," whether there should be fewer, or whether the current number is "just about right." Table 3.1 demonstrates that people are generally supportive of more women in elected office, with 58 percent saying that there should be more women in office, 37 percent of respondents saying that current numbers of women in office are about right, and only 6 percent saying that there should be fewer. This is in line with other public opinion surveys, which tend to find that people believe more women in government would be a good thing for our system (Dolan and Sanbonmatsu 2009; Sanbonmatsu 2003; Simmons 2001).

At the same time, that 42 percent of respondents say that the current underrepresentation of women is "just right" or even too high might be a cause for concern among those who seek more representation of women. Of course, without knowing whether respondents have an accurate sense of the level of women's underrepresentation, it is difficult to know what

Table 3.1. ATTITUDES ABOUT WOMEN IN POLITICS

Number of women in office...	All	Men	Women	
Should be more	57.85%	50.31%	64.96%	
Is about right	36.52%	42.60%	30.80%	
Should be fewer	5.62%	7.10%	4.24%	
N	2,999	1,539	1,460	

Number of women in office by percent women in Congress	Underestimate	Correct	Overestimate	N
More	61.76%	62.24%	51.90%	1,728
About right	33.46%	34.63%	40.72%	1,019
Fewer	4.78%	3.13%	7.38%	142
N	1,090	791	1,008	2,889

Percent women in government should be...	All	Men	Women	
0–25	15.89%	17.86%	14.04%	
26–40	14.19%	16.38%	12.13%	
41–49	1.91%	2.23%	1.61%	
50	60.13%	58.33%	61.81%	
50+	7.89%	5.20%	10.41%	
N	2,914	1,496	1,418	

Baseline gender preference	All	Men	Women
Man candidate	49.26%	65.05%	34.49%
Woman candidate	50.74%	34.95%	65.51%
N	2,870	1,466	1,404

Same-sex representation is...	All	Men	Women
Not at all important	47.62%	58.15%	37.72%
Only somewhat important	42.69%	35.69%	49.27%
Very important	9.69%	6.16%	13.01%
N	3,046	1,562	1,484

motivates responses to this question. It might be the case that respondents who say that they would like to see more women in office do so because they underestimate women's current levels of representation. Those who think that things are fine the way they are may take this position based on an overly rosy estimate. Indeed, this appears to be the case (Table 3.1). Among respondents in the survey who underestimate the current level of women in Congress, 62 percent say that they would like to see more women in office. Among those who overestimate women's representation, 52 percent want an increase in women in office. Those who overestimate the percentage of women in Congress are more likely to say that the current number of women in office is "just right" (41 percent) than are those who underestimate women's presence in Congress (33 percent).

While understanding whether people are comfortable with the current number of women in office is important, it does not give us a concrete sense of what people mean when they support "more" or "fewer" women in office. If women currently constitute 19 percent of the members of Congress, one respondent saying "more" might like to see women constitute 25 percent, while another might want 40 percent, and still another would like 75 percent of Congress to be female. To get a better sense of how far current reality is from what people would ideally like to see, we can draw on a question in the survey that asked respondents what the percentage of women and men officeholders would be in "the best government the United States could have." Table 3.1 demonstrates that, while respondents reflect a range of opinions on the ideal level of women's representation, a majority of the sample (60 percent) call for parity—a government that is 50 percent male and 50 percent female. This finding is consistent with other recent surveys that ask people to identify their ideal gender composition (Dolan 2010; Dolan and Sanbonmatsu 2009). About 15 percent of respondents call for women to hold between 0 and 25 percent of the elected positions in government. Given that women hold approximately 19–24 percent of elected offices, depending on the level of government, these responses signal that some people are clearly comfortable with women's minority status in government. Another 15 percent of respondents say that women should be between 26 and 40 percent of officeholders. Interestingly, only a very small group, about 8 percent of respondents, calls for a female-majority government. So, while more people appear to want greater representation of women than is currently the case (about 85 percent of respondents), more people are comfortable with male-majority government (32 percent) than female-majority government (8 percent). This may be, of course, because women are so significantly underrepresented in the United States, which makes it difficult for people to imagine a world in which women hold a majority. Or it may signal a greater level of comfort with the status quo than with a government radically different than we have ever experienced.

In thinking about attitudes toward women in political life, one of the obvious assumptions is that women voters will feel differently about these issues than will men. While people's attitudes are the product of complex political considerations and life experiences, it is not unreasonable to hypothesize that sex and gender matter to how people come to think about the appropriate place for women, particularly given women's underrepresentation. When we examine respondents' beliefs about the appropriate level of women in elected office, we see that this is indeed the case. When asked whether there should be more or fewer women in office or whether the current number is just about right (Table 3.1), women are more likely than men to say that there should be more women in office (65 percent of women versus 50 percent of men) and less likely than men to see the current status of women as "just right" (31 percent versus 43 percent). Women are also more likely than men to support gender parity in office (62 percent versus 58 percent), eight percentage points less likely to favor male-majority government, and eight percentage points more likely to favor parity and female-majority government. In terms of abstract attitudes about the appropriate gender balance in government, it is not surprising that women have an easier time voicing support for more women in office. As we will see, considering sex differences in attitudes about women's place in politics remains important throughout the analysis.

Same-Sex Representation

Two other attitudes that might influence support for women candidates involve whether and how voters think about their own representation when they are choosing candidates. One of the major themes in any discussion of the status of women in elected office is the reality that women are dramatically underrepresented at every level. People who constitute 51 percent of the population make up approximately 20 percent of elected officials, and these current levels of representation are an all-time high. One of the clear consequences of this political history is that the experience of being represented by someone who shares your sex is still a novelty for women, while men probably take this for granted. As a result of this, researchers have investigated whether women and men think much about the sex of their elected representatives and whether having representatives of the same sex matters to people. In her survey of Ohio residents, Sanbonmatsu (2002a) found that a majority of respondents expressed what she calls a "baseline gender preference," an underlying predisposition to vote for and be represented by a woman or a man. Women in her sample were more likely to express a preference at all and were more likely to prefer a woman, while men were more likely to prefer a male. Cindy Simon Rosenthal (1995) also found that women were more likely to prefer same-sex representation than were men. Given women's under-representation at all levels of office, it makes sense that women voters would be more aware of this and, perhaps, interested in changing it. Men, for whom descriptive representation is merely the historical status quo, may not consciously consider a need to work to elect candidates who look like them. To examine these issues, this project includes questions that investigate whether voters have a baseline gender preference and a desire for same-sex representation.

Among the respondents in this sample, baseline gender preferences were evenly split, with 51 percent identifying a preference for women candidates and 49 percent preferring men (Table 3.1). We also see that about 66 percent of women and 60 percent of men state a baseline gender preference for a same-sex representative and 35 percent prefer representatives of the opposite sex. Another question asked respondents whether they thought sharing the sex of their representative was an important consideration or not. Just about half of the sample, 48 percent, said that this was not at all important to them, while 43 percent said that it was somewhat important. Only 10 percent of respondents described this as very important to them. As might be expected, women and men approach these considerations differently. Women are much more likely to hold a baseline gender preference for a woman candidate than are men. About 65 percent of women prefer a woman candidate, while about 35 percent of men take that position. With regard to same-sex representation, men were much more likely than women to say that sharing the sex of a representative was not at all important, 58 percent to 38 percent. Indeed, men share the sex of their representative almost all of the time, so this is probably not something that occurs to them often. Women, on the other hand, are much less likely to experience same-sex representation, making it something that they could easily value more highly. Just about half of women, 49 percent, say that having a woman representative is somewhat important, compared with 36 percent of men. And women are more than twice as likely as men to say that same-sex representation is very important, 13 percent to 6 percent. Beyond understanding how voters feel in general about the concept of same-sex representation, these attitudes could become important motivators to action. Women who have a baseline preference for women candidates and see sharing the sex of their representative as an important thing might act on these attitudes in choosing a woman candidate in an election. An assumption that attitudes are tied to action is implicit in the literature on support for women candidates but, as we will see, is not often tested empirically.

Political knowledge is often assumed to be an important basis for the attitudes and opinions people develop about political issues (Burns, Schlozman, and Verba 2001; Delli Carpini and Keeter 1996). However, it is also the case that Americans tend not to know terribly much about political issues. An extensive literature on political knowledge demonstrates that people may be able to identify the vice president or may know which branch of government can declare laws unconstitutional but that knowledge of the American system is not particularly wide or deep (Delli Carpini and Keeter 1996). One additional reality of scholarship on political knowledge is that it tends to focus on general actors, structures, and policies, aspects of our political system that are dominated by men (Delli Carpini and Keeter 2000; Dolan 2010). As a result, we do not have much of a sense of what people know about women political leaders in the United States, nor do we know whether people are aware of how underrepresented women are in elected office. This can hamper our understanding of attitudes about women, since we do not know whether these attitudes are grounded in a realistic sense of women's place in contemporary government and politics.

In an attempt to get a sense of how much people know about the status of women in American politics, I included a series of political knowledge questions on the 2010 survey. Some of these questions focused on traditional items used to measure political knowledge, while others pertained to women in American politics. Table 3.2 reports the frequencies for these questions and demonstrates that people clearly hold more information about general aspects of politics than they do about items that are specifically relevant to women's reality. In 2010, 86 percent of respondents in this sample knew that Joe Biden was the vice president of the United States. While reassuring, this probably is not terribly difficult information for most people to possess. Beyond this, 77 percent knew that the Democratic Party held a majority of the seats in the U.S. House just before the 2010 election, and 74 percent could identify the Republican Party as the more conservative of the two major parties at the national level.

When we turn to information about women, we see a clear decline in correct responses. One question asked respondents whether they thought that women serving in the U.S. Congress were likely to be Democrats or Republicans. In contemporary American politics, about 65 percent of the women who run for office do so as Democrats, and 75 percent of the women members of the 113th Congress are Democrats (CAWP 2013). In this sample, about 62 percent of respondents appear to be aware of this pattern,

Table 3.2. TRADITIONAL AND GENDERED POLITICAL KNOWLEDGE

Traditional knowledge questions	Incorrect	Correct	N
Vice president	14.50%	85.50%	2,937
House majority	23.27%	76.73%	2,845
Republican conservatives	26.24%	73.76%	2,750

Knowledge questions related to women in politics	Incorrect	Correct	N
Women Democrats	38.28%	61.72%	2,855
Women on Supreme Court	53.27%	46.73%	2,857
Percent women in Congress	73.89%	26.11%	2,966

Estimate of the percent of women in Congress by respondent sex	All	Men	Women
Underestimate	39.21%	36.93%	41.40%
Correct	26.11%	28.52%	23.79%
Overestimate	34.68%	34.55%	34.80%
N	2,965	1,529	1,436

correctly identifying women in Congress as more likely to be Democrats than Republicans. Another item asked respondents to identify the number of women on the U.S. Supreme Court. At the time of the survey, there were three women justices—Ruth Bader Ginsburg, Sonia Sotomayor, and Elena Kagan, something that 47 percent of respondents got right. Sotomayor was confirmed in 2009, and Kagan, in 2010, so it is possible that respondents in 2010 benefited from the attention to their nominations and confirmations, although this finding is virtually identical to one from a 2007 study when Ginsburg was the only woman on the court (Dolan 2010). Finally, the most difficult knowledge item regarding women appears to be the one asking respondents to estimate the percentage of seats in Congress that were held by women. In 2010, women held 17 percent of the seats in the House and Senate, so responses estimating between 15 and 20 percent were considered "correct." Only 26 percent of respondents were able to answer this item correctly. What is interesting is the fact that people were more likely to underestimate women's representation in Congress than overestimate, with 39 percent of respondents thinking women held fewer than 15 percent of seats and 35 percent saying that they held more than 20 percent. Among women and men respondents, there were two interesting differences. While 35 percent of both women and men overestimated women's presence in Congress, women were more likely than men to underestimate the actual figure (41 percent to 37 percent) and were also less likely to identify the correct percentage. Perhaps women respondents are more pessimistic about issues of representation than are men, but they are clearly less accurate in their information about women in Congress. This finding is somewhat surprising if we assume that women are more likely than men to pay attention to women's presence in government. At the same time, women's less accurate sense of women's representation in Congress is in line with the general findings that women have lower levels of overall political knowledge than men (Burns et al. 2001; Delli Carpini and Keeter 1996).

STEREOTYPES

While a host of perspectives on women's place in political office can be reasonably thought to have an impact on the fortunes of women candidates, no set of attitudes has a more prominent place in this discussion than political gender stereotypes. As blatantly sexist attitudes about women in politics recede from the public mind, or are at least less likely to be articulated, gender stereotypes have been viewed as attitudes that reveal how voters judge the competencies and abilities of women as candidates and officeholders. The key stereotypes examined have dealt with policy interests and competence, personality traits, and ideology.

Emotional Suitability

One of the long-standing arguments against women having a role in political life was that they were too emotional and did not possess the reason or dispassion to adequately provide political leadership. Indeed, this belief is thought to get at the heart of beliefs about the appropriate spheres for women and men—that women were better suited for the nurturing, emotional work of tending to families and children than the rational work of politics. To examine whether this belief still shapes voter attitudes about women in politics, respondents were asked whether they agreed or disagreed that most men are better suited emotionally for politics than are most women (Table 3.3). A significant majority (69 percent) of respondents disagreed with this statement, 55 percent saying that they disagreed and 14 percent saying that they strongly disagreed. This finding suggests that most people no longer subscribe to the worldview of women as emotionally fragile or too unstable for politics and is in line with public opinion

Table 3.3. EMOTIONAL SUITABILITY

Men better emotionally suited for politics.	All	Men	Women
Strongly agree	3.81%	4.75%	2.93%
Agree	27.63%	26.72%	28.49%
Disagree	54.76%	54.08%	55.40%
Strongly disagree	13.80%	14.45%	13.18%
N	3,006	1,540	1,466

data that find a clear trend away from the belief that women are not emotionally suited for politics. At the same time, it is interesting to note that fully 31 percent of the sample agreed that men are more emotionally well suited for politics, with about 28 percent saying that they agreed and 4 percent saying that they strongly agreed. This attitude is clearly one that has the potential to undercut support for women candidates, as people are probably unlikely to support candidates they believe to be temperamentally unsuited for the job. What is perhaps most interesting about these responses is that there was no gender difference in patterns of response—women and men held exactly the same positions on whether men were better suited emotionally for politics than women, with 31 percent of each group agreeing or strongly agreeing. Up to this point, we have seen patterns of gender difference in attitudes about women in politics, with women taking the more "pro-woman" or egalitarian position more often than men. But here we see that sex does not matter to perceptions of women's emotional suitability, with a relatively large group of women agreeing with men about women's emotional inferiority. An explanation for this discrepancy is not immediately clear.

Policy Competence and Traits

The survey data gathered in 2010 also included measures of the kinds of policy competence and personality trait stereotypes that are at the heart of the existing literature. Respondents were asked whether they saw "women and men who run for office" as better able to handle a series of policy issues—education, health care, child care, abortion, crime, economic policy, national security, immigration, and handling the deficit. They were also asked whether they thought women or men candidates were more likely to possess a series of traits—honesty, compassion, ability to build consensus, ability to change government, intelligence, decisiveness, leadership, and experience. For each set of items, respondents were able to say that women were better, that men were better, or that there was no difference between the two.

Taking policy competence first, there are a couple of things to note about the general distribution of stereotype attitudes among the sample respondents (Table 3.4). First, there are only two issues on which a majority see women or men as better than the other sex at handling the issue—child care and abortion. As is not surprising, women are seen as better able to handle both of these issues than are men. On each of the other issues, the modal response is "no difference," with anywhere from 56 percent of respondents (national security) to 76 percent of respondents (the deficit) saying that they see no difference in women's and men's ability to handle these issues. Giving respondents the "middle" option of no difference will, of course, lead to lower levels of reported stereotypes (Mondak and Davis 2001). However, there is increasing evidence from political science, as well as other disciplines, that stereotypes may be waning in contemporary life and even that women are increasingly seen as superior to men on stereotyped traits and abilities (Burrell 2008; Dolan 2010; Eagly and Carli 2007; Fridkin and Kenney 2009; Lawless 2004). In her experimental work, Deborah Brooks (2013) finds that people evaluate women and men similarly in terms of their perceived ability to handle policy issues, whether domestic, economic, or international. A recent survey of top-level business executives in the United States found women managers and executives to be consistently rated higher than their male counterparts on 15 leadership skills, including assertiveness, flexibility, persuasive ability, interpersonal

Table 3.4. ABSTRACT POLICY STEREOTYPES, ALL RESPONDENTS

	Man Better	No Difference	Woman Better	N
Female Policies				
Abortion	4.08%	45.75%	50.17%	3,059
Child care	1.56%	38.50%	59.94%	3,063
Education	4.77%	68.37%	26.86%	3,064
Health care	5.14%	70.05%	24.81%	3,055
Male Policies				
Crime	32.87%	62.18%	4.95%	3,056
Deficit	15.25%	76.27%	8.48%	3,062
Economy	18.21%	73.75%	8.04%	3,051
Immigration	19.86%	74.30%	5.83%	3,051
National security	42.06%	56.02%	1.92%	3,061

skills, and willingness to take risks (Caliper 2013). In the realm of political leadership, a recent survey done by the Pew Research Center (2008) found that 69 percent of the public evaluates women and men as equally capable of being good political leaders and even judged women to be superior to men on several traits associated with leadership, such as honesty, creativity, compassion, and intelligence. Second, for the issues on which the modal response was no difference between women and men, the next most likely response on each issue was in the expected stereotyped direction. For example, while 56 percent of respondents see no difference between women and men on national security issues, 42 percent of respondents see men as better able to handle the issue, and only 2 percent see women as better able. While 68 percent see women and men as equally able to deal with education issues, 27 percent see women as better, and 5 percent favor men. This pattern is the same for all of the remaining issues.

The same general pattern is true when we examine stereotypes about traits (Table 3.5). For each of the eight traits examined, large majorities see no difference between women and men. For most of the issues, those who hold stereotypes hold them in the expected direction—women as more compassionate, men as more decisive—with two exceptions. Women and men are seen as equally likely to be able to build consensus, and women are seen as more intelligent than men. While these findings of similar evaluations of women and men may appear to fly in the face of the traditional literature on stereotypes, they are consistent with the most recent examinations of candidate trait evaluations, from both survey and experimental data. Surveys conducted by the Pew Research Center (2008) find that trait stereotypes are easing and that women are seen as superior to men

Table 3.5. ABSTRACT TRAIT STEREOTYPES, ALL RESPONDENTS

	Man Better	No Difference	Woman Better	N
Female Traits				
Change government	11.63%	76.27%	12.10%	3,050
Compassion	2.50%	51.13%	46.36%	3,058
Consensus building	13.08%	75.44%	11.48%	3,052
Honest	2.50%	79.31%	18.19%	3,059
Male Traits				
Decisive	19.86%	72.89%	7.25%	3,050
Experience	27.06%	70.69%	2.25%	3,046
Intelligent	3.48%	88.79%	7.74%	3,055
Leadership	22.52%	72.39%	5.09%	3,054

on several traits associated with political leadership. In her experimental work on voter evaluations of candidate stereotypes, Brooks (2013) finds very little evidence that candidate sex is relevant to the trait evaluations people make about political candidates, showing that people view women and men candidates as equally intelligent, compassionate, and possessing the ability to get things done.

When we examine stereotyping by respondent sex, we see that women and men are much more similar than different with regard to their beliefs about the traits and abilities of women and men candidates and officeholders. As Table 3.6 shows, women and men do not see significant differences in the policy competence of women and men candidates, nor do they see candidates possessing markedly different traits (Table 3.7). The one issue

Table 3.6. ABSTRACT POLICY STEREOTYPES BY RESPONDENT SEX

	Man Better	No Difference	Woman Better	N
Men Respondents				
Female policies				
Abortion	4.67%	50.82%	44.51%	1,571
Child care	2.30%	43.53%	54.16%	1,569
Education	5.74%	70.41%	23.85%	1,570
Health care	6.66%	71.72%	21.62%	1,567
Male policies				
Crime	34.46%	61.10%	4.44%	1,568
Deficit	17.46%	74.87%	7.67%	1,570
Economy	20.55%	73.47%	5.98%	1,562
Immigration	22.60%	72.11%	5.29%	1,560
National security	45.63%	52.73%	1.64%	1,565
Women Respondents				
Female policies				
Abortion	3.53%	40.96%	55.51%	1,488
Child care	0.87%	33.78%	65.35%	1,494
Education	3.85%	66.46%	29.69%	1,494
Health care	3.71%	68.48%	27.81%	1,488
Male policies				
Crime	31.38%	63.20%	5.42%	1,488
Deficit	13.18%	77.58%	9.24%	1,492
Economy	16.01%	74.02%	9.97%	1,489
Immigration	17.30%	76.36%	6.34%	1,491
National security	38.74%	59.08%	2.18%	1,496

Table 3.7. ABSTRACT TRAIT STEREOTYPES BY RESPONDENT SEX

	Man Better	No Difference	Woman Better	N
Men Respondents				
Female traits				
Change government	12.13%	77.24%	10.63%	1,567
Compassion	2.81%	55.27%	41.93%	1,568
Consensus building	12.93%	75.66%	11.42%	1,566
Honest	3.96%	81.31%	14.73%	1,567
Male traits				
Decisive	24.64%	70.17%	5.19%	1,564
Experience	26.66%	71.81%	1.53%	1,562
Intelligent	5.46%	88.98%	5.56%	1,568
Leadership	25.40%	71.40%	3.20%	1,568
Women Respondents				
Female traits				
Change government	11.16%	75.36%	13.48%	1,483
Compassion	2.22%	47.27%	50.51%	1,490
Consensus building	13.22%	75.24%	11.54%	1,486
Honest	1.15%	77.44%	21.41%	1,492
Male traits				
Decisive	15.39%	75.44%	9.17%	1,486
Experience	27.43%	69.65%	2.92%	1,484
Intelligent	1.62%	88.60%	9.78%	1,487
Leadership	19.83%	73.32%	6.85%	1,486

on which a majority of the sample holds a stereotyped belief is with regard to child care, which both women and men respondents see as an area of female strength. The two places where we see women and men diverging in their beliefs are in women's greater belief that women candidates are more competent to handle abortion policy than men and their belief that women candidates are more compassionate than men. Beyond this, for those people who do hold stereotyped views, the beliefs are all in the expected stereotyped direction.

Ideology

Women and men candidates are also often stereotyped with regard to ideology. Indeed, one of the most enduring political stereotypes of women candidates is that they are more liberal than men. Several studies confirm this consistent belief in different contexts, whether among voters presented with hypothetical election scenarios or college student subjects in experiments (Alexander and Andersen 1993; Huddy and Terkildsen 1993b; McDermott 1998). David King and Richard Matland (2003) find that respondents see women candidates as more liberal than men, regardless of their party. That Republican women are viewed as more liberal than Republican men indicates that party and sex stereotypes can interact to shape the way women are perceived. Finally, in a series of studies examining the gap between voter perception and reality, Jeffrey Koch (2000, 2002) demonstrates not only that women in both parties are seen as more liberal than their male counterparts but that they are perceived as more liberal than they actually are. Koch makes the argument that this stereotype, leading to inaccurate assessments of the ideology of women candidates, can have consequences at the polls. It is important to note the impact of party here. Koch argues that Democratic women, who are perceived as the most liberal candidates, end up being seen as more extreme by moderate voters, which could hurt their vote totals. On the other hand, Republican women are seen as more "liberal" than Republican men, which results in their being seen as less extreme and closer to the average voter. While individual women candidates are clearly stereotyped ideologically, we have to be aware of the way that stereotypes about political party can influence their evaluation too.

To tap abstract ideological stereotypes, respondents in this survey were asked to rate the ideology of a "typical" woman and man member of Congress. As Tables 3.8–3.9 indicate, women are indeed seen as more liberal than men. Women members of Congress are more likely to be seen as liberal (44 percent) than moderate (41 percent) or conservative (16 percent). For male members of Congress, reactions are much more evenly dispersed, with 36 percent of respondents seeing men in Congress as liberal, 35 percent seeing them as moderate, and 28 percent judging them to be conservative. These differences between ideological placements of women and men are significant. Interestingly, ideological views of women as more liberal seem to be driven by male respondents. Men are significantly more likely than women to see women members of Congress as liberal (47 percent to 40 percent) and less likely to see them as moderate (39 percent to 42 percent) or conservative (13 percent to 18 percent). Women respondents are actually slightly more likely to see women as moderate than liberal. At the same time, women and men respondents make almost identical evaluations of men in Congress, with similar and evenly distributed placements.

Table 3.8. IDEOLOGY OF TYPICAL CONGRESSWOMAN BY RESPONDENT SEX

	All	Men	Women
Extremely liberal	4.08%	4.24%	3.93%
Liberal	18.75%	20.39%	17.19%
Slightly liberal	20.95%	23.06%	18.94%
Moderate	40.76%	39.23%	42.22%
Slightly conservative	8.75%	8.96%	8.56%
Conservative	4.99%	2.82%	7.05%
Extremely conservative	1.72%	1.30%	2.11%
N	2,977	1,535	1,442

Table 3.9. IDEOLOGY OF TYPICAL CONGRESSMAN BY RESPONDENT SEX

	All	Men	Women
Extremely liberal	4.24%	3.94%	4.52%
Liberal	15.15%	13.02%	17.16%
Slightly liberal	16.93%	18.24%	15.71%
Moderate	35.18%	35.61%	34.77%
Slightly conservative	18.23%	20.12%	16.45%
Conservative	8.21%	7.25%	9.11%
Extremely conservative	2.06%	1.82%	2.29%
N	2,977	1,531	1,446

PREDICTORS OF GENDERED ATTITUDES

Looking at a variety of attitudes toward women in politics and gender stereotypes has given us a glimpse of how people feel about women and men and their place in our system. In examining who holds various attitudes, we have seen fairly consistent differences between women and men. However, it is worthwhile broadening that examination to other characteristics of respondents and seeing how they are related to these attitudes. This allows for a more complete sense of who holds stereotypes and how we can distinguish between respondents who are positively disposed to women candidates and those who are less so (Huddy 1994). This analysis will focus on modeling the relationship between gendered attitudes and stereotypes and the characteristics of respondents—sex, race, age, education, political party, and ideology. Given general patterns of relationship between these characteristics and political values, we would expect women, nonwhites, younger people, those with more education, Democrats, and liberals to hold more support attitudes toward women in politics and to hold fewer stereotypes than other respondents.

Table 3.10 presents the data on predictors of several of the abstract attitudes about women candidates and officeholders. The first thing to notice is that there are several factors that influence whether a respondent will hold positive attitudes about women in office. The most important of these factors is the sex of the respondent, with women taking the more positive position on four of the five attitudes. Women are more likely than men to have a baseline preference for women candidates, to want more women in office, to support gender parity in elected office, and to see same-sex representation as important. The only attitude on which women do not take the more supportive position is on the question of women's emotional suitability. This pattern of women being more supportive of women candidates and officeholders was clear from the earlier discussion, but this analysis allows us to see the impact of respondent sex alongside other demographic

Table 3.10. DEMOGRAPHIC PREDICTORS OF ABSTRACT ATTITUDES

	Baseline Preference	Number of Women in Office	Gender Parity	Emotional Suitability	Same-Sex Representation
Education	0.057*	0.130***	0.040	−0.114***	−0.114***
	(0.03)	(0.03)	(0.03)	(0.03)	(0.03)
Age	0.007*	0.006	−0.000	−0.003	−0.007*
	(0.00)	(0.00)	(0.00)	(0.00)	(0.00)
Woman	1.281***	0.615***	0.390***	0.010	0.814***
	(0.10)	(0.10)	(0.10)	(0.10)	(0.10)
Party ID	0.134***	0.133***	0.086**	−0.067*	0.070*
	(0.03)	(0.03)	(0.03)	(0.03)	(0.03)
Ideology	−0.211***	−0.186***	−0.229***	0.003	−0.031
	(0.04)	(0.04)	(0.04)	(0.04)	(0.04)
White	−0.078	0.211	0.275*	−0.263*	−0.112
	(0.12)	(0.12)	(0.13)	(0.12)	(0.11)
Constant	−2.477***	−2.105***	0.204	0.934*	0.247
	(0.45)	(0.44)	(0.46)	(0.45)	(0.43)
Pseudo R^2	.11	.06	.04	.01	.05
N	2,836	2,962	2,889	2,966	3,005

*$p < .05$, **$p < .01$, ***$p < .001$, two-tailed test of significance.
Note: All models use logistic regression. Baseline preference: 0 = man, 1 = woman; number of women in office: 0 = fewer/about right, 1 = more; gender parity: 0 = majority men, 1 = parity/majority women; emotional suitability: 0 = disagree/strongly disagree men better, 1 = agree/strongly agree men better; same-sex representation: 0 = not at all important, 1 = somewhat/very important. Standard errors are in parentheses.

influences. The other patterns in these data demonstrate that positive attitudes about women are most prevalent among Democrats, people with higher levels of education, and liberals. Democrats in the sample take the more supportive position on each of the five attitudes. People with higher levels of education are more likely than those with lower levels to hold supportive attitudes about women, with the exception of supporting women's parity in government. Respondents who identify themselves as liberals are more likely than moderates and conservatives to have a baseline preference for women candidates, to want more women in office, and to support gender parity in elected office but are not different on questions of emotional suitability or same-sex representation.

We can also examine respondent demographic characteristics to determine who is more likely to hold gender stereotypes. Tables 3.11–3.14 present this analysis. Taking policies first, we see that there are several respondent characteristics that are related to holding stereotypes, but in a less consistent fashion than with the attitudes toward women in politics. Given what we know about these influences, we expect certain patterns, such as more well-educated respondents being less likely to stereotype or

Table 3.11. DEMOGRAPHIC PREDICTORS OF ABSTRACT FEMALE POLICY STEREOTYPES

	Education	Health Care	Child Care	Abortion
Education	−0.031	−0.020	−0.012	0.059*
	(0.03)	(0.03)	(0.03)	(0.02)
Age	−0.004	0.002	0.011***	0.003
	(0.00)	(0.00)	(0.00)	(0.00)
Woman	0.321**	0.323**	0.451***	0.437***
	(0.10)	(0.11)	(0.10)	(0.09)
Party ID	0.016	0.067*	0.003	0.080**
	(0.03)	(0.03)	(0.03)	(0.03)
Ideology	−0.090*	−0.056	−0.023	−0.136***
	(0.04)	(0.05)	(0.04)	(0.04)
White	0.163	−0.145	0.062	−0.183
	(0.13)	(0.13)	(0.11)	(0.11)
Constant	−0.830	−1.466**	−0.643	−1.050*
	(0.46)	(0.47)	(0.42)	(0.41)
Pseudo R^2	.01	.01	.02	.03
N	3,020	3,011	3,019	3,015

* $p < .05$, ** $p < .01$, *** $p < .001$, two-tailed test of significance.
Note: All questions: 0 = men better/no difference, 1 = women better. Standard errors are in parentheses.

Table 3.12. DEMOGRAPHIC PREDICTORS OF ABSTRACT MALE POLICY STEREOTYPES

	Crime	Economy	National Security	Immigration	Deficit
Education	−0.043	−0.020	−0.046	−0.075*	−0.028
	(0.03)	(0.03)	(0.03)	(0.03)	(0.03)
Age	0.004	0.003	0.008*	−0.006	0.001
	(0.00)	(0.00)	(0.00)	(0.00)	(0.00)
Woman	−0.139	−0.310*	−0.307**	−0.307*	−0.323*
	(0.10)	(0.13)	(0.10)	(0.12)	(0.13)
Party ID	−0.078*	−0.042	−0.037	−0.118**	−0.044
	(0.03)	(0.04)	(0.03)	(0.04)	(0.05)
Ideology	0.160***	0.105*	0.182***	0.087	0.189**
	(0.04)	(0.05)	(0.04)	(0.06)	(0.06)
White	−0.151	−0.076	−0.017	−0.037	−0.074
	(0.12)	(0.15)	(0.12)	(0.15)	(0.17)
Constant	−0.474	−1.181*	−0.328	0.241	−1.593**
	(0.45)	(0.56)	(0.43)	(0.52)	(0.61)
Pseudo R^2	.02	.01	.03	.02	.02
N	3,012	3,007	3,017	3,008	3,018

* $p < .05$, ** $p < .01$, *** $p < .001$, two-tailed test of significance.
Note: All questions: 0 = women better/no difference, 1 = men better. Standard errors are in parentheses.

older respondents being more likely to do so. Instead, we see that the influence of demographic characteristics varies across policy areas and personality traits. For example, people with higher levels of education are more likely to see women as better at handling abortion and immigration policies, one of which is the expected stereotype (abortion) and the other is not (immigration), but education is unrelated to the other policy areas. Age also only predicts holding two stereotypes, with older people being more likely to see women as better at handling child care and men as better suited for national security policy. Each of these is an expected stereotype, but the surprising finding is that older people only stereotype on two of the nine issues under consideration. Political party and ideology appear to be more related to holding stereotypes. Democrats are more likely than Republicans to stereotype women as better at abortion and health care policies, while Republicans see men as superior at crime and immigration policy. All of these are in the expected direction. A person's political ideology is clearly related to the stereotypes he or she holds, with liberals seeing women as better than men at education and abortion and conservatives stereotyping

Table 3.13. DEMOGRAPHIC PREDICTORS OF ABSTRACT FEMALE TRAIT STEREOTYPES

	Honest	Consensus Building	Compassion	Change Government
Education	−0.063*	0.102*	−0.004	−0.080*
	(0.03)	(0.04)	(0.02)	(0.03)
Age	0.001	0.011**	0.009**	0.010*
	(0.00)	(0.00)	(0.00)	(0.00)
Woman	0.394**	−0.020	0.314***	0.203
	(0.12)	(0.14)	(0.09)	(0.14)
Party ID	0.091*	0.064	−0.015	0.063
	(0.04)	(0.05)	(0.03)	(0.05)
Ideology	−0.006	−0.012	0.020	0.028
	(0.05)	(0.06)	(0.04)	(0.06)
White	0.025	0.154	0.006	−0.222
	(0.14)	(0.17)	(0.11)	(0.16)
Constant	−1.925***	−3.927***	−0.997*	−2.263***
	(0.53)	(0.70)	(0.42)	(0.58)
Pseudo R^2	.02	.01	.01	.02
N	3,016	3,009	3,015	3,007

* $p < .05$, ** $p < .01$, *** $p < .001$, two-tailed test of significance.
Note: All questions: 0 = men better/no difference, 1 = women better. Standard errors are in parentheses.

Table 3.14. DEMOGRAPHIC PREDICTORS OF ABSTRACT MALE TRAIT STEREOTYPES

	Intelligent	Decisive	Leadership	Experience
Education	−0.086	0.021	0.013	0.020
	(0.06)	(0.03)	(0.03)	(0.03)
Age	−0.011	−0.004	0.002	0.017***
	(0.01)	(0.00)	(0.00)	(0.00)
Woman	−1.349***	−0.534***	−0.290*	−0.016
	(0.29)	(0.12)	(0.11)	(0.10)
Party ID	−0.159	−0.089*	−0.132***	−0.027
	(0.09)	(0.04)	(0.03)	(0.03)
Ideology	−0.088	0.058	0.067	0.012
	(0.12)	(0.05)	(0.05)	(0.04)
White	−0.304	−0.052	−0.314*	−0.107
	(0.27)	(0.14)	(0.14)	(0.12)
Constant	1.045	−0.467	−0.543	−1.863***
	(1.07)	(0.56)	(0.52)	(0.51)
Pseudo R^2	.06	.02	.02	.01
N	3,012	3,007	3,011	3,004

* $p < .05$, *** $p < .001$, two-tailed test of significance.
Note: All questions: 0 = women better/no difference, 1 = men better. Standard errors are in parentheses.

men as better at handling crime, the economy, national security, and the deficit.

While ideology is a clear influence on the likelihood of stereotyping, the influence that had the clearest and most consistent impact on holding stereotyped attitudes is respondent sex. In this analysis, women are significantly different from men on eight of the nine policy measures. Interestingly, however, what we see here is not that women or men are more likely than the other sex to hold expected stereotypes. Instead, the pattern here is that each sex sees its own members as superior in each area. Women respondents are more likely to perceive women candidates to be better able to handle all policy areas, both the male *and* female issues, and male respondents are more likely to say that men are better at them all. The only policy on which women and men do not differ is crime policy. This notion of what we might call same-sex superiority is something of a surprise. Instead of the traditional sense that women and men had "ownership" of certain policy areas or personality traits (Hayes 2011), it would appear that women and men are both inclined to see candidates like themselves as better on every score than the opposite sex. This may be the equivalent to women respondents taking the more positive or supportive position on the gendered attitudes.

The determinants of trait stereotypes are more limited than for policies (Tables 3.13–3.14). People with higher levels of education are more likely to stereotype women as being more likely to build consensus and to see men as more honest and more likely to change government. On two of these—honesty and changing government—people with more education actually take the position opposite of the expected stereotypes. Older respondents appear to be more willing to stereotype on personality traits than on policy, holding the expected trait stereotypes of women on three of four traits (consensus, compassion, and changing government) and one for men (leadership). Interestingly, political ideology and party matter much less to holding trait stereotypes, which suggests that the greatest influence of these political variables is in shaping people's positions on policy issues. As we saw with policies, respondent sex is the most consistent influence on holding trait stereotypes and is again more about same-sex identity than about holding expected stereotypes. Women see women candidates as more likely than men to possess both the male *and* female traits—honesty, compassion, intelligence, decisiveness, and leadership—and men believe the same about men. Perhaps it is easy for people to see members of their own sex as superior in these abstract sorts of evaluations of trait and policy competence.

This examination of public attitudes about women's place in elected office demonstrates that people take a range of positions, with some people seeing women as well suited for political office and desiring greater numbers of women in office and others appearing to see women's current levels of underrepresentation as appropriate or even too high. For many years, proponents of women's inclusion in elected office, as well as academics, have raised the concern that negative gender attitudes could work to harm the electoral chances of women candidates. While this may have been the case earlier in our political history, it is clear that any negativity about women in office has been counterbalanced by increasingly egalitarian attitudes about women's roles over the last 30 or 40 years (Huddy 1994). At the same time, these assumptions about the consequences of public gender attitudes for the fate of women candidates usually come without the appropriate data to test them. Researchers and analysts often compare trends in public opinion data with trends in women's success in elections. As attitudes liberalize and women are elected at rates equal to men, we assume that the former has influenced the latter. However, to really test these assumptions, we need data that help us link voter attitudes and behaviors.

This lack of appropriate data to test for a link between gendered attitudes and vote choice in races involving women candidates is a reality that should cause us to exercise caution in drawing conclusions about these dynamics. The question here is whether abstract attitudes influence behavior. Most past work on these issues has been abstract as well, examining hypothetical candidates in fictional circumstances, which means that we do not have a clear understanding of whether and how attitudes toward women and men will influence vote choice. While, on one hand, it makes intuitive sense that the gendered attitudes voters hold should be related to their vote choice decisions when they are faced with a woman candidate, without data to support that, we are left with drawing conclusions that may not be accurate. This may not be a significant problem when voters hold egalitarian or nonsexist attitudes toward women in politics, but we run the risk of raising false alarms when attitudes are less supportive. This is a particular concern when we consider the impact of gender stereotypes on support for women. As we know, research produced by political scientists is consumed by political parties, campaign strategists, and candidates and can become part of the "conventional wisdom," potentially influencing the decision-making process of women considering candidacies (Brooks 2013; Kornblut 2009; Lawless and Fox 2010; Traister 2010).

While past work points to the importance of attitudes, and particularly stereotypes, in evaluating women candidates, methodological considerations require us to ask whether these findings accurately portray the decisions real voters make. This is, in large part, because we lack appropriate empirical tests of these findings in more realistic settings. The isolation of information in experiments and hypotheticals is different enough from a real-world election environment that we need to acknowledge the possible gap between the findings of experiments and the forces that govern actual elections. This is not just an issue in studying stereotypes but a broader methodological issue. Indeed, several recent studies are instructive in the need to more closely examine experimental findings in more realistic situations. Ben Highton (2004) tests the notion advanced by experimental work that white voters fail to support African American candidates for Congress by examining exit poll data in the 1990s. He finds very little evidence that white voters reject African American candidates. In an experimental examination of voter support for black women candidates, Tasha Philpot and Hanes Walton (2007) found that black women are much more likely to support these women candidates than are white women or men of any race. Yet, when they conducted an analysis of the vote support for black women candidates for the U.S. House in the 1990s, they found no significant relationship between sex and race and voting for black women candidates. Black women voters were no more likely to vote for black women candidates than were any other voters. Kim Fridkin and Pat Kenney (2009) counter the literature on stereotypes in their recent examination of attitudes toward incumbent U.S. senators, finding that women senators are evaluated positively by voters with regard to trait and policy competence stereotypes, while men are not seen as possessing traditionally positive male traits or expertise. Each of these studies demonstrates that we need to subject experimental findings to verification in real-world elections whenever possible.

Here I employ the survey data to provide an analysis that illustrates what we learn when we move away from hypotheticals and experiments. The findings from earlier studies would suggest that the gender stereotypes people hold are used to evaluate women in politics generally and women candidates specifically and can determine support or opposition. To demonstrate the difference between examining abstract attitudes (as in these experimental studies) and actual behaviors, I present an analysis of the relationship between gender stereotypes and two different dependent variables—gendered attitudes and vote choice. The first analysis examines whether stereotypes are related to the gendered attitudes that people hold about women in politics. This examination of the impact of stereotypes on abstract attitudes allows us to mimic the circumstances in experiments and hypothetical designs, as these attitudes—baseline gender preference, views on women's emotional suitability, desire for more women in office—are similar to the kinds of abstract declarations of support subjects in experiments are asked to give. This analysis, which replicates the sort of analysis conducted in experimental studies, can then be compared with an analysis that examines the impact of stereotypes on actual behavior—vote choice in races in which women run against men. This comparison extends our understanding of the importance (or lack thereof) of stereotypes and demonstrates the value of broadening our methodological approaches to the study of stereotypes.[1]

Races for the U.S. House are employed here because they offer a large number of respondents available for analysis across a large number of elections that span a range of electoral contexts—incumbent races, open seats, high-spending and low-spending contests, competitive and less competitive races. This investigation of whether stereotypes have an impact on real-world behavior offers a contrast to the analysis of stereotypes and the abstract attitudes. The expectation is that stereotypes are more likely to be related to the abstract gendered attitudes than to vote choice in U.S. House elections. The attitudes examined here—such as baseline gender preference and desire for more women in elected office—represent respondents' thinking about relatively abstract concepts about women in politics. As such, we would assume that people would draw upon their stereotypes about "women and men" in developing an orientation to women in political life. All of these issues are working at the level of abstraction, so it would make sense that they be related to each other. Vote choice, on the other hand, is an actual, tangible behavior that requires voter to consider the choice between the two candidates in front of them. There are no abstractions here but, instead, specific individuals, about whom voters may have additional pieces of information. Voters must decide not whether they want more "women" in office but whether they want that particular woman who is on the ballot in their election. The calculations that must be made in choosing among real candidates are likely to limit the ability of stereotypes to have a major impact on vote choice.

Do Gender Stereotypes Shape Attitudes toward Women in Politics?

To provide a comparison between examining abstract attitudes and voting behavior, I first present the analysis of the relationship between gender stereotypes and attitudes about women in politics—baseline gender preference for a woman candidate or man, whether there should be more or fewer women in office, support for gender parity in office, and whether women are emotionally suited for politics. Each of these attitudes will be analyzed separately. The major explanatory variables in the models are gender stereotypes. Here I have taken the individual female and male policy and trait items and created four summary variables that measure the different stereotypes—male policy, female policy, male traits, and female traits.[2] In addition, to account for individual differences in these attitudes, I consider the impact of respondent sex, race, age, education, party identification, and ideology.

The primary relationships of interest are between each of these attitudes and the four variables measuring gender stereotypes. If stereotypes are an important way by which people think about women's suitability for politics, we should see stereotypes influencing attitudes toward women. In looking at this analysis (Table 3.15), it is clear that gender stereotypes are strongly related to the abstract attitudes that people hold about women candidates and women's place in politics. All four stereotype measures are related to all of the attitudes except whether women are emotionally suited for politics. All of the relationships are in the expected direction. Holding traditional female policy and trait stereotypes generally increases the likelihood that respondents will have a baseline gender preference for women, believe that there should be more women in office, and be in favor of greater numbers of women in office than there are now. Holding traditional male stereotypes leads to the opposite, with those people being less likely to prefer women candidates and having less interest in more women in office. Interestingly, in each of these models, the impact of male stereotypes is a stronger negative influence on the attitude than the female stereotype is a positive influence. Stereotypes are less closely related to beliefs about women's emotional suitability, with only a respondent's male policy stereotypes being a significant predictor here. Respondents who hold male policy stereotypes are more likely to see men as better suited emotionally than women. This analysis of abstract gender attitudes suggests that political gender stereotypes help shape people's attitudes about women candidates and women in government. Each of these findings is in the expected direction for each stereotype, and the stronger negative impact of male stereotypes is consistent with previous research (Dolan 2010). Taken together, this analysis illustrates the concerns raised by researchers who suggest that women candidates can be hurt by the gender stereotypes people hold.

Table 3.15. PREDICTORS OF ABSTRACT GENDER ATTITUDES

	Baseline Preference	Number of Women in Office	Gender Parity	Emotional Suitability
Female policy stereotypes	0.249***	0.368***	0.187***	0.041
	(0.05)	(0.05)	(0.05)	(0.04)
Male policy stereotypes	−0.554***	−0.398***	−0.646***	0.289***
	(0.06)	(0.06)	(0.06)	(0.05)
Female trait stereotypes	0.262***	0.273***	0.061	0.047
	(0.07)	(0.06)	(0.07)	(0.05)
Male trait stereotypes	−0.350***	−0.194**	−0.286***	−0.009
	(0.07)	(0.06)	(0.07)	(0.06)
Education	0.068*	0.135***	0.036	−0.106***
	(0.03)	(0.03)	(0.03)	(0.03)
Age	0.008*	0.004	0.002	−0.006
	(0.00)	(0.00)	(0.00)	(0.00)
Woman	1.226***	0.383***	0.173	0.017
	(0.12)	(0.11)	(0.12)	(0.11)
Party ID	0.068	0.090**	0.030	−0.070*
	(0.04)	(0.03)	(0.04)	(0.03)
Ideology	−0.193***	−0.154**	−0.186***	−0.034
	(0.05)	(0.05)	(0.05)	(0.05)
White	−0.073	0.240	0.297*	−0.304*
	(0.14)	(0.14)	(0.14)	(0.13)
Constant	−13.596***	−11.803***	−8.476***	2.317**
	(1.21)	(1.03)	(0.99)	(0.70)
R^2	.24	.17	.19	.04
N	2,641	2,764	2,699	2,768

$* p < .05, ** p < .01, *** p < .001$, two-tailed test of significance.
Note: All models except the model for number of women in government use logistic regression. The model for number of women in government employs ordinary least squares regression. The logistic regressions use a pseudo R^2, while the number of women in government uses an adjusted R^2. Baseline preference: 0 = man, 1 = woman; number of women in office: 0 = fewer/about right, 1 = more; gender parity: 0 = majority men, 1 = parity/majority women; emotional suitability: 0 = disagree/strongly disagree, 1 = agree/strongly agree. Standard errors are in parentheses.

Do Stereotypes Influence Vote Choice?

This analysis of attitudes clearly suggests that abstract gender stereotypes are related to people's general ideas about women in the political world. These results closely mimic the findings of experiments and surveys that conclude that stereotypes matter to the success of women candidates. However, this analysis of abstract attitudes is incomplete because candidates in real elections are not abstractions. In the absence of real political information, it may make sense that people draw on gender stereotypes to develop their thoughts about women candidates. But once voters are faced with actual candidates, I expect that stereotypes would take a back seat to all of the traditional forces that generally influence vote choice in elections. To demonstrate the gap that can exist between findings drawn from abstract election situations and those from real-world elections, the next analysis investigates whether these stereotypes that seem so important to abstract gender attitudes matter to the vote choice decisions people make when they are faced with women candidates.

The dependent variable in this next analysis is whether the respondent voted for the woman candidate or her male opponent. Because analyzing real elections allows us to examine different aspects of the elections themselves, the models presented in Table 3.16 are somewhat different from those in Table 3.15. As with the analysis of the relationship between gender stereotypes and the abstract attitudes, the primary explanatory variables of interest are the four measures of gender stereotypes. Also included are the measures of respondent characteristics. Beyond these variables, we also need to consider two of the primary influences on vote choice in House elections— political party and incumbency. The vote choice analysis includes a variable that measures the incumbency status of the woman candidate. Finally, party identification is measured differently. In the analysis of the impact of stereotypes on gender attitudes, the measure of political party was a traditional measure of whether the respondent was a Democrat or a Republican. In the vote choice analysis, the important measure of party is whether a respondent shares the party of the woman candidate or not. Since political party is often the most important influence on vote choice, I assume that people who share a woman candidate's party will vote for her and those of the other party will not. Measuring party correspondence between the respondent and the woman candidate allows us to tap into that dynamic. I also include a variable for respondents who identify as Independents.

Because of the primacy of political party in shaping thinking about politics and because we know that voters can hold partisan stereotypes as well as gender stereotypes, we need to analyze vote choice separately for Democratic and Republican women candidates. Indeed, recent studies of women candidates have demonstrated that political party is relevant to the way these candidates are perceived by voters and that outcomes are different for Democratic and Republican women (Koch 2000, 2002; Lawless and Pearson 2008; Sanbonmatsu and Dolan 2009). As a result, each analysis is conducted for respondents who were faced with a Democratic woman running against a Republican man and, separately, for those facing a Republican woman running against a Democratic man.

Table 3.16. IMPACT OF ABSTRACT STEREOTYPES ON HOUSE VOTE CHOICE

	Democratic Women versus Republican Men	Republican Women versus Democratic Men
Female policy stereotypes	−0.008	−0.556
	(0.12)	(0.30)
Male policy stereotypes	0.021	0.057
	(0.10)	(0.10)
Female trait stereotypes	0.306	0.688*
	(0.16)	(0.32)
Male trait stereotypes	−0.185	0.435
	(0.10)	(0.25)
Education	0.230**	−0.266
	(0.08)	(0.14)
Age	0.006	0.022
	(0.01)	(0.01)
Woman	0.473	0.128
	(0.32)	(0.41)
Share party	2.285***	3.390***
	(0.46)	(0.61)
Independent	−0.169	–
	(1.26)	–
Ideology	−0.449*	0.242
	(0.22)	(0.18)
White	−1.050*	1.792***
	(0.45)	(0.54)
Incumbent	1.642***	0.584
	(0.45)	(0.45)
Constant	−5.887*	0.283
	(2.33)	(3.86)
Pseudo R^2	.44	.52
N	465	216

* $p < .05$, ** $p < .01$, *** $p < .001$, two-tailed test of significance.
Note: Clustered standard errors are in parentheses.

It is immediately clear from this analysis that gender stereotypes have very little relationship to actual vote choice decisions when respondents are faced with real candidates. In looking at the two models, we see that none of the four stereotypes is related to voting for a Democratic woman candidate and only one, female trait stereotypes, is related to voting for Republican women. Voters who hold traditional stereotypes about the traits of women candidates are more likely to vote for Republican women than their Democratic male opponents. It would appear that these women gained some advantage among respondents by being seen as more likely than their Democratic male opponents to possess female traits such as compassion and honesty. But this is the only time abstract gender stereotypes appear to have an impact on voting for women candidates. In all, people's abstract ideas about female and male policy competence or personality traits did not inform their decision in choosing between a Democratic woman and a Republican man for the House. In races with Republican women, only stereotypes about women being more likely to possess honesty and compassion helped in shaping voting for these women.

Beyond the fact that stereotypes are not related to vote choice in these House elections, we see the first sign of the importance of real-world political forces in shaping vote choice for women candidates. Far and away, the most important determinant of whether a voter will choose a woman candidate is whether that voter shares her political party. For women of either party, the party correspondence measure is strongly related to voting for the woman candidate and is the strongest influence in the model, particularly for Republican women candidates. For Democratic women, being an incumbent also increases the likelihood that voters will choose her over the male opponent. Incumbency is not related to vote choice in races with Republican women.[3] Beyond these important political influences, we see that liberals are more likely to vote for the Democratic women than their Republican male opponents. However, ideology is not significantly related to voting in races with Republican women, indicating that conservatives are no more likely to vote for Republican women in these races.

One final relationship to examine here is that of the sex of the respondent and vote choice in races involving women candidates. Recall that the earlier analyses of the determinants of stereotypes demonstrated clearly that women and men saw things differently. Women were more likely to see women as better than men at handling all policy areas, male and female, and as more likely than men to hold both male and female traits. Men took the opposite position, essentially seeing men as superior to women on all of the traditional stereotyped dimensions. However, when we look at voting patterns, we see that women are no more likely to vote for women candidates than are men. This would appear to confirm that stereotypes are not doing much to structure people's candidate choices. Women in this sample clearly see "women" as better than "men" on a number of measures, but this sense of women's superiority does not make them more likely than men voters to support women candidates at the ballot box.

Taken together, the analysis provided in Tables 3.15 and 3.16 demonstrates support for the notion that, while gender stereotypes may be significantly related to abstract or hypothetical attitudes that people have about women candidates and leaders, there is much less evidence that they are important in shaping vote choice. One contribution of this is that it gives us a way to see why there may be a gap between experimental findings and real-world elections. Abstract gender stereotypes about women and men do appear to influence the ways in which people think about women in politics, but these attitudes themselves are abstractions. These findings are similar to those from much of the experimental literature on stereotypes. But when we move to examining a real-world political behavior, vote choice, we see that stereotypes no longer play a significant role. Indeed, these different results should not be surprising. Experimental subjects who are asked about their support for "women" or "men" running for office do not have much information beyond candidate sex and may well rely on stereotyped attitudes in forming positions. However, we know that real elections provide voters with that additional context, allowing them to move beyond the abstract and draw on traditional influences on politics such as political party and incumbency in making decisions. We also see this in the fact that voters make distinctions between women candidates by reacting to Democratic and Republican women differently.

Do Gender Attitudes Influence Vote Choice?

One result of the analysis comparing the impact of stereotypes on gender attitudes and vote choice is the understanding that we should expand our attempts to test the findings and assumptions of earlier work on real election situations whenever possible. The data in this project allow us to continue in that vein by questioning the link between the gender attitudes that people hold and their willingness to support women candidates. One of the basic assumptions in the literature on public reaction to women who run for office is that the presence of supportive attitudes among members of the public is an important precursor to electoral success. However, given the primacy of traditional political variables, it may be the case that these sorts of abstract attitudes about women in politics are not necessarily related to behavior. An individual voter may prefer to see more women in office but, when faced with two candidates in an election, may employ other, more immediate factors beyond the sex of the candidates when deciding for whom to vote. The data from this survey allow for an examination of whether people act on the abstract attitudes they hold, whether these attitudes motivate them to vote for or against women when they have the opportunity, or whether other considerations are more central.

To investigate this possibility, I analyze the impact of gendered attitudes on vote choice in races involving women candidates. The dependent variable is voting for the woman candidate. I analyze the impact of each of the attitudes separately—baseline gender preference, whether there should be more or fewer women in office, support for gender parity, beliefs about women's emotional suitability, and beliefs about the importance of same-sex representation. Beyond the attitude, the other explanatory variables include the respondent demographics—sex, race, age, and education. The political variables include political party correspondence between the woman candidate and the respondent, Independents, political ideology, and the incumbency status of the woman candidate. As with the earlier analysis, vote choice is examined separately for Democratic women running against Republican men and Republican women running against Democratic men. Finally, because of the nature of the variable, the analysis of the importance of same-sex representation to respondents is conducted separately for women and men.

Table 3.17 examines the impact of having a baseline gender preference on vote choice. Taking Democratic women candidates first, we see that people

Table 3.17. BASELINE GENDER PREFERENCE AND HOUSE VOTE CHOICE

	Democratic Women versus Republican Men	Republican Women versus Democratic Men
Baseline gender preference	0.934**	−0.963*
	(0.34)	(0.38)
Education	0.156*	−0.191
	(0.07)	(0.12)
Age	0.010	0.018
	(0.01)	(0.01)
Woman	0.121	0.413
	(0.29)	(0.32)
Share party	2.161***	3.014***
	(0.43)	(0.66)
Independent	–	–
	–	–
Ideology	−0.453*	0.174
	(0.21)	(0.19)
White	−1.040*	1.364**
	(0.44)	(0.47)
Incumbent	1.588***	0.665
	(0.41)	(0.48)
Constant	−1.773	−2.363
	(1.49)	(1.43)
Pseudo R^2	.45	.44
N	470	217

* $p < .05$, ** $p < .01$, *** $p < .001$, two-tailed test of significance.
Note: Baseline preference: 0 = man, 1 = woman. Clustered standard errors are in parentheses.

who express a baseline preference for women candidates are more likely to vote for the Democratic woman candidate over her Republican male opponent. This would support the notion that having a baseline gender preference for women candidates can be important in motivating action when a voter has a chance to act on this belief. At the same time, we see that this attitude is significantly related to voting in races with Republican women candidates, but in the opposite direction. Respondents who have a baseline preference for women are more likely to choose the Democratic man candidate in these races, not the Republican woman. Instead it is the people with a baseline preference for men who are voting for the Republican woman. The most likely explanation for that is that people who have a baseline preference for men are probably more traditional on gendered attitudes, which may be more likely linked to their voting for Republican candidates. Here these Republican candidates happen to be women, but voters are unlikely choosing them for their sex. This finding clearly suggests that respondents view women candidates differently based on their political party and that the impact of these attitudes is tied up with broader ideological beliefs, rather than just candidate sex.

Table 3.18 reveals that a belief that there should be more women in office than is currently the case is related to vote choice in the same way. Respondents who believe that there should be more women in office are *more* likely to vote for the Democratic women and *less* likely to vote for a Republican woman. Instead, the voters more likely to choose the Republican woman candidate are actually those who think that there should be fewer women in office than there currently are. Again, we must assume that partisan and ideological forces are at work here. Voters who want more women in office are likely to be voters who would support Democrats anyway, so they can vote for the woman candidate and experience alignment between partisan and ideological goals. Those who want fewer women in office are faced with conflicting partisan and ideological goals—voting for a woman Republican or a Democratic man. For these voters, it appears that partisan considerations are more central.

To this point, the impact of these two attitudes about women's place in office seems to be about partisan and ideological influences as much as anything else. People with more egalitarian attitudes toward women in office are significantly more likely to vote for Democratic women running against Republican men but are less likely to vote for Republican women running against Democratic men. This would suggest that these voters are not looking to support women candidates per se but, instead, a particular *kind* of woman candidate—a Democratic woman. This makes sense when we recall the earlier analysis that showed Democrats and liberals to be the

Table 3.18. NUMBER OF WOMEN IN OFFICE AND HOUSE VOTE CHOICE

	Democratic Women versus Republican Men	Republican Women versus Democratic Men
Number of women in office	0.635*	−0.667*
	(0.29)	(0.32)
Education	0.193*	−0.168
	(0.08)	(0.12)
Age	0.009	0.014
	(0.01)	(0.01)
Woman	0.432	0.162
	(0.32)	(0.34)
Share party	2.217***	2.823***
	(0.46)	(0.61)
Independent	−0.364	–
	(1.25)	–
Ideology	−0.449*	0.244
	(0.21)	(0.17)
White	−1.094**	1.649***
	(0.42)	(0.48)
Incumbent	1.456***	0.785
	(0.39)	(0.43)
Constant	−3.383	−1.588
	(1.78)	(1.51)
Pseudo R^2	.44	.44
N	488	228

* $p < .05$, ** $p < .01$, *** $p < .001$, two-tailed test of significance.
Note: Number of women in government: 1 = should be fewer, 2 = current number is about right, 3 = should be more. Clustered standard errors are in parentheses.

respondents more likely to hold a baseline gender preference for women and to want more women in office. So while these respondents are happy to act on their gender attitudes when there is a Democratic woman candidate present in their election, they are not likely to cross party lines to vote for a woman of the other party. The same is true in the reverse for Republican respondents. While they might prefer male candidates and want fewer women in office, they will vote for a woman Republican as opposed to crossing party lines to vote for a man. The primacy of shared party identification is clear in each of the models and is consistent with what we know about the influence of party on vote choice.

Tables 3.19–3.21 show that none of the other gender attitudes are related to voting for women candidates. Neither peoples' support for gender parity, nor beliefs about women's emotional suitability for politics,

Table 3.19. GENDER PARITY IN GOVERNMENT AND HOUSE VOTE CHOICE

	Democratic Women versus Republican Men	Republican Women versus Democratic Men
Gender parity in government	0.259	–0.169
	(0.37)	(0.34)
Education	0.182*	–0.159
	(0.08)	(0.12)
Age	0.009	0.012
	(0.01)	(0.01)
Woman	0.493	0.113
	(0.30)	(0.34)
Share party	2.280***	2.917***
	(0.50)	(0.62)
Independent	–0.018	–
	(1.32)	–
Ideology	–0.428	0.230
	(0.22)	(0.17)
White	–1.034*	1.449**
	(0.44)	(0.44)
Incumbent	1.474***	0.945*
	(0.40)	(0.48)
Constant	–2.057	–2.990*
	(1.49)	(1.27)
Pseudo R^2	.44	.42
N	480	222

* $p < .05$, ** $p < .01$, *** $p < .001$, two-tailed test of significance.
Note: Gender parity in government: 0 = majority men, 1 = gender parity, 2 = majority women. Clustered standard errors are in parentheses.

nor thoughts about the importance of same-sex representation appear to be linked to their voting for women candidates, indicating that although people may hold attitudes in favor of a particular political outcome, they do not always act in pursuit of that outcome. For example, women respondents who believe that same-sex representation is important to them are no more or less likely to vote for a woman candidate than a women who does not value this representation. People who see women as emotionally less well suited for politics do not appear to be factoring in this belief when they chose a candidate. On one hand, this may seem surprising—people with a particular belief are failing to take action to put that belief into action. At the same time, we can see this as evidence that the impact of gender attitudes on vote choice pales in comparison to the more centrally important influences on vote choice, such as party and incumbency. This

Table 3.20. EMOTIONAL SUITABILITY AND HOUSE VOTE CHOICE

	Democratic Women versus Republican Men	Republican Women versus Democratic Men
Emotional suitability	0.029	−0.531
	(0.23)	(0.37)
Education	0.190*	−0.200
	(0.08)	(0.13)
Age	0.009	0.016
	(0.01)	(0.01)
Woman	0.514	0.140
	(0.32)	(0.35)
Share party	2.239***	2.904***
	(0.46)	(0.61)
Independent	0.039	–
	(1.30)	–
Ideology	−0.437*	0.259
	(0.20)	(0.15)
White	−0.990*	1.413**
	(0.42)	(0.52)
Incumbent	1.421***	1.022*
	(0.36)	(0.48)
Constant	−1.937	−1.753
	(1.81)	(1.39)
Pseudo R^2	.42	.44
N	486	225

* $p < .05$, ** $p < .01$, *** $p < .001$, two-tailed test of significance.
Note: Men better suited emotionally: 1 = strongly agree, 2 = agree, 3 = disagree, 4 = strongly disagree. Clustered standard errors are in parentheses.

could cut both ways for women candidates. On one hand, knowing that people who see women as emotionally unsuitable for politics are not turning that concern into votes against women candidates may allay concerns about the negative impact of stereotypes. But, at the same time, it may be that women candidates miss out on the possibility of support among those who hold positive attitudes toward women in politics. While voters who have a baseline preference for women candidates or who believe that there should be more women in elected office may seek to put those beliefs into practice when they have the chance to vote for a woman, these attitudes are less central to vote decisions than other, more central considerations.

In focusing on these more central considerations, we see that a shared party affiliation with the candidate and the incumbency status of the candidate are the two most important influences on vote choice. In each of

Table 3.21. SAME-SEX REPRESENTATION AND HOUSE VOTE CHOICE

	Democratic Women Candidates— Men Respondents	Democratic Women Candidates— Women Respondents	Republican Women Candidates— Men Respondents	Republican Women Candidates— Women Respondents
Importance of same-sex representation	−0.333	−0.369	−0.120	−0.512
	(0.24)	(0.50)	(0.69)	(0.58)
Education	0.124	0.124	−0.065	−0.232
	(0.10)	(0.09)	(0.12)	(0.17)
Age	0.015	−0.008	0.000	0.017
	(0.01)	(0.01)	(0.02)	(0.01)
Share party	1.853***	3.042***	3.242***	2.491***
	(0.42)	(0.91)	(0.85)	(0.74)
Independent	−0.607	–	–	–
	(1.06)	–	–	–
Ideology	−0.577***	−0.341	.331	0.217
	(0.16)	(0.40)	(0.26)	(0.20)
White	−1.231***	−0.488	1.109	2.872**
	(0.37)	(0.35)	(0.69)	(0.92)
Incumbent	1.049**	2.014***	0.228	1.117
	(0.36)	(0.59)	(0.58)	(0.67)
Constant	0.188	−0.742	−3.461	−2.695
	(1.19)	(2.67)	(2.10)	(2.39)
Pseudo R^2	.41	.49	.46	.46
N	285	211	125	108

** $p < .01$, *** $p < .001$, two-tailed test of significance.
Note: Same-sex representation: 0 = not at all important, 1 = somewhat/very important. Clustered standard errors are in parentheses.

the five models, sharing the party of the candidate is the overwhelming influence on voting for that candidate, whether the candidate is a woman or a man, a Democrat or a Republican. Incumbency works the same way. Incumbents, whether women or men, Democrats or Republicans, are more likely to win people's votes than are challengers. Even when attitudes such as baseline gender preference and support for more women in office are related to vote choice, their impact is far more limited than that of party and incumbency.

Finally, as we saw in the analysis of the impact of gender stereotypes on vote choice, we see that women are no more likely to vote for women candidates here than are men. Earlier analysis indicated that women took the most supportive gender position on each of these five attitudes and also on each of the policy and trait stereotypes, seeing women as superior to men on each item. Yet, in the two vote choice analyses, women do not appear to be carrying many of those beliefs into action by voting for women candidates when they have the chance. Conventional wisdom often assumes that women voters will serve as an automatic base of support for women candidates. Instead, while women may be more likely than men to support abstract ideas about women's place in politics, the evidence here supports the notion that people, including women, can hold abstract attitudes about women in politics but not necessarily employ them in real-world political calculations. Instead, voters here clearly rely on traditional political influences in making their choices among candidates.

CONCLUSION

Scholarly thinking on women in politics has long assumed that public support for these women would be critical to their success. Indeed, for much of our nation's history, public antipathy was a significant limitation on women's political opportunities. Yet today we have evidence of greater support for women in political life than ever before. Gender stereotypes appear to be easing, and general attitudes about women's integration into politics are largely positive or neutral.

Respondents in this survey are generally supportive of women in political life. While there is certainly not unanimity on these issues, there is more support than less for the idea that having women in office is a good thing and that our government might be better off with more women in office. Women respondents are clearly more supportive of a political role for women than are men. With regard to stereotypes, respondents see fewer differences among women and men than more, mirroring what appears to be a trend in lessening of stereotypes. Again, women are more supportive of women than are men, with women seeing women candidates as superior to men on every policy and trait dimension examined. The reverse is true as well, with male respondents seeing men candidates as uniformly better than women.

While, on its face, this trend in supportive public attitudes should be a positive for women who seek office, the other important finding here is that attitudes are generally not important to shaping concrete actions such as vote choice. This is an important finding, since scholars and political leaders have long assumed that positive attitudes toward women were important to their success and negative attitudes could stand in their way.

Gender stereotypes are clearly related to abstract attitudes about women in politics but are not often related to vote choice decisions that voters make when faced with real candidates. Only two of the gendered attitudes—baseline gender preference and a desire for more women in office—are related to vote choice. This suggests that, while attitudes toward women in politics may have ideological or personal value to voters, they have relatively little role to play in structuring vote choice, particularly in comparison to the more traditional and primary political influences on the vote, such as political party and incumbency.

The analysis in this chapter also demonstrates that gendered attitudes are related to women Democrats and Republicans in different ways. None of the gender stereotypes were related to voting for Democratic women, but people who voted for Republican women factored female trait stereotypes into their choice. People who have a baseline gender preference for women candidates and those who want more women in elected office are significantly *more* likely to vote for Democratic women but significantly *less* likely to vote for Republican women. Instead, those with a baseline gender preference for men candidates and those who see no need for more women in office are the ones who vote more often for Republican women than their Democratic male opponents. It is probably safe to assume that people who prefer women candidates are more likely to vote for Democrats regardless of sex and those who have more traditional views and prefer men candidates are more likely to be voting for Republicans. Since these voters are acting at cross purposes with their gender preference, it is clear that these gender attitudes are not a central influence and that the pull of political party is stronger. Gender attitude positions are clearly not strong enough to get voters to cross party lines to vote for their preferred sex.

In sum, these data contain mixed news for women candidates. It is clear that attitudes about the role of women in political life, while not unanimous, are more supportive now than they have ever been. The good news is that people appear to want more women in office. At the same time, we have to acknowledge that these gendered attitudes and stereotypes appear to have less impact on political decisions than has been assumed, which means that they are both less helpful and less harmful to women candidates than they could be. It also appears that how we examine these questions matters. When we move beyond hypothetical situations and make efforts to connect voter attitudes with their actions toward women candidates, we see that examining candidates and elections in the real world matters. The preliminary evidence presented here stands in contrast to the findings of some earlier works and demonstrates that concerns about the impact of abstract stereotypes and attitudes on the fate of women candidates may have been overstated.

CHAPTER 4

Do Stereotypes Shape Evaluations of Candidates?

I don't really like her. She seems too masculine, I guess, not enough feminine.

Scott Smith, a New York City voter, on Christine Quinn

If you're tough enough to run New York City, you're too tough to be considered acceptably feminine.

Gloria Steinem, women's rights activist, on Christine Quinn

When Christine Quinn sought the Democratic Party's nomination for mayor of New York City in 2013, she was faced with some number of voters who found that her hair, her clothing, and her voice did not match their expectations of a woman candidate. In campaigning on issues, she was often faced with questions about her tepid support for a family leave policy being considered by the City Council and a proposal for universal preschool floated by one of her male opponents. Despite her 14 years on the New York City Council, her work on a myriad of issues, and her many public appearances, her campaign for mayor was shaped, at least in part, by expectations of what she would do and say and wear because she is a woman. Public reaction to Quinn was also no doubt shaped, in part, by the fact that she is a lesbian.

Quinn's experience in this regard is not unusual. When voters are faced with a choice between candidates running for office, the first thing they have to do is form impressions and make evaluations of those candidates. These evaluations can be based on any number of different criteria and can be critical to later vote choice decisions. Indeed, it seems obvious that positive evaluations of a candidate would be linked to voting for that candidate and negative evaluations probably lead people to choose someone else. In evaluating candidates, voters rely on myriad characteristics and properties, some relevant and others perhaps less so, ranging from traditional political influences such as party identification, incumbency, and issue position to personal characteristics such as race, sex, or age, and even physical appearance (Campbell et al. 1960; Hillygus and Shields 2008; Kinder and Sears 1981; McDermott 1998; Rahn 1993; Riggle et al. 1992).

While traditional political influences such as partisanship and issue position are thought to be the primary drivers of candidate evaluations, research over the last few decades has focused on the role that candidate sex and gender-related attitudes such as stereotypes can play in shaping evaluations. Experimental work of this type tends to find that voters evaluate women in ways that are consistent with gender stereotypes—seeing them as more liberal than men, less capable on terrorism and foreign affairs, and less well suited to the presidency (Lawless 2004; McDermott 1998; Smith et al. 2007). Voters who hold sexist attitudes are more likely to prefer male candidates to female candidates (Swim et al. 1995). Findings from research on real-world candidates are less clear cut, with some research finding that candidate sex can influence evaluations of candidates and others finding a much more limited role. For example, Jeff Koch (2002) finds that people use candidate sex to infer the ideology of women candidates for U.S. House but not for male candidates. Women candidates are seen as more liberal, but men are not viewed through a correspondingly gendered lens. Koch suggests that the uniqueness of women candidates causes voters to pay attention to their sex and use it in developing evaluations. He finds much the same dynamic present in U.S. Senate races, where women candidates were routinely evaluated as more liberal than men and were judged to be even more liberal than they actually were based on objective measures of ideology. Kim Fridkin and Pat Kenney (2009) find that voters in 2006 evaluated incumbent women U.S. senators as superior to their male counterparts across a number of dimensions. With regard to traits, women senators were judged to be more honest, caring, and able to exercise leadership than men senators and were given higher overall favorability ratings than men. In terms of policy, women were seen as superior to men on both economic and health care issues. What is most interesting about these findings is that women senators were seen as superior on traditionally female dimensions (honesty, caring, health care) as well as traditionally male dimensions (leadership, economic issues).

Other recent work finds that candidate sex and gender-related attitudes have a much more limited influence on candidate evaluations. In examining the impact of race and sex in the 2008 presidential elections, Caitlin Dwyer, Daniel Stevens, and Barbara Allen (2009) found that racist attitudes were strongly related to evaluations of Barack Obama but that sexist attitudes were not related to evaluations of Sarah Palin at all. In their conclusion, the authors suggest that sexism did not have an impact because the images of Palin as a warm, nurturing mother figure might have protected her from attitudes about women's inappropriateness for high office. They suggest that a woman candidate with a "stronger" personal image, like Hillary Clinton, may not fare as well with voters who hold sexist attitudes. While the authors do not test this directly, it may also be the case that people who hold more sexist attitudes are more likely to be conservative and/ or Republican voters, people who would have been more supportive of Palin despite their general attitudes about women in society. Danny Hayes (2011) finds a similar potential role for political party in his examination of U.S. Senate elections in 2006. In this work he finds that all candidates are much more likely to be viewed in line with partisan stereotypes than with gender stereotypes. Finally, in examining candidate evaluations in U.S. House races in 2010, Jennifer Lawless and Danny Hayes (2013) find that voter evaluations of candidates are primarily driven by party, ideology, and incumbency. They find no sex differences in candidate evaluations and conclude that assumptions about the inevitability of stereotyping in elections with women candidates are misplaced.

As is generally the case with research on gender stereotypes, the results of work from experiments and hypotheticals tend to paint a more consistent portrait of the impact of stereotypes than does research that examines real-world elections. This is, no doubt, because of the complexity of the real world of elections and candidates and the presence of multiple potential influences on voter decisions. Previous work represents a strong beginning at helping us understand how candidate sex and gender stereotyping work in elections. However, there is still an important limitation in this work—it tends to focus on evaluations as an outcome without giving attention to what factors or attitudes shape those evaluations. For example, much of this research asks survey respondents whether a series of traits—trustworthy, empathetic, a strong leader—applies to candidates for election and then examines whether women and men candidates are evaluated differently on these traits. While this approach is appropriate for determining whether candidates are stereotyped, it does not allow us to understand the basis on which these evaluations are made.

This chapter takes a different approach. Much of the research on gender stereotypes assumes that people take their stereotypes of women and men and transfer them to the women and men candidates in their world, leading to stereotyped evaluations of these candidates. However, one of the current limitations in our understanding of gender stereotypes is that we have a lot of research that documents their existence but much less work that examines whether the stereotypes people hold have any impact on their political attitudes and behaviors. With regard to evaluations of candidates, we might assume that people who hold gender-stereotyped attitudes would evaluate women and men candidates differently with regard to traits and abilities, but current research does not examine whether people actually employ the stereotypes they hold when they evaluate candidates. The analysis of gendered attitudes and stereotypes in chapter 3 strongly suggested that there is reason to question whether people employ these sorts of attitudes in their political decisions, which means that we should consider whether people actually do rely on their gender stereotypes when evaluating candidates.

Data from the two-wave panel study conducted in 2010 make these explorations possible. Recall that the first wave of the survey measured the trait and policy stereotypes respondents held about "women and men in elected office"—what I call *abstract gender stereotypes*. In the second wave, respondents were asked to evaluate the specific candidates in their House, Senate, or governor race on these same trait and policy dimensions—what I call *specific candidate evaluations*. Asking the stereotype and evaluation questions in separate waves of the survey minimizes the possibility of question order problems. Taken together, these measures allow us to examine whether voters employ the abstract gender stereotypes they hold about women and men when they are asked to evaluate the specific and individual candidates running in an election. This important step allows us to move from abstract and hypothetical situations to a consideration of real candidates, something that most research is not able to do.

ABSTRACT STEREOTYPES VERSUS SPECIFIC EVALUATIONS

The first step in understanding the relationship between abstract gender stereotypes and evaluations of individual candidates is to examine the patterns of these responses among respondents. Here I present the four summary variables that measure female policy, male policy, female traits, and male traits for abstract gender stereotypes and specific candidate evaluations. Table 4.1 presents the distributions for each measure of abstract stereotypes. As we first saw in chapter 3, respondents were more likely to report seeing no difference between abstract "women and men who run for office" than they were to take a stereotyped position on these measures,

Table 4.1. DISTRIBUTION OF ABSTRACT STEREOTYPES

	Men Better	No Difference	Women Better	N
Female policy	2.92%	32.23%	64.85%	3,043
Male policy	45.47%	48.03%	6.50%	3,007
Female traits	7.11%	52.46%	40.43%	3,019
Male traits	37.08%	55.28%	7.63%	3,006

with the exception of female policy stereotypes. As I have argued, this makes sense when we are asking people to respond to abstract candidates and are not providing them with any information or context in which to make a judgment. "No difference" is the modal category on three of the four summary measures, with approximately 50–55 percent of respondents taking that position on male policies and female and male trait stereotypes. For female policy stereotypes, 65 percent of respondents take the stereotype-expected position of seeing women as better at these issues than men. After accounting for the "no difference" position, we see that respondents are then most likely to take the stereotype-expected position on each variable. People who do indicate that "women" or "men" are better at certain policy areas are most likely to say that women are better at female policies such as education and health care and men are better at male policies such as the economy and foreign affairs. The same patterns hold for traits. While most respondents see no difference between women and men on key personality traits, those who do take a position tend to see women as more likely than men to possess female traits such as compassion and the ability to reach consensus and see men as more likely to exhibit male traits such as decisiveness and leadership.

However, when we examine the distributions on the specific candidate evaluations that people make, we begin to see evidence that people come to different conclusions when they are evaluating real candidates. Table 4.2 presents the distribution of specific candidate policy and trait evaluations for respondents who experienced a U.S. House race in which a woman ran against a man. The first thing we see here is that the percentage of respondents who see no difference between the women and men candidates in these races drops to, on average, about 35 percent. This is an approximately 20-percentage-point difference from the distributions on the abstract gender stereotypes, which indicates that respondents were much more likely to see policy and trait differences between the real candidates in their election than they were between abstract "women and men." So while about 35 percent of respondents saw no difference between the woman and man

Table 4.2. DISTRIBUTION OF SPECIFIC EVALUATIONS OF HOUSE CANDIDATES

Mixed Sex	Men Better	No Difference	Women Better	N
Female policy	28.10%	32.45%	39.45%	811
Male policy	33.71%	33.33%	32.97%	806
Female traits	27.51%	37.68%	34.82%	807
Male traits	30.57%	35.89%	33.53%	803

Male Only	Republican Better	No Difference	Democrat Better	N
Female policy	28.99%	37.40%	33.61%	1,488
Male policy	33.62%	35.01%	31.37%	1,476
Female traits	27.99%	41.59%	30.43%	1,483
Male traits	28.80%	39.91%	31.28%	1,471

in their House race across the four evaluation measures, about 65 percent of respondents did choose one of the candidates as better at certain policies or more likely to possess a particular trait. The patterns of response also indicate that respondents who did see differences between candidates were not just choosing the stereotype-expected candidate—say, the woman on female policies or the man on male traits. Instead, we see that responses are fairly evenly distributed, with generally equal numbers of people choosing the woman or the man on each of the four variables. So, for example, we see that about 33 percent of respondents see no difference between women and men on male policy issues. Beyond that, the 67 percent of respondents who did see differences were evenly divided between seeing the women candidates as better at these policies and seeing men as better. The same is true for female policies and for both female and male traits. Finally, we see that respondents are more likely to see differences between their candidates on policy issues than they are on traits.

A strength of the data for this project is that they allow us to examine whether gender stereotypes and evaluations are present only when women candidates run or whether they shape the experiences of male candidates as well. To examine this, we can also look at patterns of candidate evaluation in male-only House races (Table 4.2). In these races, respondents were asked to evaluate which of the two candidates in a race was better at a particular issue or more likely to possess a particular trait. These male candidates were evaluated on both the male and female policies and traits. Here we see very similar patterns of evaluation to those in the mixed-sex races. Levels of "no difference" are much lower here than in the abstract stereotyped distributions and are similar to those in the woman-versus-man races at about 35–40 percent. Beyond the "no difference" category, respondents are about equally likely to see male Democrats and Republicans as better at policies and possessing specific traits. Respondents see Democrats as a bit better at female policies than Republicans and see Republicans as a bit better at male policies than Democrats, but the differences are small. Again, as with the races between women and men, respondents in male-only races are making distinctions between actual candidates and are not simply defaulting to expected stereotypes.

Moving to evaluations of Senate candidates, we see that the conventional wisdom that voters tend to know more about Senate candidates is borne out (Table 4.3). In the mixed-sex races, respondents are even less likely to choose the "no difference" position in evaluating women and men running for the Senate. Here the range is between 24 and 32 percent of people seeing no difference, with 68–76 percent of respondents seeing differences between the candidates. We again see the slight tilt toward women on female policies and toward men on male policies, but the difference is small. Plenty of respondents see candidates as better suited to handle issues or more likely to possess traits that do not align with expected gender stereotypes. As with the House candidates, voters in Senate races perceive more differences between candidates on policies than on traits. In looking at the male-only Senate races, one minor difference is that respondents appear to be a bit more likely to see no difference between the candidates in these races, with about 35–40 percent of respondents consistently taking this position across the four variables. Beyond this, though, evaluations in male-only races are very similar to those in the mixed-sex races.

Table 4.3. DISTRIBUTION OF SPECIFIC EVALUATIONS OF SENATE CANDIDATES

Mixed Sex	Men Better	No Difference	Women Better	N
Female policy	32.35%	24.20%	43.45%	818
Male policy	43.14%	23.99%	32.87%	812
Female traits	31.57%	29.08%	39.36%	822
Male traits	35.48%	31.84%	32.86%	813

Male Only	Republican Better	No Difference	Democrat Better	N
Female policy	34.09%	35.08%	30.83%	830
Male policy	40.85%	33.38%	25.77%	832
Female traits	32.40%	40.83%	26.77%	837
Male traits	36.02%	39.11%	24.87%	832

Respondents generally see Democratic and Republican men in fairly equal terms on both policy and trait dimensions, although each evaluation here favors the Republican candidate. This is most likely a function of the fact that six of the 10 Republican male Senate candidates represented here ran as incumbents.

Finally, we see that evaluations of candidates for governor are similar to those for Senate candidates (Table 4.4). Respondents are able to identify that one or the other candidate is superior on some trait or policy measure and only choose the "no difference" evaluation option approximately 30 percent of the time. In mixed-sex governor elections, voters see the women and men candidates as equally capable of handling female policies and favor men on male policies by a small margin. Female trait evaluations are quite evenly distributed across women and men candidates, although men are seen as being more likely to possess male traits a bit more often than are their women opponents. In male-only races, Democratic candidates are evaluated to be a bit better at handling female policy issues, and Republican candidates are thought to be stronger on male policies. This is, of course, in line with expectations based on partisan stereotypes about the issue ownership patterns of each party. Interestingly, with regard to trait evaluations, Democratic men are seen as more likely to possess both female and male traits than are Republican candidates, although the margins are not large. In general, Democratic and Republican candidates are evaluated fairly consistently.

Table 4.4. DISTRIBUTION OF SPECIFIC EVALUATIONS OF GOVERNOR CANDIDATES

Mixed Sex	Men Better	No Difference	Women Better	N
Female policy	36.23%	31.09%	32.68%	901
Male policy	38.40%	29.99%	31.61%	898
Female traits	34.88%	33.40%	31.72%	895
Male traits	41.39%	31.68%	26.94%	902

Male Only	Republican Better	No Difference	Democrat Better	N
Female policy	29.53%	32.28%	38.19%	1,058
Male policy	35.69%	30.01%	34.30%	1,059
Female traits	29.51%	33.99%	36.51%	1,053
Male traits	29.50%	32.33%	38.17%	1,055

In general, the data presented here demonstrate that abstract gender stereotypes are different from specific candidate evaluations in their distribution and patterns. Respondents see more differences in the abilities and traits of real candidates than they do between abstract "women and men." These perceived differences between women and men candidates do not always follow predicted patterns and, in some cases, are driven by political party as much as by candidate sex. Evaluations appear to be consistent across races, regardless of the sex of the candidate pairs, with evaluation patterns being similar in mixed-sex and male-only races. Level of office also appears to matter, with perceived differences between candidates being larger in Senate and governor races than in House elections.

ABSTRACT STEREOTYPES AND SPECIFIC EVALUATIONS IN CONTEXT

The comparison of stereotypes and evaluations offers evidence in support of the argument that abstract stereotypes are distinct from evaluations of specific candidates in real elections. This analysis is a good first step but is not a conclusive discussion of the relationship between stereotypes and evaluations. Indeed, the next step in the analysis is to determine whether voters employ the gender stereotypes they hold when they are faced with evaluating actual candidates for office, while controlling for other important influences. In doing so, there are several things to consider. First, an important element of this analysis is the recognition that studying real-world elections is different from experimental and hypothetical work in the complexity of actual election situations. Indeed, one of the primary arguments I make is that gender stereotypes pale in comparison to the traditional political influences at play in elections. As a result, we have to account for these important influences in the analysis of candidate evaluations and examine the influence (or lack thereof) of stereotypes in this context. Primary among these influences is political party identification. If political party identification is the most important influence on reactions to political candidates, we should expect this to be the case even in the presence of women candidates. Respondents who share the party identification of the woman candidate should be more likely to evaluate the woman candidate more positively than other respondents. Other potential influences on candidate evaluations include the incumbency status of the candidates, the competitiveness of the race, and how much money candidates spent on their campaigns. Incumbents, with their resource advantages and name recognition, are likely to be more well known and liked than challengers, which could translate into better evaluations. Candidates who spend more money should get more positive evaluations. Competitive elections and those between candidates who spend large amounts of money are usually races in which information is more freely available. The information exchanged in campaigns is then available for voters in forming evaluations of candidates.

Other important considerations include the level of office being sought and the political party of the woman candidate. Work on gender stereotypes assumes that they will be most useful in low-information elections in which voters may have little information and less necessary in more high-visibility races where more might be known about the candidates (Conover and Feldman 1989; McDermott 1998). If this is the case, we should see abstract stereotypes being more useful to voters as they develop evaluations of candidates for the House and less useful in considering candidates for higher-visibility, statewide offices such as the Senate and governor. To account for this possibility, I examine the candidate evaluations made by respondents who took part in elections for U.S. House, U.S. Senate, and governor separately. With regard to the impact of political party, we need to acknowledge that several recent studies have found that voters interact differently with Democratic and Republican women candidates (King and Matland 2003; Koch 2002; Sanbonmatsu and Dolan 2009; Winter 2010). As Nicholas Winter (2010) has demonstrated, gender and partisan stereotypes have become closely intertwined, resulting in the possibility of multiple influences on impressions of women and men candidates depending on their party identification. Currently in American politics, both women and Democrats are seen as best able to deal with feminine issues such as education, child care, and family issues and as people more likely to compromise and work to build consensus. Men and Republicans are both thought to be superior on economic and military issues and to be people who can provide strong, decisive leadership. Overlap of the stereotypes of women and Democrats, and those of men and Republicans, has led Winter to refer to "feminized Democrats" and "masculinized Republicans." Given the consistent direction that stereotypes of women and Democrats take, we might expect that it would be "easier" for voters to employ abstract gender stereotypes in their evaluation of Democratic women. Republican women, for whom the stereotypes of "woman" and "Republican" send more inconsistent signals, may be less likely to experience gender-stereotyped evaluations. To account for this possibility, the analysis is presented separately for Democratic women who ran against Republican men and Republican women who ran against Democratic men.

In gauging whether abstract stereotypes are related to the specific candidate evaluations voters make, the dependent variables analyzed are the policy and trait evaluations that people made of the specific candidates in elections in their state/congressional district. These are the four summary variables that capture how respondents evaluate their candidates on possessing male and female traits and ability to handle male and female policy areas.[1] These variables are coded to reflect whether respondents thought that the woman candidate or her male opponent was more likely to possess female and male traits or policy competence or whether there was no difference between the two. The primary independent variables of interest are the measures of abstract policy and trait gender stereotypes that were asked in the first wave of the survey. If people's abstract stereotypes are important to shaping their specific political attitudes and behaviors, these measures should be related to specific candidate evaluations when individuals are participating in an election contested between a woman and a man. Included here are the four summary measures of abstract gender stereotypes, one each for the perceived policy competence of "women and men who run for office" on male and female issues and one each for beliefs about whether "women and men who run for office" possess typical male and female personality traits. These variables are coded to measure whether respondents hold what would be the expected stereotyped position.[2] The other independent variables in the analysis account for traditional political and contextual influences on evaluations. In this analysis, there are two measures of party identification—one coded to measure whether the respondent shares the party of the woman candidate, and the other coded to measure whether the respondent is an Independent. Other variables measure the incumbency status of the woman candidate, the competitiveness of the race, the percentage of total campaign spending that was spent by the woman candidate, whether the election was for an open seat, and how closely the respondent followed the House/Senate/governor race in his or her district or state. I hypothesize that abstract gender stereotypes will be less likely to shape candidate evaluations than will traditional influences such as party identification and incumbency.

ANALYSIS

U.S. House of Representatives

Taking evaluations of women Democratic House candidates first, Table 4.5 demonstrates that stereotypes exhibit almost no impact at all on evaluations of the policy abilities and traits of these women candidates. Across

Table 4.5. POLICY AND TRAIT EVALUATIONS OF DEMOCRATIC WOMEN IN MIXED-SEX HOUSE RACES

	Evaluation of Female Policy	Evaluation of Male Policy	Evaluation of Female Traits	Evaluation of Male Traits
Female policy	0.095	−0.037	−0.022	−0.112
stereotypes	(0.09)	(0.10)	(0.08)	(0.08)
Male policy stereotypes	−0.144	−0.258*	0.003	−0.018
	(0.09)	(0.12)	(0.08)	(0.08)
Female trait stereotypes	−0.119	0.033	0.030	0.105
	(0.12)	(0.15)	(0.11)	(0.11)
Male trait stereotypes	−0.091	−0.082	−0.169	−0.187
	(0.13)	(0.16)	(0.10)	(0.10)
Same party	2.695***	3.484***	2.353***	2.290***
	(0.27)	(0.33)	(0.25)	(0.25)
Independent	0.290	0.345	−0.396	−0.530
	(0.58)	(0.70)	(0.62)	(0.57)
Woman incumbent	0.568	1.087	0.644	0.905
	(0.50)	(0.61)	(0.50)	(0.51)
Open seat	−0.143	0.478	0.070	0.260
	(0.45)	(0.52)	(0.42)	(0.44)
Percent of spending by	0.750	0.549	0.675	0.958
woman	(0.61)	(0.77)	(0.61)	(0.66)
Competitive race	−0.307	−0.093	−0.036	−0.051
	(0.30)	(0.38)	(0.30)	(0.32)
Interest in House race	−0.079	−0.009	−0.002	0.010
	(0.13)	(0.16)	(0.13)	(0.13)
Constant	4.635***	4.215**	4.910***	4.439***
	(1.18)	(1.58)	(1.23)	(1.29)
Adjusted R^2	.36	.36	.32	.34
N	516	512	513	515

* $p < .05$, ** $p < .01$, *** $p < .001$, two-tailed test of significance.
Note: This table contains ordinary least squares regressions for policy and trait evaluations. Standard errors are in parentheses.

the four dependent variables, the only significant relationship between an abstract stereotype and a specific candidate evaluation involves attitudes about male policy competence. In this analysis, respondents who hold traditional stereotypes about men's superiority at handling male issues are less likely to evaluate the actual woman candidate in their House race as the better of the two candidates to handle these issues. This is in line with the findings of earlier work that raises concerns about the potential negative impact of stereotypes on the fate of women candidates. Here respondents who see men in the abstract as better able to handle male policy issues appear to be transferring that belief to the specific candidates in their House elections, which results in the Democratic women candidates being evaluated as less well suited to these policy issues than their male Republican opponents. At the same time, we see that respondents who do not hold traditional stereotypes about male policy competence are the ones who evaluate the woman candidate in their race higher on these issues than her male opponent. These more positive evaluations from those who do not hold traditional stereotypes may provide a counterbalance in support of women candidates. Beyond this, respondents do not appear to be employing stereotypes in their evaluations of individual candidates. Abstract stereotypes about female policies and male and female traits are not related at all to the policy and trait evaluations of Democratic women candidates. Indeed, stereotypes only matter in one of 16 possible relationships between abstract stereotypes and specific candidate evaluations. Given that both women and Democrats are generally seen as less competent on male policy issues than men and Republicans, it may be that the overlap of party and gender stereotypes makes Democratic women most vulnerable to being stereotyped on this dimension. Yet, despite the concerns raised by previous experimental research that attitudes about women's traditional limitations and strengths will work to the detriment of women candidates, this first analysis of attitudes toward specific candidates provides only very limited support for that concern. Instead, we see that abstract stereotypes do not appear to be particularly useful to voters as they develop evaluations of specific women candidates.

While this first look fails to provide much support for the notion that abstract gender stereotypes shape attitudes toward specific women candidates, the other point of this analysis is to place stereotypes alongside other important political influences. Indeed, the analysis here speaks to the central importance of political party to these candidate evaluations. On each of the four dependent variables, the strongest influence on specific evaluations, by far, is whether the respondent shared the political party of the woman candidate. Given what we know about the impact of party on attitudes and behavior, this is not surprising. When people approach the task of evaluating candidates in an election, their party is among the most important cues. Partisans are clearly disposed to evaluate their party's candidate positively. This finding contrasting the power of stereotypes with the impact of party suggests that stereotypes may not be as problematic for women candidates as some have suggested, at least not among fellow partisans. None of the other political and contextual influences appear to shape candidate evaluations here. While in general we might be surprised by the lack of an impact for incumbency, given the dynamics of the 2010 election and the success of Republican candidates in general, this finding probably makes sense in this case.

In looking at evaluations of Republican women House candidates (Table 4.6), we see a similar pattern to that of evaluations of Democratic women. First, the most important thing to note is the complete absence of an impact for abstract gender stereotypes in respondent evaluations of Republican women House candidates. These women appear to gain no

Table 4.6. POLICY AND TRAIT EVALUATIONS OF REPUBLICAN WOMEN IN MIXED-SEX HOUSE RACES

	Evaluation of Female Policy	Evaluation of Male Policy	Evaluation of Female Traits	Evaluation of Male Traits
Female policy stereotypes	−0.095 (0.14)	−0.192 (0.18)	−0.105 (0.14)	−0.031 (0.15)
Male policy stereotypes	0.126 (0.11)	0.162 (0.13)	0.101 (0.11)	0.049 (0.12)
Female trait stereotypes	0.158 (0.18)	0.072 (0.23)	0.034 (0.17)	−0.055 (0.17)
Male trait stereotypes	0.181 (0.16)	−0.240 (0.17)	−0.124 (0.12)	−0.120 (0.12)
Same party	3.385*** (0.34)	4.427*** (0.39)	2.873*** (0.33)	2.377*** (0.33)
Independent	4.859*** (0.75)	5.597*** (1.32)	3.086*** (0.66)	3.176*** (0.65)
Woman incumbent	2.614** (0.84)	2.489** (0.92)	1.813* (0.83)	2.279** (0.87)
Open seat	−0.449 (1.27)	0.918 (0.51)	0.693 (0.56)	0.651 (0.51)
Percent of spending by woman	−2.723* (1.18)	−2.373 (1.42)	−1.448 (1.18)	−0.754 (1.23)
Competitive race	0.123 (0.38)	−0.349 (0.47)	−0.109 (0.38)	−0.063 (0.40)
Interest in House race	0.376* (0.16)	0.349 (0.21)	0.403* (0.16)	0.360* (0.17)
Constant	7.970*** (2.02)	8.291*** (2.24)	6.435*** (1.73)	5.683** (1.74)
Adjusted R^2	.42	.46	.37	.34
N	228	226	227	221

* $p < .05$, ** $p < .01$, *** $p < .001$, two-tailed test of significance.
Note: This table contains ordinary least squares regressions for policy and trait evaluations. Standard errors are in parentheses.

benefit nor suffer any consequence from stereotyped thinking on the part of voters. While we do not have a direct test of this, it may be that conflicting gender and party stereotypes make evaluating Republican women a "harder" task for voters, particularly in lower-visibility House elections. If this is the case, voters may not be able to easily call on their gender stereotypes in forming evaluations of these women. However, as with Democratic women, a shared political party is the most significant influence on respondent likelihood of evaluating the Republican woman candidate higher than her male opponent. Interestingly, Republican women candidates also attracted more positive evaluations from Independent voters and those most interested in the House race in their district, and incumbent Republican women House members clearly received more positive evaluations than did their Democratic male opponents. This finding, which seems in keeping with the general tenor of the 2010 elections as a positive year for Republican candidates, indicates the importance of traditional political variables and campaign context to the fate of individual candidates.

U.S. Senate

The analysis of evaluations of House candidates indicated that voter gender stereotypes had almost no impact on these evaluations. Given that these races are generally considered low-visibility races, this is somewhat surprising. In examining Senate races, we would expect a continuation of that pattern, since the greater visibility and statewide nature of Senate races should provide voters with more specific information about individual candidates and decrease reliance on stereotypes.

Taking the analysis of Democratic women Senate candidates first (Table 4.7), we see results that differ considerably from those for House candidates. Here we see that several of the stereotypes are significantly related to evaluations of these Democratic women. Respondents who hold traditional stereotypes about women's superiority on female policies are more likely to evaluate the Democratic woman candidate as better able to handle female policies and more likely to possess stereotyped female traits than her male opponent. This may be a continuation of the impact of the overlap of party and gender stereotypes, as the perceived strengths of women and Democrats align here. This relationship between general stereotypes and evaluations of specific candidates works to help these Democratic women candidates by shaping positive evaluations of their policy capabilities and personality traits. However, the impact of male policy stereotypes works

	Evaluation of Female Policy	Evaluation of Male Policy	Evaluation of Female Traits	Evaluation of Male Traits
Female policy	0.292***	0.053	0.169*	0.129
stereotypes	(0.08)	(0.10)	(0.07)	(0.07)
Male policy stereotypes	−0.150*	−0.339***	−0.141*	−0.153*
	(0.07)	(0.09)	(0.06)	(0.07)
Female trait	0.227*	0.286*	0.217*	0.140
stereotypes	(0.09)	(0.12)	(0.09)	(0.09)
Male trait stereotypes	0.160	0.086	0.058	−0.061
	(0.10)	(0.13)	(0.09)	(0.10)
Same party	3.104***	3.759***	2.685***	2.552***
	(0.24)	(0.29)	(0.20)	(0.21)
Independent	2.047***	2.104***	1.523***	1.553***
	(0.54)	(0.42)	(0.31)	(0.32)
Woman incumbent	−1.292	−2.674*	−1.221	−0.969
	(1.03)	(1.08)	(0.62)	(0.59)
Open seat	−0.628	−1.198*	−0.267	−0.258
	(0.43)	(0.47)	(0.30)	(0.30)
Percent of spending by	3.334	5.447**	3.015**	3.334***
woman	(1.82)	(1.87)	(1.04)	(0.93)
Competitive race	0.372	0.531	0.136	0.088
	(0.46)	(0.52)	(0.32)	(0.32)
Interest in Senate race	−0.146	−0.370**	−0.129	−0.054
	(0.11)	(0.13)	(0.10)	(0.11)
Constant	1.629	6.849***	3.663**	5.076***
	(1.36)	(1.85)	(1.20)	(1.39)
Adjusted R^2	.40	.39	.39	.36
N	606	601	610	601

* $p < .05$, ** $p < .01$, * $p < .001$, two-tailed test of significance.
Note: This table contains ordinary least squares regressions for policy and trait evaluations. Standard errors are in parentheses.

in the opposite direction. Here we find that people who hold traditional stereotypes of men's superiority on male policies give Democratic women Senate candidates lower evaluations than their male opponents on all four policy and trait measures. This is similar to the impact of male policy stereotypes on evaluations of Democratic women House candidates. For these Democratic women Senate candidates, abstract policy stereotypes have the greatest impact on specific candidate policy evaluations, but the influence is present for evaluations across the board. Finally, female trait stereotypes also influence evaluations. Respondents who see women as more likely than men to possess traditional female traits evaluate the Democratic woman candidate more positively than her male opponent on both male and female policy abilities and on possession of female traits.

At first, finding that abstract stereotypes have this impact on Democratic women candidates for the Senate may seem surprising given that the literature suggests people will be less likely to rely on stereotypes in these high-information elections. However, there are a couple of things to keep in mind. First, the impact of female and male stereotypes appears to result in offsetting influences on candidate evaluations for Democratic women. These women candidates receive positive evaluations from respondents who hold traditional stereotypes about women's areas of superiority and lower evaluations among respondents who hold traditional stereotypes about men, which is consistent with Leonie Huddy's (1994) notion of the offsetting influence of stereotypes. Second, the impact of stereotypes on evaluations pales in comparison to the influence of the political and contextual variables at play. Sharing the political party of the woman results in respondents evaluating the woman candidate higher than her male opponent across the board—on both male and female policy and trait dimensions. The same relationship is true among respondents who identify as Independents, with these respondents evaluating women higher than men on all four variables. Interestingly, when Democratic women candidates spend more, they tend to receive higher evaluations than their Republican male opponents on both male and female dimensions. This would seem to indicate that women are successful at using their campaigns to garner favorable evaluations from voters.

While the extent to which abstract stereotypes shape voter evaluations of women Democratic candidates for the Senate is considerable, taking a look at the results for Republican women reminds us that all women candidates are not evaluated in the same way (King and Matland 2003; Koch 2002). As Table 4.8 demonstrates, stereotypes have a much more limited impact on evaluations of these women. Indeed, only female trait stereotypes are significantly related to any evaluations, with respondents who see women as more likely to possess stereotypically female traits being more likely to evaluate the Republican woman candidate as more competent on male policy issues than her Democratic male opponent. While we do not have a direct test of this, one explanation for this finding might again involve the relevance of party stereotypes. The Republican women candidates may be seen as better able to handle male policy areas than their Democratic male opponents based on party stereotypes, since Republicans are stereotyped as better at these issues than are Democrats (Winter 2010). Beyond this

Table 4.8. POLICY AND TRAIT EVALUATIONS OF REPUBLICAN WOMEN IN
MIXED-SEX SENATE RACES

	Evaluation of Female Policy	Evaluation of Male Policy	Evaluation of Female Traits	Evaluation of Male Traits
Female policy	0.074	−0.266	0.066	0.173
stereotypes	(0.25)	(0.21)	(0.18)	(0.17)
Male policy	0.214	0.309	0.119	0.087
stereotypes	(0.18)	(0.20)	(0.14)	(0.15)
Female trait	0.035	0.683*	0.294	0.132
stereotypes	(0.38)	(0.26)	(0.29)	(0.27)
Male trait stereotypes	−0.050	0.139	0.156	0.241
	(0.25)	(0.28)	(0.19)	(0.19)
Same party	4.218***	5.280***	3.651***	3.265***
	(0.53)	(0.68)	(0.55)	(0.57)
Independent	–	0.436	3.001***	1.542
	–	(1.65)	(0.74)	(0.96)
Open seat	0.919	1.412	0.254	0.483
	(0.79)	(0.99)	(0.66)	(0.70)
Percent of spending by	−1.548	−1.188	−0.280	−1.977
woman	(2.06)	(2.38)	(2.04)	(1.97)
Interest in Senate race	−0.301	−0.293	−0.160	−0.325
	(0.23)	(0.33)	(0.28)	(0.28)
Constant	3.881	−0.325	0.590	1.584
	(2.92)	(3.33)	(2.67)	(2.90)
Adjusted R^2	.42	.53	.41	.36
N	135	137	137	136

*$p < .05$, ** $p < .01$, *** $p < .001$, two-tailed test of significance.
Note: This table contains ordinary least squares regressions for policy and trait evaluations. The woman incumbent variable is excluded because none of the Republican women were incumbents. The competitive race variable is excluded because the only race that was competitive (Nevada) is also the only race where that was not an open seat. Independents are not included in the evaluation of female policy model because of the small number of respondents. Standard errors are in parentheses.

finding, abstract stereotypes do not appear to influence candidate evaluations on the other three dimensions. As we saw with House candidates, the evaluation of Republican women appears to be less sensitive to the influence of abstract gender stereotypes.

As we saw with the analysis of Democratic women, the most important influence on evaluations of Republican women Senate candidates is a shared political party identity. Republicans in the sample are overwhelmingly more likely to evaluate the Republican women candidates as superior to their male opponents on each of the four trait and policy dimensions. Clearly respondents are not employing gender stereotypes if they see women candidates as better at male *and* female policy areas and more likely to possess male *and* female traits. Instead, what we are seeing is partisans who see their own candidate as superior to the opposing party's candidate. This is not surprising at all, but it does provide evidence that traditional political variables are the most important influences on political attitudes and that these dynamics perform as expected even when women candidates are present.

There are several things to note about this analysis of the impact of gender stereotypes on evaluations of women Senate candidates. First, while we see stereotypes having a greater impact in these races than in races for the House, we have to keep in mind that stereotypes are still a minor influence on evaluations compared with political party and other contextual variables. This role for stereotypes in Senate races is somewhat counterintuitive, since past work suggests that stereotypes should be more useful to people in low-information environments such as House races. However, it may be that the higher visibility of these elections actually makes people more aware of the candidates, which then allows them to evaluate the candidates more fully. This suggestion is supported by the analysis that shows a markedly different role for stereotypes based on the political party of the woman candidate. Stereotypes have a greater impact on evaluations of Democratic women candidates than for Republican women. This difference may well be more about the power of partisan stereotypes than it is about gender. As Hayes and others have demonstrated, voters do see women Democrats and Republicans differently, with consequences for the way these women are evaluated (Hayes 2011; Koch 2002). Hayes (2011) argues that partisan stereotypes are more powerful than gender stereotypes and go a long way to explaining public reaction to women. The key here is the way that partisan and gender stereotypes interact. It is clear that the American public holds stereotypes about the policy abilities and personal traits of Democratic and Republican candidates and even extends these stereotypes out to parties themselves (Hayes 2010; Winter 2010). Democrats are seen as best able to handle female issues such as education, health care, and the environment, while Republicans are seen as better suited for defense, economic, and military policies. Democrats, often thought of as the "Mommy party," are thought to be more compassionate and concerned about the less fortunate, while "Daddy party" Republicans are seen as tougher and more focused on individual rights. The parallels between stereotypes of women and stereotypes of Democrats are obvious, as are the parallels between stereotypes of men and of Republicans. When women candidates run for office, voters are presented with multiple signals and identities on which they can draw to evaluate them. With regard to women candidates, it may be the case that Democratic women are an "easier" evaluation task for voters, since the stereotypes of Democrats and those of women overlap and reinforce each other. In this analysis, gender stereotypes may have been more influential because the consistency of party and gender signals makes it easier for voters to draw on that information in forming an evaluation, just as with the impact of male policy stereotypes on evaluations of Democratic women House candidates. This same thinking can explain the almost complete lack of a role for stereotypes in the evaluations of Republican women candidates. If Democratic women present a more consistent set of signals to voters, Republican women send signals that are at cross purposes. Stereotypes of women are at odds with stereotypes of Republicans. This may make evaluating women Republicans harder for voters—Are these candidates perceived as women or Republicans? In the end, the contradictory stereotypes may end up cancelling each other out and resulting in a situation in which these stereotypes are less useful to people. Indeed, the only time that stereotypes are related to evaluations of Republican women is when they are seen as better able to handle male issues than their Democratic male opponents, which would speak to the power of the party signal over the gender signal.

The last point to make about this Senate analysis is that we have to acknowledge the real world. The value of an examination like this is that we can get a look at how voters size up real candidates—individuals who run in particular states for particular offices in a particular election year. This means that there will be idiosyncrasies of candidates, context, and election dynamics that we have to consider—for example, that 2010 was a "wave" year for Republicans, with control of the House of Representatives going to Republicans along with a large number of governor offices. One thing to note is that there are many fewer women who ran for Senate than for House in 2010, as in all years. In all, there were 15 women Senate candidates, two of whom ran against each other in California. Eleven of the remaining 13 women are reflected in this data set. While these data include all but two of the women Senate candidates who ran against men, these women ran in 11 states, which means that there is less variation with regard to electoral context than in the House analysis. The other reality is that some of the women candidates who ran for Senate in 2010 were particularly visible, idiosyncratic candidates. This is certainly true for the Republican women, who were, for the most part, fairly conservative candidates, some of whom ran with Tea Party support and most of whom lost—for example, Sharron Angle, Linda McMahon, and Christine O'Donnell. Only six of the 15 women who ran for the Senate in 2010 (three of the 11 included in these data) were elected, and five of the six were incumbents seeking re-election. As a result, we have to keep in mind that this analysis illustrates the evaluations of that particular mix of candidates and electoral context.

Governors

Examining evaluations of candidates for governor provides an important contrast to races for the House and Senate. Our expectations for how people react to women running for governor are less clear because past research gives less guidance here than for legislative office. There are fewer executive offices than legislative in the United States and, as a result, fewer women candidates for these offices over time. Most of the work done on the impact of stereotypes of women running for executive offices has focused on the presidency. Given the unique nature of that office and the fact that no woman has ever run as a major-party candidate for president, extending the lessons of that research is problematic. Governors are, of course, executives, and earlier work suggests that voters see executive office as more "male" than legislative office, which could have an impact on whether women candidates are deemed appropriate for the position. Rosenwasser and Dean (1989) find that people see executive offices at every level as more prestigious and more "masculine" than legislative offices. Huddy and Terkildsen (1993a) demonstrate that a "good politician" for executive office is thought to need more male traits (assertive, active, rational) than for legislative office. These beliefs about the requirements for success in executive office can shape the candidate pool, as Richard Fox and Zoe Oxley (2003) find that women are much less likely to run for executive offices that align with male policy areas (governor, attorney general, treasurer) than with female or neutral policy areas (superintendent of education, secretary of state, Board of Elections). Interestingly, women are no less likely to win the "male" executive offices they do seek, but they are less likely to be candidates in the first place.

In 2010, a record-tying 10 women ran for governor. Of these 10 women, four ran in woman-only races in Oklahoma and New Mexico. Of the remaining six women candidates for governor, five of them are included in this analysis. This leaves us with a smaller number of woman-versus-man races, requiring us to exercise caution in interpreting the results of evaluations of candidates for governor. Taking Democratic women candidates first (Table 4.9), we see that only female trait stereotypes are significantly related to evaluations of women candidates for governor but that these stereotypes influence evaluations on all four policy and trait dimensions. Interestingly, holding female trait stereotypes results in respondents

Table 4.9. POLICY AND TRAIT EVALUATIONS OF DEMOCRATIC WOMEN IN MIXED SEX GOVERNOR RACES

	Evaluation of Female Policy	Evaluation of Male Policy	Evaluation of Female Traits	Evaluation of Male Traits
Female policy	0.264	0.118	0.147	0.210
stereotypes	(0.14)	(0.11)	(0.12)	(0.13)
Male policy	−0.258	−0.297	−0.218	−0.300
stereotypes	(0.17)	(0.15)	(0.19)	(0.18)
Female trait	−0.354*	−0.314*	−0.391*	−0.481**
stereotypes	(0.17)	(0.15)	(0.16)	(0.17)
Male trait	0.315	0.207	0.145	0.154
stereotypes	(0.18)	(0.14)	(0.18)	(0.18)
Same party	3.019***	2.522***	2.672***	2.666***
	(0.35)	(0.28)	(0.33)	(0.31)
Independent	1.712*	1.322***	1.346***	1.738***
	(0.78)	(0.25)	(0.37)	(0.41)
Interest in governor	0.201	0.099	0.287	0.395*
race	(0.17)	(0.14)	(0.17)	(0.16)
Constant	6.137*	6.361**	8.590***	8.897***
	(2.42)	(2.02)	(2.34)	(2.30)
Adjusted R^2	.32	.34	.30	.32
N	243	243	244	246

* $p < .05$, ** $p < .01$, *** $p < .001$, two-tailed test of significance.
Note: This table contains ordinary least squares regressions for policy and trait evaluations. The variables for woman incumbent, open seat races, spending, and competitiveness are excluded due to the small number of races and the lack of contextual variation. Standard errors are in parentheses.

evaluating these candidates lower than their male opponents on all four measures. One explanation for this may be that stereotypical female traits do not fit with people's perceptions of being an executive, which results in these stereotypes harming evaluations of women who run for governor across the board. At the same time, we have to exercise caution in drawing conclusions here, as there are only two Democratic women candidates in the data set—Alex Sink (FL) and Leslie Petersen (WY)—and these more negative evaluations may be a function of voter reactions to them specifically, particularly because each of them lost to their Republican male opponent. These two women candidates took part in very different races. Sink, who had previously won statewide office in Florida in being elected chief financial officer in 2006, lost a very competitive governor's race to Rick Scott by less than 1 percent. Leslie Petersen was the Democratic nominee for governor in an overwhelmingly Republican state and only received 23 percent of the vote. At the same time, when we look at the other major influences on evaluations of these women, we see that political party is far and away the most significant influence on voter reactions. Respondents who share the Democratic identification of the women candidates evaluate these women higher than their male opponents on each of the four policy and trait measures. Interestingly, both of these women also received more positive evaluations from Independent voters.

The three Republican women candidates for governor in this analysis—Jan Brewer (AZ), Nikki Haley (SC), and Meg Whitman (CA)—receive voter evaluations that are less affected by gender stereotypes (Table 4.10). Indeed, the only significant impact for stereotypes on evaluations involves female trait stereotypes. Here, voters who hold traditional female trait stereotypes evaluate these women candidates as more likely to possess female

Table 4.10. POLICY AND TRAIT EVALUATIONS OF REPUBLICAN WOMEN IN MIXED-SEX GOVERNOR RACES

	Evaluation of Female Policy	Evaluation of Male Policy	Evaluation of Female Traits	Evaluation of Male Traits
Female policy	0.016	−0.102	−0.118	−0.097
stereotypes	(0.08)	(0.06)	(0.07)	(0.07)
Male policy	0.208	0.153	0.137	0.142
stereotypes	(0.13)	(0.09)	(0.11)	(0.11)
Female trait	0.162	0.155	0.239*	0.185
stereotypes	(0.12)	(0.09)	(0.12)	(0.11)
Male trait stereotypes	0.016	−0.066	0.057	−0.027
	(0.11)	(0.09)	(0.10)	(0.10)
Same party	2.438***	2.229***	2.252***	2.004***
	(0.26)	(0.20)	(0.25)	(0.24)
Independent	0.812	0.904**	0.665	0.759*
	(0.62)	(0.34)	(0.51)	(0.39)
Percent of spending by	−1.583	−0.825	−2.198*	−3.701***
woman	(0.95)	(0.75)	(0.96)	(0.99)
Competitive race	0.461	−0.096	0.076	−0.253
	(0.40)	(0.30)	(0.39)	(0.42)
Interest in governor	−0.158	−0.140	−0.157	−0.215
race	(0.12)	(0.10)	(0.12)	(0.11)
Constant	5.086**	5.065***	6.470***	8.458***
	(1.62)	(1.34)	(1.57)	(1.53)
Adjusted R^2	.24	.29	.25	.24
N	572	568	566	571

* $p < .05$, ** $p < .01$, *** $p < .001$, two-tailed test of significance.
Note: This table contains ordinary least squares regressions for policy and trait evaluations. The variable for woman incumbent is excluded because only one race (Arizona) featured a woman incumbent. Standard errors are in parentheses.

traits than their male opponents. This is an interesting finding given these women candidates, each of whom ran a tough, no-nonsense campaign. Brewer was the incumbent governor of Arizona, who supported and signed the controversial state law requiring residents to carry papers to prove their immigration status or risk deportation. Haley survived a bruising Republican primary campaign in which she was accused of having an extra-marital affair. Whitman is the founder and former CEO of eBay and has a reputation as a no-nonsense business executive. Beyond this, gender stereotypes about policies and male traits are not related to candidate evaluations at all. Instead, as we have seen before, a shared party identification is the most important influence on evaluations. Republicans evaluate their party's women candidates higher than the Democratic male opponents on all four policy and trait measures. Independents evaluate these Republican women as superior to their Democratic male opponents on male policy and male trait measures. This could indicate the greater impact of party stereotypes over gender stereotypes, as these findings are in line with what we would expect people to conclude about Republicans in general. The other interesting finding here is the negative impact of campaign spending by Republican women candidates on evaluations of their female and male traits. Here we see that voters judged Republican women candidates more harshly on their trait evaluations in races where the women candidates spent more money than their male opponents. While it may seem counter-intuitive at first, this result is largely driven by Meg Whitman's candidacy for governor of California. Whitman broke all records for campaign spending in a nonpresidential race in the United States, spending $177 million, $144 million of it her own money, in losing to Jerry Brown by 13 percentage points (Mehta and Reston 2011). This would indicate that, despite her campaign spending, Whitman was not successful in making herself personally appealing to voters.

Analyzing evaluations of women candidates for governor reveals patterns that are similar to those seen in the analysis for the Senate. Stereotypes appear to matter more to evaluations of Democratic women candidates than for Republican ones, but stereotypes are always dwarfed by the importance of political party in shaping voter response to women. Party differences in reaction to women candidates may be a result of the different ways in which gender stereotypes interact with partisan stereotypes. These differences may also be a result of the particular races and candidates who ran for governor in 2010. There were 10 such women candidates that year, four of whom won their elections. Five of the 10 are reflected in these analyses. Of the five other women candidates for governor, four are excluded here because they ran in same-sex races with two women candidates in

Oklahoma and New Mexico. As with Senate candidates, the relatively small number of women who run for governor requires that we exercise some care in drawing conclusions.

WHAT ABOUT MEN?

Scholars and political practitioners have long expressed concern that the gender stereotypes people hold about women and men can create difficulties for women candidates if they are not perceived to be capable of handling the issues and tasks of governing. In examining the impact of people's gender stereotypes on evaluations of women candidates who run against men, we have seen only limited evidence that stereotypes influence evaluations of women candidates. In House elections, stereotypes mattered very little. In Senate and governor races, gender stereotypes created more favorable evaluations of women candidates as often as they lowered them. Instead, what became obvious is the important role of political party and other contextual variables. Partisans embrace their party's women candidates. Incumbents are often evaluated positively. Campaign spending matters in some cases. Beyond this, we also learned that voters evaluate Democratic and Republican women candidates differently, clearly employing partisan stereotypes in various situations. These findings are all important expansions of our understanding of how voters evaluate women candidates. But they do not tell the whole story. Past research on gender stereotypes has always focused on their impact on women candidates, with almost no attention at all to whether these attitudes influence reaction to men running for office. If gender stereotypes are about what women *and* men are good at or what they are like, we should assume that stereotypes can influence reactions to men who run for office. Indeed, we need to know more about whether these stereotypes are relevant to men, as failing to do so implies that gendered considerations are not important to men. Examining the experiences of men candidates allows us to determine if voter reliance on gender stereotypes is only activated in the presence of a woman candidate. By examining the influence of gender stereotypes in races *without* women present, we learn more about what governs reaction to both women and men. Indeed, if stereotypes matter in male-only races, this may be an example of the connections between stereotypes and political party images.

The sample that was created for this project was stratified to include races in which a woman ran against a man and those in which two men ran against each other. Respondents in male-only races were asked the same sets of questions about abstract gender stereotypes and specific candidate evaluations. As a result, we can conduct the same analysis of voter evaluations of these candidates that was presented for women running against men. Because both candidates here are men, the dependent variables measure evaluations of the Democratic candidate. The analysis is conducted separately for each of the three offices.

House Races

The analysis of the determinants of evaluations for Democratic men running for the House presented in Table 4.11 provides an interesting take on the utility of gender stereotypes in elections when women are not candidates. Much of the past work on stereotypes assumes that gender stereotypes are activated when women candidates seek office, which means that we have little understanding of whether the experiences of male candidates are shaped by these attitudes. The analysis of male-only House races suggests that this can be the case. First, both male and female policy stereotypes are significantly related to how voters evaluate Democratic male candidates. People who hold traditional female policy stereotypes evaluate the Democratic man more positively than his Republican opponent on all four policy and trait dimensions. Holding traditional male policy stereotypes leads to lower evaluations of Democratic men on all four dimensions. There are two things to take from these results. First, an impact for policy stereotypes here provides support for the assumption that stereotypes will matter more in low-information races such as the House, which differs from the results we saw for mixed-sex House races. The other important aspect of these results is that they underscore the degree to which partisan and gender stereotypes can interact—female issues are Democratic issues, and male issues are Republican issues. Recall that the questions measuring gender stereotypes asked people to judge "women and men officeholders" with regard to policy and trait characteristics. Yet here we see people linking these gender stereotypes in the way that *partisan* stereotypes would predict—Democrats appealing more to those who see women as better at female policy areas and Republicans being seen more positively by voters who see men as better at male policies. Again, the overlap of partisan and gender stereotypes seems clear, and voters appear to be likely to hold consistent partisan and gender stereotypes and employ them even in the absence of women candidates.

Beyond this, other variables perform as expected. As with races between women and men, respondent partisanship is the strongest predictor of

TABLE 4.11. POLICY AND TRAIT EVALUATIONS OF THE DEMOCRATIC CANDIDATE IN MALE-ONLY HOUSE RACES

	Evaluation of Female Policy	Evaluation of Male Policy	Evaluation of Female Traits	Evaluation of Male Traits
Female policy	0.145*	0.141*	0.126*	0.158**
stereotypes	(0.06)	(0.07)	(0.05)	(0.05)
Male policy	−0.181***	−0.237***	−0.174***	−0.199***
stereotypes	(0.05)	(0.06)	(0.05)	(0.05)
Female trait	0.007	0.022	0.006	−0.039
stereotypes	(0.07)	(0.09)	(0.07)	(0.06)
Male trait	0.097	0.088	0.051	0.028
stereotypes	(0.07)	(0.09)	(0.07)	(0.07)
Democrat	2.445***	3.281***	2.231***	2.085***
	(0.16)	(0.21)	(0.16)	(0.16)
Independent	1.479***	2.083***	1.383***	1.193***
	(0.29)	(0.38)	(0.25)	(0.30)
Democrat incumbent	−0.067	−0.332	−0.408	0.109
	(0.36)	(0.47)	(0.36)	(0.35)
Open seat	0.067	0.400	−0.252	0.149
	(0.28)	(0.35)	(0.28)	(0.26)
Percent of spending	1.609***	2.492***	2.010***	2.048***
by Democrat	(0.47)	(0.62)	(0.47)	(0.45)
Competitive race	−0.023	0.041	0.027	−0.048
	(0.19)	(0.25)	(0.19)	(0.19)
Interest in House	−0.094	−0.290**	−0.109	−0.062
race	(0.09)	(0.11)	(0.08)	(0.08)
Constant	3.845***	4.418***	3.858***	3.203***
	(0.72)	(0.90)	(0.72)	(0.72)
Adjusted R^2	.31	.34	.31	.33
N	1,372	1,361	1,367	1,358

* $p < .05$, ** $p < .01$, *** $p < .001$, two-tailed test of significance.
Note: This table contains ordinary least squares regressions for policy and trait evaluations. Clustered standard errors are in parentheses.

candidate evaluations. Democratic respondents evaluate Democratic male candidates higher than their Republican opponents on all four policy and trait variables. Interestingly, Independent voters also evaluate Democratic candidates higher than Republicans on each of the four measures. Finally, higher levels of campaign spending by the Democratic candidate result in more positive evaluations across the board, which would indicate that these candidates were successful in using their campaigns to achieve positive evaluations from voters. These findings are all consistent with expectations and with the general pattern of the political influences on evaluations of women candidates in mixed-sex races.

Senate Races

The analysis of male-only Senate races is fairly straightforward and conforms to broad expectations about when stereotypes are useful to voters (Table 4.12). Here we see that voter stereotypes are not related to

Table 4.12. POLICY AND TRAIT EVALUATIONS OF THE DEMOCRATIC CANDIDATE IN MALE-ONLY SENATE RACES

	Evaluation of Female Policy	Evaluation of Male Policy	Evaluation of Female Traits	Evaluation of Male Traits
Female policy stereotypes	0.050	0.022	−0.014	0.031
	(0.09)	(0.12)	(0.10)	(0.10)
Male policy stereotypes	−0.060	−0.073	−0.035	−0.063
	(0.07)	(0.10)	(0.08)	(0.08)
Female trait stereotypes	−0.121	−0.013	−0.003	−0.050
	(0.09)	(0.10)	(0.09)	(0.08)
Male trait stereotypes	−0.036	−0.012	−0.051	−0.021
	(0.09)	(0.11)	(0.09)	(0.09)
Democrat	2.520***	3.219***	2.282***	2.074***
	(0.22)	(0.27)	(0.21)	(0.20)
Independent	2.316***	3.235***	1.617***	1.698***
	(0.55)	(0.85)	(0.44)	(0.46)
Democrat incumbent	−0.193	−0.291	−0.184	1.444
	(0.85)	(1.09)	(0.83)	(0.87)
Open seat	−0.362	−0.313	−0.574	0.676
	(0.56)	(0.71)	(0.56)	(0.58)
Percent of spending by	3.131*	2.546	2.208	0.426
Democrat	(1.54)	(2.05)	(1.57)	(1.64)
Competitive race	−0.522	−0.532	−0.110	−0.340
	(0.31)	(0.40)	(0.31)	(0.31)
Interest in Senate race	−0.098	−0.280*	−0.053	−0.110
	(0.10)	(0.13)	(0.10)	(0.10)
Constant	5.925***	6.933***	5.794***	5.563***
	(1.13)	(1.45)	(1.18)	(1.22)
Adjusted R^2	.28	.28	.25	.24
N	771	772	777	772

* $p < .05$, *** $p < .001$, two-tailed test of significance.
Note: This table contains ordinary least squares regressions for policy and trait evaluations. Standard errors are in parentheses.

candidate evaluations at all. This contrast to the findings for the male-only House races is in line with conventional wisdom that information cues such as gender stereotypes are less important in higher-visibility elections where voters are likely to have more specific information about candidates. Interestingly, it is the male-only races that conform to this expected pattern, while in the woman-versus-man races, stereotypes were more influential on the candidate evaluations of Senate candidates. What does matter to evaluations of Democratic male Senate candidates is partisanship. As we saw with House races, Democrats and Independents evaluate Democratic male Senate candidates as better than their Republican opponents on all four evaluation variables. Male Democrats also benefit from their campaign spending, which results in higher evaluations from voters on female policy dimensions. As we saw with the male-only House races, this finding that male Democrats are seen as superior to their Republican opponents on female policy issues no doubt signals the operation of partisan stereotypes about Democrats having "ownership" of these issue areas.

Governor Races

Table 4.13 presents the final analysis, that of evaluations of Democratic male candidates for governor in male-only races. These results are very similar to those for Senate candidates, with one exception. Here we see that evaluations of the male policy competence of Democratic men are lower than for Republican men among respondents who hold traditional stereotypes about men being better at these issues.[3] This again highlights the interaction of gender and partisan stereotypes. If gender stereotypes were an important influence here, the party of the male candidate would be irrelevant. Instead we see that Democratic men are not given credit for possessing typical male policy competences in the same way Republican men are. As with women, we see that candidates are evaluated differently based on their political party. It also may be the case that policy stereotypes are most relevant to evaluations of governor candidates because of the executive nature of the position. With regard to the more traditional political influences on evaluations, we continue to see the impact of the expected influences. As all of the previous analysis has demonstrated, a shared partisanship is the most important influence on candidate evaluations. Democrats and Independents evaluated Democratic men running for governor more positively than their Republican opponents. Also, Democratic men who spent more money received the benefit of higher evaluations across the board on policies and traits. However, in competitive races for

Table 4.13. POLICY AND TRAIT EVALUATIONS OF THE DEMOCRATIC
CANDIDATE IN MALE-ONLY GOVERNOR RACES

	Evaluation of Female Policy	Evaluation of Male Policy	Evaluation of Female Traits	Evaluation of Male Traits
Female policy	0.096	0.057	0.022	0.040
stereotypes	(0.06)	(0.05)	(0.06)	(0.06)
Male policy	−0.180	−0.174*	−0.108	−0.094
stereotypes	(0.10)	(0.08)	(0.10)	(0.11)
Female trait	−0.107	−0.102	−0.060	−0.083
stereotypes	(0.08)	(0.07)	(0.08)	(0.08)
Male trait stereotypes	−0.051	−0.109	−0.036	−0.042
	(0.09)	(0.07)	(0.08)	(0.10)
Democrat	2.759***	2.336***	2.536***	2.473***
	(0.19)	(0.15)	(0.18)	(0.18)
Independent	0.766	0.876*	1.025**	1.177**
	(0.57)	(0.44)	(0.35)	(0.36)
Democrat incumbent	0.228	−0.040	−0.036	0.003
	(0.21)	(0.16)	(0.19)	(0.21)
Percent of spending	2.315**	1.471*	2.563**	3.266***
by Democrat	(0.86)	(0.67)	(0.82)	(0.78)
Competitive race	−0.355	−0.511*	−0.282	−0.391
	(0.28)	(0.22)	(0.27)	(0.26)
Interest in governor	0.049	−0.002	−0.068	−0.006
race	(0.10)	(0.07)	(0.09)	(0.09)
Constant	4.195***	2.733**	5.153***	4.859***
	(1.10)	(0.85)	(1.05)	(1.09)
Adjusted R^2	.33	.36	.31	.31
N	981	980	980	979

* $p < .05$, ** $p < .01$, *** $p < .001$, two-tailed test of significance.
Note: This table contains ordinary least squares regressions for policy and trait evaluations. Standard errors are in parentheses.

governor in 2010, Democratic men were evaluated less positively than their Republican opponents on male policy competence.

CONCLUSIONS: EVALUATIONS OF WOMEN AND MEN

While the primary focus of this project is to examine the role that gender stereotypes might play in shaping the fortunes of women candidates, considering the experiences of male candidates provides additional leverage for understanding these dynamics. The benefit to including the male-only races is that we can begin to address the implicit assumption that gender stereotypes are only relevant to voters when women candidates are present.

In examining whether voters employ their abstract gender stereotypes of women and men when they are faced with the task of evaluating specific, individual women and men candidates, we find that the evidence is mixed. First, and perhaps most central, gender stereotypes are not uniformly and consistently present as an influence on evaluations of candidates of either sex. Stereotypes play next to no role in evaluations of women running for the House. They appear to have a greater impact on evaluations for women Senate and gubernatorial candidates, but only for Democratic women. For men, the reverse is true. Gender stereotypes have a limited impact on policy evaluations of male House and governor candidates but not on those running for Senate. Beyond this, we see strong evidence that what appears to be an influence for gender stereotypes is mediated by political party considerations. Stereotypes have a limited relationship to evaluations of Democratic women running for Senate and governor but no impact on Republican woman candidates for those offices. Gender stereotypes are significantly related to evaluations of male candidates for the House, but in ways that clearly represent the intersection of party and gender stereotypes. Democratic men are favored by voters who hold traditional stereotypes about female policy issues, and Republican men are favored by those who carry male policy stereotypes, indicating that people can employ their stereotypes of women and men even when they are only faced with male candidates through the process of linking gender and party impressions.

Finally, even though gender stereotypes appear to influence evaluations in some situations, their impact always pales in comparison to the strong and significant influence of party correspondence between voters and candidates. Voters evaluate candidates of their party as superior to candidates of the opposing party in all circumstances and across all four policy and trait evaluation measures. Indeed, this influence is not so much one of stereotyping along party or gender lines but, instead, a belief that one's party's candidates are always superior to candidates of the other party. In the end, then, these results indicate that women and men are sometimes viewed through the lens of stereotypes but that these stereotypes are not often purely about reactions to women and men. Instead they are bound up with the overlay of people's impressions about political parties. These findings support a recent and growing body of research that demonstrates the way that gender and party images have become interconnected in contemporary American politics (Hayes 2010, 2011; Koch 2002; Sanbonmatsu and Dolan 2009; Winter 2010).

As we have seen, candidate evaluations are shaped by a myriad of influences at work in the electoral environment. The evaluations that voters make are an important part of assessing the viability of a candidate for elected office and reflect the sum total of important elements of voter attributes, the candidates themselves, and the context of the given election. But evaluations are not the end of the process. Instead they are an important influence on the most central consideration in elections—vote choice. Whether gender stereotypes are a barrier to the election of women is the key question and is one to which we now turn.

CHAPTER 5

The Role of Stereotypes in Vote Choice Decisions

Although we weren't able to shatter that highest, hardest glass ceiling this time, thanks to you, it's got about 18 million cracks in it.

Hillary Clinton, U.S. Senator (D-NY)

In June 2008, when Hillary Clinton conceded the Democratic nomination for president to then-senator Barack Obama, she made reference to the "18 million cracks" her supporters had helped her put in the glass ceiling standing between a woman candidate and the U.S. presidency. These 18 million cracks represented the 18 million votes she received in becoming the first woman candidate to win a presidential primary. For all of the symbolism of her candidacy, these 18 million votes are its most important legacy, since, at the end of the day, it is votes that determine whether candidates win or lose. Clinton did indeed lose the Democratic nomination, but the 18 million votes she received demonstrated loudly and clearly that Americans will vote for a woman candidate for president. This is, of course, the heart of the question about women candidates in the United States—Will people vote for them? Will they be seen as viable candidates, or will something about their sex, related gender issues, or historical concerns about women in politics limit their opportunities? In this next examination of the role of gender stereotypes in the success of women candidates in 2010, we consider whether stereotypes have any influence on voting patterns in races involving women candidates.

In thinking about whether voters will support women candidates at the polls, it is important to note that much of the information we have focuses on public reaction to a woman running for president. This is ironic, since in 2014 we still have never had a woman major-party candidate for president in the United States, which means that all women candidates are running for subpresidential office. As a result, we have a fairly large body of work that examines people's reaction to the hypothetical situation of a woman president and much less work that gauges voter reaction to the women who actually do run. Beginning in 1936, the Gallup Organization began asking people the following question: "Would you vote for a woman for president if she was qualified in every other respect?" At that time, 65 percent of the public said no (Smith 1979). Note, of course, that the structure of the question implies that the major way in which she is not qualified is as a woman. This question wording has changed over time, reflecting a move away from an automatic assumption.that a woman's sex was her disqualifying trait, to the present form that asks, "If your party nominated a generally well-qualified person for president who happened to be a woman, would you vote for that person?" Responses to this newer question clearly show that the American people have steadily changed their thinking about whether they would vote for a woman candidate for our nation's highest office, as the vast majority (95 percent) in the contemporary period indicate that they would do so. Of course, the more recent form of the question highlights the primacy of political party in decision making in American politics, as people are asked to consider whether they would support a woman candidate of their own party. Given that party identification overwhelmingly shapes vote choice in elections, this makes sense, but it is important to recognize that polling data on this issue do not tap general support for a woman president but, instead, support that is tied to a respondent's political identification. Levels of support for this idea of a woman president, already high, have not changed much since the high-visibility candidacies of Hillary Clinton and Sarah Palin in 2008, when their quests for the presidency and vice presidency, respectively, stimulated broad societal conversations about the possibility of a woman in the White House. Indeed, in 2009, after these historic candidacies, 92 percent of Americans said that they would vote for a woman, although 56 percent said that they thought that "America was not ready for a woman leader" (Pew Research Center 2008).

Most recent data on the question of a woman president continue to suggest high levels of support among Americans. A 2013 poll of voters in nine competitive "battleground" states conducted for Emily's List found that 90 percent of respondents said they would vote for a "qualified woman candidate" from their political party (Emily's List 2013).[1] Beyond this, 86 percent of respondents now believe that the United States is ready for a woman president, and 72 percent predicted that a woman will be elected in 2016. The survey found positive attitudes toward women in office beyond the presidency, with 51 percent of voters surveyed saying that the women elected to Congress in 2012 are making a positive difference in government and politics. In terms of evaluating women and men as possible presidents, respondents perceived a woman to be as capable as or more capable than a man on a range of policy and personal actions. In contrast to research that has found women to be disadvantaged compared with men, this survey found that respondents rated a woman president as likely as a man to exercise good judgment, rise above partisan bickering, and stand up to party leaders.

Several analyses of voting returns of elections involving women candidates who run for office below the level of the presidency find that their sex is not a direct impediment to success. Work by Jody Newman (1994) declared that "when women run, women win," demonstrating that women candidates for congressional and statewide office won as often as male candidates in comparable circumstances. Work that examines voting in races in which women ran against men as far back as the 1970s and 1980s found no disadvantage for women running for local, statewide, or congressional office (Burrell 1994; Darcy, Welch, and Clark 1987; Eckstrand and Eckert 1981; Karnig and Walter 1976; Zipp and Plutzer 1985). Darcy and Schramm (1977) also find that political party can matter, finding that women and men had similar success rates in running for Congress but Democratic women won more often than did Republican women. Examining more recent elections, I (Dolan 2004) found that voting for women candidates for Congress in the 1990s was explained by the same factors that explained voting for men—primarily party identification and incumbency status. Smith and Fox (2001) report similar support for women running for Congress, but they find evidence of an electoral advantage for women over men in running for open seats in the House.

While evidence from election results suggests that women candidates win at least as often as men, this work is contradicted by experimental work and studies of hypothetical candidates, which tend to find that voters can harbor biases against women candidates. Many of these works focus on gender stereotypes and the implications they can have for voter decision making. For example, Paul and Smith (2008) found that potential women candidates for president, Hillary Clinton and Elizabeth Dole, "lost" every hypothetical matchup with a series of male rivals—John Edwards, Rudy Guiliani, and John McCain. Fox and Smith (1998) conducted an experiment in which they found that some college students were less willing to say that they would vote for hypothetical women candidates for Congress. Some work demonstrates that voters devalue candidate characteristics when they are associated with women candidates, although these studies do not ask respondents directly about their willingness to vote for women candidates (Huddy and Terkildsen 1993b; Rosenwasser and Dean 1989; Smith et al. 2007). Lawless (2004) demonstrated that concerns about women's abilities to fight terrorism in the immediate aftermath of September 11th led people to express less support for the idea of a woman president. While this research can be instructive, the lack of information about people's willingness to vote for actual women candidates means that we do not know whether stereotypes do indeed push people away from voting for women.

Whether implicitly or explicitly, the literature on gender stereotypes suggests that women candidates are perceived differently than men by voters and that these differences result, on balance, in concerns about women's electoral viability. However, the disconnect between types of analyses remains here—research that focuses on voting returns generally does not have information about voter gender stereotypes. Research that examines stereotypes is generally conducted on hypothetical candidates or in experimental treatments. And public opinion polls tend not to ask questions about supporting women candidates for offices where women are actually running. As a result, we are still lacking an ability to directly test whether voters use gender stereotypes in making choices among candidates.

STEREOTYPES AND VOTING IN 2010

The analysis in chapter 4 demonstrated that gender stereotypes have a limited and inconsistent impact on the candidate evaluations that voters make. The next step is to examine whether and how voters employ stereotypes in their vote choice decisions. The data analyzed here allow me to address several important aspects of these decisions. First, we can consider the potential impact of stereotypes alongside other important political influences such as party, incumbency, and candidate spending. Beyond this, we can examine whether voter willingness to vote for a woman candidate depends on the office she seeks by examining races for House, Senate, and governor. Finally, we can compare the dynamics of vote choice in races with women candidates with those in male-only races to see whether the presence of women changes the calculations voters make.

Chapter 4 argued that candidate evaluations are an important step in the process of voters deciding whether they can support a particular candidate. The analysis examined whether abstract gender stereotypes shape the evaluations that voters make of specific candidates for office. Fully accounting for the potential impact of gender stereotypes on vote choice, then, requires an acknowledgment that stereotypes could influence vote choice directly or indirectly through an impact on evaluations. At the same time, we know that candidate evaluations themselves can be an important influence on vote choice, as voters are more likely to vote for candidates they evaluate positively and less likely to vote for those whom they evaluate more negatively. For this reason, the vote choice analysis proceeds as follows. First, to examine whether gender stereotypes have a direct impact on voting for women, the stereotype variables are used to predict vote choice alongside the political variables of interest. Then, to account for the possibility that the impact of stereotypes on vote choice is mediated through candidate evaluations, vote choice is estimated a second time as a function of the abstract stereotypes, the specific candidate evaluations, and the political variables (Malhotra and Krosnick 2007).

The primary independent variables of interest here are the four measures of the male and female policy and trait stereotypes employed in previous analyses. If, as much of the literature suggests, people use gender stereotypes in deciding whether to support women candidates, these stereotypes should be significantly related to vote choice. In the second model, I also employ the four variables that measure the evaluations respondents made about the specific women and men candidates in their elections. Since the other major assumption of this research is that stereotypes will matter less to vote choice when we consider them alongside traditional contextual factors thought to exert an impact on evaluations and vote choice, I include a series of important political and contextual influences on vote choice. These include whether the respondent shares the party of the woman candidate, whether the respondent is an Independent, the incumbency status of the woman candidate, the competitiveness of the race, the percentage of total campaign spending that was spent by the woman candidate, and whether the election was for an open seat. The vote choice analysis is run separately for each of the three offices. Within office type, I analyze the determinants of vote choice for Democratic women and Republican women separately.

As suggested earlier, gender stereotypes can influence vote choice decisions directly or indirectly through their influence on candidate evaluations. To test both of these possibilities, Table 5.1 presents the results of two separate analyses of the determinants of vote choice in mixed-sex House races. The first examines a direct effect for stereotypes on vote choice and includes the four measures of abstract stereotypes (female and male policies and traits) and the political context variables. The second model considers the possibility of mediation and tests the impact of abstract stereotypes and specific candidate evaluations side by side, along with the political variables.

Turning to an analysis of the potential for a direct impact of gender stereotypes on vote choice in races involving Democratic women House candidates (Column 1), we see that none of the respondent stereotypes have an impact on vote choice. Put another way, people's abstract gender stereotypes about whether women or men are better at handling policy areas such as education or foreign affairs or which sex is able to provide greater leadership or compassion are *not* related to their vote choice when they choose between women and men candidates in their local House election. Instead, there is one primary and dominant influence on people's vote choice here—political party. People who share the same party as the woman are more likely to vote for her than for the male candidate of the other party. And, of course, the same is true for the men candidates—party identifiers vote for them more often than the woman candidate of the opposing party.

Column 2 examines the impact of stereotypes alongside the variables measuring the specific candidate evaluations. Here the analysis indicates that the important attitudes are those that people form toward specific candidates, not abstract stereotypes about women and men in general. Again we see that none of the abstract stereotypes are related to choosing a Democratic woman House candidate but, instead, that the candidate evaluations are important. Not surprisingly, respondents who saw the woman candidate as better than her male opponent at handling both female and male policy issues were more likely to vote for her over her male opponent. The same is true for people who saw the woman candidate as exhibiting traditional male traits. Evaluations of female traits are not significantly related to vote choice, suggesting that voters may place a lower value on these considerations when choosing for whom to vote. As with the analysis in Column 1, we see that political party remains the most important influence on vote choice for Democratic women. The lack of an impact for stereotypes on vote choice demonstrated here, along with the absence of

Table 5.1. HOUSE VOTE CHOICE IN MIXED-SEX RACES

	Democrat Women	Democrat Women	Republican Women	Republican Women
Stereotypes				
Female policy	−0.051	0.125	−0.535**	−0.468
	(0.13)	(0.18)	(0.20)	(0.28)
Male policy	0.026	0.096	0.153	−0.141
	(0.13)	(0.17)	(0.14)	(0.29)
Female trait	0.287	0.205	0.623**	0.563
	(0.16)	(0.35)	(0.21)	(0.42)
Male trait	−0.188	−0.269	0.397	0.451
	(0.14)	(0.23)	(0.20)	(0.33)
Evaluations				
Female policy	–	0.362*	–	0.813**
	–	(0.17)	–	(0.30)
Male policy	–	0.497**	–	0.537
	–	(0.18)	–	(0.30)
Female trait	–	0.382	–	0.013
	–	(0.34)	–	(0.43)
Male trait	–	0.717*	–	0.230
	–	(0.33)	–	(0.48)
Same party	2.966***	2.233***	3.939***	2.528**
	(0.35)	(0.47)	(0.52)	(0.96)
Independent	−0.295	1.318	–	–
	(1.21)	(1.18)	–	–
Woman incumbent	0.742	1.451	2.335	1.400
	(0.63)	(0.96)	(1.29)	(1.83)
Open seat	−0.028	0.383	1.712	3.453*
	(0.51)	(0.87)	(0.93)	(1.63)
Percent of spending by woman	1.430	0.182	−1.729	−1.252
	(0.81)	(1.16)	(1.86)	(3.55)
Competitive House race	−0.321	−0.581	0.578	0.397
	(0.39)	(0.58)	(0.70)	(1.05)
Interest in House race	−0.038	0.252	0.563*	−0.020
	(0.19)	(0.35)	(0.25)	(0.38)
Constant	−5.569**	−23.076***	0.414	−14.160*
	(2.15)	(6.23)	(2.27)	(6.57)
Pseudo R^2	.40	.73	.49	.74
N	469	438	214	197

* $p < 0.05$, ** $p < 0.01$, *** $p < .001$, two-tailed test of significance.
Note: Standard errors are in parentheses.

an impact of stereotypes on Democratic candidate evaluations (Table 4.1), also reveals that there is no influence for stereotypes that is being mediated through an impact on candidate evaluations.[2]

In turning to the analysis of vote choice for races with Republican women, the model in Column 3 appears to indicate that, at first glance, abstract gender stereotypes can influence people's decision making. Here we see that people who hold traditional stereotypes about women's superiority in handling female issues such as education and health care are less likely to vote for the Republican woman candidate in their House race. It is likely that this finding is being driven, at least in part, by party stereotypes. While women are often seen as better at female issues than are men, Republicans are not usually identified with strength in these policy areas. So it may be the case that respondents are seeing these women as Republicans first and are assuming that they do not have the same competence on these issues as their Democratic male opponent. The other significant impact for stereotypes surrounds female traits, with people who see women as more likely than men to be compassionate consensus builders being more likely to vote for the Republican woman.

However, the more complete test of the impact of stereotypes offered in Column 4 suggests again that specific evaluations of individual candidates are more important to voter decision making than are abstract stereotypes. Once we include the measures of specific candidate evaluations, the impact of stereotypes disappears completely. Instead, what matters to people's choice of Republican women candidates is policy. As with Democratic women candidates, respondents who evaluated the Republican woman as better on female policy areas were more likely to vote for the woman than her male opponent. Trait evaluations are not significant to voters here. And as with Democratic women candidates, a shared party identity is the most important influence in choosing the woman Republican candidate. As with the analysis for Democratic candidates, there is also no evidence that stereotypes are indirectly influencing vote choice through candidate evaluations.[3]

U.S. Senate

While there is a clear lack of evidence of an impact for stereotypes in voting for the House, we cannot assume that the same dynamics are at play for other offices. Indeed, the analysis in chapter 4 demonstrated that the link between gender stereotypes and candidate evaluations differed by office. As work by Huddy and Terkildsen (1993a) suggests, people can have different expectations about the requirements for elected officials based on the level or type of office. Here we can also consider whether stereotypes are important to voting for the U.S. Senate and for governor. If we would expect stereotypes to have a greater impact on vote choice for lower-visibility offices such as the House (McDermott 1997, 1998), then we would not expect to see them matter much to vote choice in Senate elections. Table 5.2 provides the analysis of voting for women candidates for the Senate in 2010.

While one of the strengths of this project is the analysis of real-world reactions to women candidates, we have to acknowledge that, at times, the real world does not provide ideal circumstances for analysis. This challenge is visible in analyzing races for the U.S. Senate in 2010. As has been clear in earlier analyses, it is important to examine the determinants of support for Democratic and Republican women separately. However, when there are fewer races and candidates to be analyzed, this can become more difficult. Of the 11 women Senate candidates who ran in mixed-sex races, only four are Republicans. These four ran in states with smaller populations (Connecticut, Delaware, New Hampshire, and Nevada), which limits the number of respondents from these states included in the sample. Beyond this, none of the women were incumbents, and only one of them took part in a competitive race, which limits the contextual diversity of the races. Taken together, this reality means that analysis of the Senate races is limited to those elections in which a Democratic woman ran against a Republican man.[4]

Analysis of these races is presented in Table 5.2. Recall that several gender stereotypes were related to evaluations of Democratic women Senate candidates (Table 4.3). At first glance, the same pattern is visible here with regard to vote choice. Column 1 of the table suggests that female policy, male policy, and female trait stereotypes are related to voting for women Democrats, with voters who hold the expected female stereotypes being more likely to vote for these women and those who hold the expected male policy stereotypes being more likely to support their Republican male opponents. However, when we look at the more complete model in Column 2, we see that stereotypes are no longer related to vote choice when we introduce the specific candidate evaluations. Here we see that respondent evaluations of the candidates with regard to their competence on male policy issues and their likelihood of possessing female traits are significantly related to choosing the woman candidate over her male opponent. As should not be surprising, respondents who evaluated the woman candidate in their race as better able than her male opponent to handle traditionally male issues such as crime and the economy were more likely

Table 5.2. SENATE VOTE CHOICE, DEMOCRATIC WOMEN VERSUS REPUBLICAN MEN

	Vote for Woman	Vote for Woman
Stereotypes		
Female policy	0.314**	0.294
	(0.11)	(0.16)
Male policy	−0.357**	−0.313
	(0.12)	(0.16)
Female trait	0.303*	0.268
	(0.13)	(0.25)
Male trait	0.175	0.070
	(0.15)	(0.20)
Evaluations		
Female policy	–	0.283
	–	(0.15)
Male policy	–	0.523***
	–	(0.13)
Female trait	–	0.665**
	–	(0.25)
Male trait	–	−0.024
	–	(0.20)
Same party	3.851***	3.107***
	(0.35)	(0.53)
Woman incumbent	−0.533	3.126*
	(1.18)	(1.57)
Open seat	−0.488	0.667
	(0.52)	(0.76)
Percent of spending by woman	3.463	−1.725
	(2.15)	(2.66)
Competitive Senate race	−1.130	−3.606***
	(0.64)	(0.92)
Interest in Senate race	−0.120	0.290
	(0.15)	(0.22)
Constant	−5.892**	−16.827***
	(1.92)	(4.36)
Pseudo R^2	.47	.74
N	577	524

* $p < .05$, ** $p < .01$, *** $p < .001$, two-tailed test of significance.
Note: This table contains logistic regression for candidate vote choice. Independent respondents are excluded due to the small number of Independent identifiers. Standard errors are in parentheses.

to vote for her. People who saw the woman candidate as more honest and compassionate than her opponent also were more likely to vote for her. Because male policy and female trait stereotypes were significantly related to evaluations of Democratic women Senate candidates (Table 4.7) and these stereotype variables are also significant in the vote choice model in Column 1, the significance of the specific male policy and female trait evaluations for vote choice suggests that the influence of these stereotypes is being mediated through the candidate evaluations. This is evidence that stereotypes can have an indirect impact on vote choice through their ability to shape the way in which voters are evaluating these women candidates. These Democratic women candidates are more likely to receive vote support from voters who hold expected stereotypes about women's superiority on female traits and also from those who hold counterstereotype beliefs that women are better able to handle male policy issues. Given that fewer voters hold this counterstereotypic view, this may not help these women much and may even hurt them a bit among voters who see men as better at these issues. But the relatively limited impact that these evaluation variables have on vote choice should signal that this is not a major concern.[5]

Beyond the stereotypes, Table 5.2 continues to demonstrate the central importance of political and contextual variables in explaining vote choice. As we have seen in several analyses to this point, sharing the party of the woman candidate is the primary explanation for choosing her over her male opponent. Respondents are also significantly more likely to choose the Democratic woman candidate when she is an incumbent. Finally, the influence of competitiveness indicates that Democratic women were more likely to draw votes in less competitive races. In 2010, five of the seven Democratic women Senate candidates represented here either won or lost their race by more than 10 percentage points, which indicates a less competitive race.

Governors

The last office we consider involves races for governor. Earlier work suggests that the public may view executive offices differently than legislative ones, so we need to determine whether respondents employ gender stereotypes differently when they consider legislative and executive candidates (Huddy and Terkildsen 1993a). The assumption in the literature is that the single-executive nature of the office of governor may raise people's concerns about a woman's ability to hold the position successfully. Also, as Fox and Oxley (2003) suggest, many executive offices are focused on specific policy areas that may be stereotyped (law enforcement, education, agriculture), and executives, as single-person branches of government, may draw a different level of scrutiny from voters.

As with Senate races, the number of women candidates in each party brings limitation to the analysis. Here the issue is that there are only two Democratic women candidates, one of whom comes from Wyoming, which has very few respondents in the sample. As a result, the analysis of Democratic women candidates running for governor really reflects the dynamics of the race in Florida between Alex Sink and her Republican opponent, Rick Scott. Given that this severely hampers my ability to make any generalizations about Democratic women candidates for governor, I focus here on vote choice in races in which Republican women ran against Democratic men.[6]

As with the other vote choice analysis, the first model examines whether abstract stereotypes directly influence people's voting for a woman Republican candidate for governor (Table 5.3). At first glance, the findings in Column 1 would suggest that people employ their stereotypes about female personality traits in deciding to vote for a woman. Here we see that voters who hold traditional stereotypes about women being compassionate, consensus-oriented, and honest are more likely to vote for the woman Republican. However, when we account for the important influence of candidate evaluations on vote choice, we see that stereotypes have no impact on vote choice. Instead, what matters more is the specific evaluations that people made about the candidates in their race. People who evaluated the Republican woman candidate for governor as better able to handle female and male policies than her opponent were significantly more likely to vote for her. Interestingly, the impact of male policy evaluations is the stronger of the two influences. Beyond the evaluations, we see that political party continues to be the most important influence on vote choice, with Independent voters and those sharing her party being most likely to choose the woman candidate. One last note to make is of the outsized importance of candidate spending on vote choice for governor in these races. The negative coefficient signifies that, as Republican women spent more money than their male opponents, they attracted fewer votes. This finding is driven by the California governor's race in which the Republican candidate, Meg Whitman, spent $177 million in losing to Jerry Brown by almost 10 percentage points.

Table 5.3. GOVERNOR VOTE CHOICE, REPUBLICAN WOMEN VERSUS DEMOCRATIC MEN

	Vote for Woman	Vote for Woman
Stereotypes		
Female policy	−0.087	0.011
	(0.09)	(0.16)
Male policy	0.043	−0.198
	(0.17)	(0.27)
Female trait	0.339*	0.242
	(0.14)	(0.31)
Male trait	0.009	0.083
	(0.14)	(0.24)
Evaluations		
Female policy	–	0.467**
	–	(0.17)
Male policy	–	1.001***
	–	(0.22)
Female trait	–	0.604
	–	(0.46)
Male trait	–	0.254
	–	(0.25)
Same party	2.727***	1.647**
	(0.31)	(0.52)
Independent	1.725	3.125**
	(1.02)	(1.11)
Percent of spending by woman	−3.204*	−8.088***
	(1.47)	(2.32)
Competitive governor race	0.242	−0.068
	(0.39)	(0.57)
Interest in governor race	0.096	0.296
	(0.17)	(0.25)
Constant	−2.011	−14.189
	(1.99)	(8.14)
Pseudo R^2	.30	.73
N	506	480

* $p < .05$, ** $p < .01$, *** $p < .001$, two-tailed test of significance.
Note: Incumbent governors are excluded because only one Republican gubernatorial candidate (Jan Brewer, AZ) was an incumbent. Standard errors are in parentheses.

VOTING IN MALE-ONLY RACES

The analysis of vote choice in races with women candidates suggests that abstract gender stereotypes do not have a significant direct impact on people's vote choice decisions or an indirect impact by shaping candidate evaluations. One additional way we can examine whether stereotypes matter in elections is by looking at vote choice decisions in male-only races. The literature on gender stereotypes generally assumes that they are relevant in the presence of women candidates. But in an age when the political parties have become so closely associated with female and male images, it is worth exploring whether stereotypes shape vote choice along partisan lines.

House Races

Table 5.4 presents the determinants of vote choice in male-only House races. In Column 1, we see that female policy stereotypes appear to be related to voting for Democratic men, with those who hold the expected stereotype of women's superiority on these issues to be more likely to vote for the Democrat. This finding makes sense from the perspective of partisan stereotypes, in that Democrats are most often seen as better at female issues such as education and health care than are Republicans. People who hold the traditional gender stereotype about female policies may well identify Democratic candidates, male or female, as the best people to handle these issues. This result is also in line with the finding from chapter 4 (Table 4.11) indicating that female policy stereotypes were related to evaluation of Democratic male candidates in House races.

In moving to the full model in Column 2, we see that female policy stereotypes are no longer related to vote choice. Instead, each of the four candidate evaluation variables is related to vote choice. The positive direction on each coefficient indicates that respondents who evaluated the Democratic man in their race as better than his Republican opponent on female and male policies are significantly more likely to vote for the Democratic candidate. The same is true for respondents who see the Democratic man as being more likely to possess a range of female and male attributes. Given that evaluations are an important step in considering a candidate, we should expect them to be related to vote choice. While it appears clear that female policy stereotypes are not directly influencing vote choice for Democrats in these male-only races, one additional step requires us to examine whether there is an indirect impact through evaluations. Indeed, this appears to be the case. A test of mediation reveals that the impact of female policy stereotypes on vote choice is an indirect one—female policy stereotypes influence the evaluations people make about the candidates in their House races, resulting in them evaluating Democratic men higher on this dimension.[7] This more positive evaluation is then significantly related to voting for Democratic men. In this analysis, Democratic men get a boost

Table 5.4. VOTE CHOICE IN MALE-ONLY HOUSE RACES

	Vote for Democrat	Vote for Democrat
Stereotypes		
Female policy	0.210**	0.153
	(0.08)	(0.10)
Male policy	−0.138	0.005
	(0.08)	(0.10)
Female trait	−0.017	0.009
	(0.08)	(0.14)
Male trait	−0.021	−0.104
	(0.11)	(0.14)
Evaluations		
Female policy	–	0.332***
	–	(0.10)
Male policy	–	0.261**
	–	(0.08)
Female trait	–	0.519**
	–	(0.18)
Male trait	–	0.518**
	–	(0.17)
Democrat	3.140***	2.271***
	(0.22)	(0.28)
Independent	1.946**	1.586
	(0.74)	(1.16)
Democrat incumbent	−0.763	−0.929
	(0.40)	(0.71)
Open seat	−0.370	−0.430
	(0.30)	(0.44)
Percent of spending by Democrat	2.999***	2.259**
	(0.55)	(0.84)
Competitive House race	−0.079	−0.078
	(0.26)	(0.38)
Interest in House race	−0.143	0.161
	(0.11)	(0.16)
Constant	−5.554***	−17.643***
	(0.91)	(2.44)
Pseudo R^2	.39	.66
N	1,290	1,191

** $p < .01$, *** $p < .001$, two-tailed test of significance.
Note: This table contains logistic regression for candidate vote choice. Clustered standard errors are in parentheses.

in vote support from being seen as better than Republican men at handling female policy issues.

Beyond the stereotypes and evaluations, we continue to see the strong and central influence of political variables. The two most significant influences on voting for a Democrat in these House races are being a Democrat and taking part in a race in which the Democratic candidate spent more money than his Republican opponent. Both of these findings are in line with the expected influence of these variables. These political variables are more central to the explanation of vote choice in these races than are the stereotypes and candidate evaluations. Interestingly, Democratic incumbents do not fare any better than nonincumbents in this analysis. While this contradicts our general expectation that incumbents do well, this finding makes sense in the context of the 2010 election, which saw the Republican Party take majority control of the House of Representatives.

Senate Races

The determinants of vote choice in male-only Senate races conform very closely to traditional explanations (Table 5.5). As the literature would suggest, none of the measures of abstract stereotypes are related to vote choice in these higher-visibility elections. Indeed, the stereotype variables are not significant in either of the two models. Instead, how voters evaluate their two candidates on male policy and female and male trait dimensions is important in shaping vote choice. Voters who see the Democratic candidates as better on these three evaluations are more likely to vote for them than their Republican opponents. Since there were no significant relationships between stereotypes and candidate evaluations for male Senate candidates, we can be confident that the evaluations influencing vote choice here are not being affected by stereotypes. As we have seen in all of the other analyses to this point, the political variables are the most important determinants of vote choice. Here, Democratic men running for the Senate did well among Democratic voters, although, overall, they did less well in competitive races. As with House races, we see that 2010 was a tough year for Democratic incumbents, with Democratic incumbents not experiencing the usual boost at the ballot box.

Governor Races

Male-only governors races look very much like the Senate races described above (Table 5.6). Abstract stereotypes are not related to vote choice in

Table 5.5. VOTE CHOICE IN MALE-ONLY SENATE RACES

	Vote for Democrat	Vote for Democrat
Stereotypes		
Female policy	0.101	0.143
	(0.14)	(0.12)
Male policy	0.112	0.063
	(0.10)	(0.12)
Female trait	−0.089	0.040
	(0.12)	(0.18)
Male trait	−0.068	−0.055
	(0.10)	(0.16)
Evaluations		
Female policy	–	0.242
	–	(0.15)
Male policy		0.316*
	–	(0.13)
Female trait	–	0.517*
	–	(0.20)
Male trait	–	0.398*
	–	(0.18)
Democrat	3.237***	2.709***
	(0.30)	(0.36)
Independent	1.693	−0.959
	(0.88)	(1.76)
Democrat incumbent	−0.387	−0.718
	(1.02)	(1.50)
Open seat	−0.698	−0.881
	(0.67)	(0.98)
Percent of spending by Democrat	3.923*	4.431
	(1.78)	(2.58)
Competitive Senate race	−0.913*	−1.183*
	(0.41)	(0.53)
Interest in Senate race	−0.044	−0.062
	(0.13)	(0.20)
Constant	−1.996	−15.840***
	(1.52)	(3.26)
Pseudo R^2	.35	.66
N	705	651

* $p < .05$, *** $p < .001$, two-tailed test of significance.
Note: This table contains logistic regression for candidate vote choice. Standard errors are in parentheses.

Table 5.6. VOTE CHOICE IN MALE-ONLY GOVERNOR RACES

	Vote for Democrat	Vote for Democrat
Stereotypes		
Female policy	0.090	0.068
	(0.08)	(0.13)
Male policy	−0.219	−0.193
	(0.14)	(0.18)
Female trait	−0.101	0.213
	(0.11)	(0.21)
Male trait	−0.085	−0.179
	(0.12)	(0.16)
Evaluations		
Female policy	–	0.879***
	–	(0.17)
Male policy	–	0.880***
	–	(0.16)
Female trait	–	0.344
	–	(0.25)
Male trait	–	0.410
	–	(0.24)
Democrat	3.278***	2.061***
	(0.23)	(0.34)
Independent	2.020*	2.629*
	(0.94)	(1.06)
Democrat incumbent	0.465	0.716
	(0.27)	(0.38)
Percent of spending by Democrat	3.047***	4.044**
	(0.86)	(1.30)
Competitive governor race	−0.674*	0.211
	(0.30)	(0.48)
Interest in governor race	0.007	0.166
	(0.12)	(0.18)
Constant	−4.791***	−26.930***
	(1.45)	(4.56)
Pseudo R^2	.39	.76
N	901	860

* $p < .05$, ** $p < .01$, *** $p < .001$, two-tailed test of significance.
Note: This table contains ordinary least squares regressions for policy and trait evaluations. Standard errors are in parentheses.

the model in Column 1, nor are they significant in the model with evaluations included (Column 2). This would indicate that voters are not bringing their stereotypes to bear in selecting among male candidates for governor. Both male and female policy evaluations matter to voting, with people who see the Democratic candidate in their race as better at these issues being more likely to vote for him than his male Republican opponent. Beyond this, partisanship and campaign spending are the most significant influences on vote choice. As Democratic candidates for governor account for a higher percentage of campaign spending, they are more likely to be chosen by voters. Democrats and Independent voters are more likely to vote for the Democrat, but Democratic incumbents do not receive any additional benefit.

CONCLUSION

In examining the literature on the impact of gender stereotypes on support for women candidates, it becomes clear that current knowledge is incomplete. Findings based largely on experimental and hypothetical candidates and election scenarios reveal at least two areas of uncertainly. First, we have little information on whether the stereotypes people hold matter at all to their vote choice decisions. Second, we can only guess at whether stereotypes matter differently for women candidates across a range of different elective offices. The research presented here is an attempt to address these gaps in our knowledge by examining whether and when people employ gender stereotypes when deciding to vote for women candidates for Congress and governor. In all, the evidence for the influence of stereotypes is limited. There are very few places where we see stereotypes influencing vote choice for women candidates. The stereotypes people hold do not appear to have a direct impact on their vote choice decisions, nor, in most cases, do they have an indirect impact through candidate evaluations. Interestingly, when we do see an indirect influence for stereotypes as mediated through candidate evaluations, it is only for Democratic candidates. Vote choice for Democratic women Senate candidates is influenced by male policy and female trait stereotypes, while vote choice for Democratic male House candidates reveals the influence of female policy stereotypes. Candidate evaluations, not surprisingly, do matter to vote choice, with positive evaluations leading respondents to vote for the favored candidate.

Beyond stereotypes, we see the strong and consistent influence of traditional factors—political party, incumbency, competitiveness—shaping vote choice. Political party is the dominant influence on vote choice, whether women candidates are present or not. There is no evidence that people cross party lines to avoid voting for a woman candidate of their party; instead, high levels of support among party voters is the rule regardless of the sex of the candidates in a matchup. In the context of real-world elections, stereotypes clearly are dwarfed by the expected political variables.

The second conclusion to draw is that stereotypes, when they do appear, can act to influence vote choice differently for different offices. Here we see stereotypes in a couple of instances in voting for House candidates but not at all in Senate or gubernatorial elections. However, before we make firm conclusions based on this analysis, we have to acknowledge that there are fewer women candidates for Senate and governor in the sample than there are women candidates for House and that the findings here may be influenced by the particular mix of candidates and issues in those races, as opposed to broader trends. More research should be conducted on women candidates for Senate and governor before we conclude that stereotypes affect legislative and executive candidates differently.

CHAPTER 6

Gender Stereotypes in Other Places?

Candidate Quality and Issue Campaigns

There are lots of reasons women make great candidates. It's not just because they can talk about abortion.

Anna Greenberg, pollster, Greenberg Quinlan Rosner Research

To this point, the results of this project demonstrate in a number of ways and in a variety of contexts that political gender stereotypes do not appear to have much of a clear or consistent impact on the fortunes of women candidates. The gender stereotypes that voters hold do not appear to play a central role in shaping the evaluations they make of candidates or the vote choice decisions they make when faced with women candidates running against men. Instead they have an impact on some candidates, female and male, in some limited circumstances. What we have seen is the steady and strong influence of political party—through both partisan identity and political party stereotypes—on the evaluations and vote choice decisions people make. The analysis conducted here points to two conclusions: The stereotypes people hold do not seem to be as useful to their political decisions as researchers have assumed, and, even when stereotypes have an impact, it is minimal when considered alongside the traditional influences on candidate evaluations and vote choice.

However, as I discussed in the first chapter, the gender stereotypes that voters hold about women and men are not the only way in which candidate sex and gendered considerations can influence the fortunes of women candidates. Women candidates exist in a gendered environment that often leads them to make different calculations than men about their political opportunities. One clear example of this is the process of candidate emergence. As Jennifer Lawless and Richard Fox (2010) have carefully documented, women are less likely than men to run for office for a variety of reasons. Among these are women's tendency to underestimate their credentials as candidates, their lesser likelihood of being encouraged or recruited to run by those around them, and a belief that sexism in the political world still handicaps women. These findings are all examples of the ways in which gendered consideration can still shape our political world. These are not the only points, however. Other aspects of the process of becoming and being candidates can be experienced differently by women and men. Indeed, the data gathered in the survey of voters in the 2010 election allow me to examine two other points in the process where candidate sex can have an influence on political outcomes. The first is the debate about how candidate sex influences candidate quality. The second involves examining the decisions candidates make about how to present themselves in their campaigns. As a way of rounding out our understanding of the impact of candidate sex on the candidates in 2010, we now turn to these additional considerations.

CANDIDATE QUALITY

Recent work on whether and when women choose to become candidates for office has focused on the higher standards of evaluation to which women subject themselves. Lawless and Fox (2010) demonstrate time and again that women are much more likely than men to devalue their own credentials and to delay their candidacies until they have passed a rather high bar of qualifications. In short, men see themselves as viable candidates much more easily and more often than do women. They suggest that women delay candidacies because of concerns that they may not possess enough of the appropriate skills and experiences to be successful candidates. At the same time, women who do run for office win at the same rate as men in similar circumstances. Some scholars have begun to focus on the inconsistencies between these sets of findings, examining whether women candidates are of higher quality than similarly situated men. This notion of candidate quality is important because if women candidates are of higher quality than men, their winning at equal rates might signal some measure of bias in the political world, whether on the part of voters, the media, or other actors. Work by Sarah Fulton (2012) and Kathryn Pearson and Eric McGhee (2013) finds that women candidates for the House of

Representatives tend to be of higher quality than men candidates, particularly in having held office prior to running for Congress.

The respondents in this survey participated in 275 House races, 22 Senate races, and 20 races for governor. In all, there are about 650 candidates represented in this data set. Beyond the survey responses, I gathered background data on all of these candidates. Relevant here is information about the education level, previous political experience, and campaign fundraising of each candidate. These are three variables by which we can get a sense of the quality of the candidates. In the United States, the vast majority of candidates who run for Congress or governor have at least a college degree, and those with some previous political experience are usually considered to be more qualified for high-level office. Fundraising ability is also a sign that a candidate is credible and can attract enough money to run a viable campaign. I also coded the results of each election, which allows me to examine the rates at which women and men won their races. Comparing the women and men candidates for each of the three levels of office examined here will allow for a test of whether the women and men are of different levels of quality and whether they are winning at comparable rates. Examining these factors can help us determine whether there are hidden or subtle biases in the system that might work against women's success.

Table 6.1 presents a breakdown of the highest levels of education of women and men candidates by the office they sought. In general, there are

Table 6.1. CANDIDATE EDUCATION BY SEX

	Man Candidate	Woman Candidate
House		
Less than bachelor's	12.68%	11.11%
Bachelor's	31.46%	34.26%
Graduate degree	55.87%	54.63%
N	426	108
Senate		
Less than bachelor's	–	–
Bachelor's	29.03%	38.46%
Graduate degree	70.97%	61.54%
N	31	13
Governor		
Less than bachelor's	6.45%	22.22%
Bachelor's	12.90%	44.44%
Graduate degree	80.65%	33.33%
N	31	9

fewer differences than more, and the data support the notion that women and men who run for office have similar educational credentials. There are no significant differences among candidates for the House or Senate. For House candidates, there is very clear parity. Women are slightly more likely than are men to hold a bachelor's degree, 34 percent to 31 percent, and equally likely to have earned both a bachelor's degree and a graduate degree of some kind, 55 percent for women and 56 percent for men. Among Senate candidates, it appears that women are more likely than men to hold a bachelor's degree as their terminal degree (38 percent to 29 percent) and less likely to hold both a bachelor's and a graduate degree (62 percent to 71 percent), but these differences are not significant. We see the same pattern among candidates for governor, with women being significantly more likely than men to have a bachelor's degree (44 percent to 13 percent) and significantly less likely to hold a graduate degree (33 percent to 81 percent).

With regard to candidate experience (Table 6.2), we see support for the finding that women tend to have more experience than men when they make a first run for the House (Pearson and McGhee 2013). Among the House candidates represented in this project, 43 percent of men and 29 percent of women running had no previous political experience, a statistically significant difference. This indicates that these women were more likely than men to prepare for a run for the House by accruing political and elected office experience, while for men, running for the House was more likely to be a first political step. Beyond these newcomers, when we look at women and men who had political experience before running for the House, we see no differences in the kinds of positions held. Women and men were equally likely to have local, state legislative, and statewide elected office, indicating that women with experience are coming to House races with the same range of experiences as men.

In looking at candidates for the Senate, we find that women candidates are the ones with less previous political experience. Here, only 13 percent of the male candidates had no previous experience, compared with 38 percent of the women. Here we have to recognize that these data reflect the particular circumstances of the 2010 Senate elections, a cycle in which there were a number of high-visibility "nonpolitical" women candidates, such as former Hewlett-Packard CEO Carly Fiorina, WWE founder Linda McMahon, and public relations executive Christine O'Donnell. These differences are more visible in Senate races since it might be more likely to have nonpolitical amateur or "celebrity" candidates for a higher-visibility office such as Senate than for the House. Among Senate candidates with previous political experience, we see some small differences between women and men. Men who ran for the Senate in 2010 were more likely

Table 6.2. CANDIDATE EXPERIENCE BY SEX

	Man Candidate	Woman Candidate
House		
No experience	42.56%	29.36%
Local office	6.18%	8.26%
State legislator	6.86%	9.17%
Statewide elected (attorney general, lieutenant governor)	0.23%	0.92%
U.S. House	43.94%	52.29%
N	437	109
Senate		
No experience	12.90%	38.46%
Local office	9.67%	–
State legislator	3.23%	7.69%
Statewide elected (attorney general, lieutenant governor)	12.90%	23.08%
Statewide administrative	3.23%	–
U.S. House	29.03%	–
U.S. Senate	29.03%	30.77%
N	31	13
Governor		
No experience	16.13%	11.11%
Local office	12.90%	22.22%
State legislator	19.35%	11.11%
Statewide elected (attorney general, lieutenant governor)	12.90%	22.22%
Statewide administrative	3.23%	11.11%
U.S. House	6.45%	11.11%
U.S. Senate	3.23%	–
Governor	25.81%	11.11%
N	31	9

than women to have held local office (10 percent for men, none of the women), and women were more likely to run after having held a statewide elected office such as lieutenant governor or attorney general. This finding would seem to echo that of Lawless and Fox (2010), who found that men see themselves as more qualified to run for office than do women. Running for a U.S. Senate seat after having held local office is perhaps a bit more of a stretch than running after having held statewide elective office and may reflect men's greater risk-taking and women's overpreparedness. Finally, in looking at candidates for governor, we see that women and men exhibited no significant differences with regard to political background. They are equally likely to have had political experience when they ran for governor, and while women were more likely to have "higher-level" experience (statewide elected, statewide administrative, U.S. House) than men, the differences are not dramatic.

In terms of campaign fundraising, women candidates often struggle against the conventional wisdom that it is more difficult for them to raise money than it is for men (Lawless and Fox 2010). Burrell and others have produced a significant body of work that refutes this belief and have demonstrated that women have been raising as much money as, if not more than, men for the past two decades. The data from 2010 support the finding that women are as successful as men in their fundraising ability (Table 6.3). Among this group of candidates, there are no significant differences in the amounts of money that women and men raised for any of the three offices, indicating that women candidates are able to raise the money they need to run campaigns. Median figures for money raised are presented here for women and men candidates instead of the more traditional means, as there were several women candidates who spent such large amounts of money that means would provide a distorted view of things. Women and men candidates for the House demonstrate parity in spending. It is among candidates for Senate and governor that we see the impact of some number of high-spending candidates. Among the women who spent significant amounts of money were Barbara Boxer and Carly Fiorina, who spent a combined $50 million in their race for the Senate seat in California; Linda McMahon, who spent $50 million of her own money in running for a Senate seat in Connecticut; and eBay founder Meg Whitman, who spent $177 million ($144 million of it her own money) in running for governor of California. Campaign spending for men running for governor reflects the candidacy of Rick Scott, who spent $85 million ($73 million of it from family money) in winning election in Florida.

Table 6.3. MEDIAN CANDIDATE SPENDING BY SEX

	Man Candidate		Woman Candidate	
	Spending	N	Spending	N
House	$911,036	437	$942,489	109
Senate	$7,702,566	31	$11,515,567	13
Governor	$8,319,207	31	$4,099,098	9

In terms of the measures of candidate quality examined here, it is clear that women and men are at least of equal quality. Women candidates for the House have more political experience than do men, but this is the only place where women are significantly more well qualified than men. In this sample, women and men have equivalent educational credentials, and they have concomitant political experience and, with a few high-visibility, wealthy exceptions, spend equal amounts of money on their campaigns. On these dimensions, they represent the contemporary status of women candidates as professional, well-credentialed, and well-resourced candidates, which suggests that women should win their elections at comparable rates to similarly situated men.

Indeed, the women candidates in this sample are excellent examples of the adage that "when women run, women win." As Table 6.4 demonstrates, the women and men candidates in the sample won and lost their races at similar rates. Tables 6.4–6.6 group candidates for each level of office by the type of candidacy—incumbent, open seat, and challengers. Within each category, candidates are presented by political party. Taking the House candidates first, we see that incumbents of all types were elected with comfortable, and comparable, margins. Democratic men incumbents had an average vote share of 59 percent, while Democratic women received 63 percent of the vote. Republican women and men incumbents received 65 percent and 66 percent, respectively. In these races, as in most House

Table 6.4. HOUSE RACE OUTCOMES

	Vote Share	Races
Incumbent		
Democratic man	59.47%	115
Democratic woman	62.75%	49
Republican man	66.36%	73
Republican woman	65.10%	10
Open Seat		
Democratic man	37.88%	17
Democratic woman	50.11%	9
Republican man	58.08%	25
Republican woman	53%	1
Challenger		
Democratic man	33.28%	68
Democratic woman	36.13%	15
Republican man	39.52%	139
Republican woman	39.74%	25

Table 6.5. SENATE RACE OUTCOMES

	Vote Share	Races
Incumbent		
Democratic man	50.67%	3
Democratic woman	52.50%	4
Republican man	63.17%	6
Republican woman	–	0
Open Seat		
Democratic man	48%	7
Democratic woman	35.50%	2
Republican man	57.67%	6
Republican woman	49%	3
Challenger		
Democratic man	35.75%	4
Democratic woman	39%	2
Republican man	49.20%	5
Republican woman	46%	2

Table 6.6. GOVERNOR RACE OUTCOMES

	Vote Share	Races
Incumbent		
Democratic man	52.88%	5
Democratic woman	–	0
Republican man	–	0
Republican woman	56%	1
Open Seat		
Democratic man	47.22%	10
Democratic woman	40.50%	4
Republican man	55.78%	10
Republican woman	52%	4
Challenger		
Democratic man	44%	1
Democratic woman	–	0
Republican man	47.12%	5
Republican woman	–	0

races, incumbency benefits candidates of both sexes and both parties. In looking at open-seat races, we see that Republican men in those races earned the biggest average vote share, at 58 percent.[1] Among Democrats, women who ran for open seats did considerably better than Democratic men in open races, 50 percent to 38 percent. This is the first place we see women candidates doing considerably better than men and may be related to the higher candidate quality we saw among women House candidates. With regard to challengers, the candidates here experienced the typical fate of a challenger—defeat. Republican women and men received similar vote shares—40 percent—and did slightly better than did Democratic challengers. Among Democratic challenging candidates, women received 36 percent of the vote to men's 33 percent. But for all of these candidates, these differences are largely irrelevant, since all challengers received an average below 40 percent of the vote totals.

It is more difficult to detect patterns among candidates for U.S. Senate and governor, as the smaller number of candidates represented in the data set means fewer candidates in each of the different race type and party categories (Tables 6.5 and 6.6). This is particularly true of races for governor, but we can say a few things about Senate races. Here we see the same general patterns as were visible with the House races—incumbents of each sex and party received average vote shares of at least 50 percent, with Democratic women and men incumbents receiving very similar totals.[2] Challenging candidates all received less than 50 percent of the vote on average, with Republicans doing a bit better than Democrats and women and men within each party receiving comparable vote shares. We see more variance among the open-seat candidates, with Republican men doing quite a bit better—receiving 58 percent of the vote on average—than Republican women (49 percent), Democratic men (48 percent), and Democratic women (36 percent). This pattern makes sense given the Republican victories in the 2010 midterms, although the number of open-seat races with women candidates is too small to draw firm conclusions.

The additional secondary data collected for each candidate in the data set allow us to examine additional points in the electoral process where gender might matter. With regard to candidate quality and electoral success, the women candidates in these races provide evidence in support of the contemporary view that women candidates are at least of equal quality to men and, as with the House candidates, may have some stronger credentials. Overall, however, there were few differences between women and men on these quality indicators. If the women candidates represented in this sample were of consistent and significantly higher quality than the men candidates, their winning election at equal rates might indicate a concern. But with regard to election returns, the women House candidates here perform at the same level as their similarly situated male candidates. Overall, these findings do not raise concerns about hidden biases against women candidates.

To this point in the analysis, it has been clear that voters are not engaging in clear and consistent stereotyping of women candidates. While this is most likely explained by the attitudes and behaviors of voters themselves, there may be an additional explanation for the lack of impact of stereotypes and the primary impact of political party, one that involves the kind of information that candidates make available to voters through their election campaigns. This points to sources of stereotypes beyond the internal stereotypes that voters possess. Indeed, in terms of thinking about women candidates, the literature has long focused on three potential sources—the individual-level stereotypes voters bring to politics, the ways in which candidates are covered and portrayed by the media, and, to a lesser degree, the ways in which candidates present themselves to voters through their campaigns and media messages.

Research on the relationship between women candidates and the media has grown considerably over the past 30 years or so. Examinations of the role of the media in creating or downplaying stereotypes in the electoral environment have also been extensive. While the media have long been seen as a source of bias against women candidates, providing less coverage and "softer" coverage of women candidates (Braden 1996; Bystrom et al. 2004; Carroll and Schreiber 1997; Fowler and Lawless 2009; Kahn 1992, 1996; Smith 1997), more recent work suggests that media coverage of women candidates may be changing, with evidence demonstrating that remaining gender differences in coverage are much smaller than in years past (Atkeson and Krebs 2008; Banwart, Bystrom, and Robertson 2003; Kittilson and Fridkin 2008; Smith 1997). One extensive study of newspaper coverage of candidates for the U.S. House in 2010 finds that differences in tone and amount of coverage are not explained by candidate sex but, instead, by candidate differences in partisanship, ideology, and incumbency status (Lawless and Hayes 2013).

The third potential source of stereotyped information in elections is candidates themselves. Discussions of the impact of voter gender stereotypes on evaluations of candidates rightly raise questions about the role that candidate decisions have in shaping reactions to their candidacies. Whether voters employ stereotyped thinking about women candidates can certainly be influenced by the issues on which candidates choose to campaign or the images candidates work to create. Evaluating a woman candidate based on stereotypes about female policy competence on education and health care policies is not necessarily sexist if that candidate campaigns unstintingly on those issues. Women candidates are often counseled to keep gender stereotypes in mind when they campaign (Witt et al. 1994). Since an extensive literature finds that people see women as better suited to handle some issues than others, it would not always be irrational for a woman candidate to "play to her strengths" by emphasizing competence on the issues where voters expect it. Conscious or unconscious attempts by women candidates to meet voter expectations and foster positive images based on stereotypes could then contribute to voters and the media perceiving women in these stereotyped ways. Given this, a more complete understanding of how women candidates are perceived requires us to think about the information candidates present and whether this information is gendered in some way.

WOMEN CANDIDATES AND CAMPAIGNS

Current media research demonstrates that people's evaluations of women candidates can be shaped by the information candidates include in their campaigns. Chingching Chang and Jacqueline Hitchon (2004) caution that voters often default to gender stereotypes to "fill in" gaps in their information about candidates. Their research finds that, when campaign ads do not contain information about particular policy areas, voters use gender as a cue to discern a candidate's abilities or position in those areas. However, when information about a candidate's strengths in a policy area is provided, voters readily rely on that concrete information in making judgments. They also find that women candidates are most well served by keeping the tone of campaign ads neutral, as overly positive or negative emotional tones are evaluated as less appropriate (Hitchon et al. 1997). Another concern along these lines has involved the use of negative advertising by women candidates. Some early researchers feared that negative ads would violate stereotyped expectations of women as kinder, less aggressive candidates (Gordon et al. 2003). However, women candidates have come to employ negative advertising in equal proportions with men and have had success in using attack ads to bolster their own issue competence (Gordon et al. 2003; Kahn 1996). Beyond that, Kim Fridkin, Pat Kenney, and Gina Woodall (2009) find that negative advertising is less successful at shaping people's evaluations of women candidates than it is in influencing attitudes toward men.

While some research suggests that women should think carefully about campaign strategy and play to their stereotyped strengths to benefit from positive stereotypes (Herrnson et al. 2003; Iyengar et al. 1997; Witt et al. 1994), there is relatively little evidence that women behave differently from men in presenting themselves to the public, at least with regard to the issues on which they campaign. These findings are consistent whether considering television advertisements or campaign websites. Dianne Bystrom and her colleagues (2004) examine both ads and websites for Senate and gubernatorial candidates in the 1990s and early 2000s and find very few differences in issue presentation between women and men candidates. Relying on data from the Wisconsin Ads Project for congressional races in 2000 and 2002, Virginia Sapiro and her coauthors (2011) find much more similarity among women and men in their campaign ads and suggest that the limited differences are explained by race-specific electoral context. In examining the potential impact of the September 11th attacks on the way candidates campaign, Patricia Strach and Virginia Sapiro (2011) find that Republican men were more likely to give attention to military and foreign affairs issues in 2002 as compared with 2000 than were Democratic men or women of both parties. However, this gender difference, which is also driven by political party considerations, is the only difference they identify in campaigns immediately following the tragedy. Finally, in examining congressional candidate websites in 2000 and 2002, I find the same pattern of no differences among women and men candidates in their issue presentations (Dolan 2005). Instead, these data demonstrate that candidates, both women and men, are strategic actors who campaign on the important issues of the day. Any differences in candidate issue presentation are generally explained by political party or incumbency, which is in line with other works in this area (Bystrom et al. 2004; Sapiro et al. 2011). Based on these data, it does not appear that candidates, women or men, attempt to play to voter stereotypes in any significant way. This would suggest that any remaining voter stereotyping or media coverage bias is not a result of significant or overt attempts by candidates to ensure that they are perceived in gender-stereotypic ways.

DATA AND METHODS

As discussed in chapter 2, one of the main goals of this project is to contribute to a recent body of work that seeks to provide new sources of data on the impact of gender stereotypes in real-world elections with actual women and men candidates (Fridkin and Kenney 2009; Hayes 2011; Lawless and Hayes 2013). In addition to the survey data from 2010 that examine voter stereotypes in the presence of women candidates are data that examine whether the women and men candidates for Congress and governor in 2010 presented themselves in gender-stereotyped ways with regard to their issue campaigns through their campaign ads and websites. These data allow us to examine whether candidates contribute to being perceived in gender-stereotyped ways because of the messages they send through their campaigns. This could occur as a result of a decision to highlight or downplay particular issues. Based on recent work, the expectation here is that candidates will not create issue representations based on gender stereotypes. For example, women will not present issue campaigns dominated by education, health care, or children's issues, and men's campaigns should not overrepresent economic or military issues. Instead, I expect that candidates will present similar issue emphases and will represent the issues that dominate the particular election cycle. In 2010, those issues were the economy, jobs, taxes, government spending, and health care. Finally, I anticipate that any significant differences among candidates should be more closely related to political party than to candidate sex.

Among the primary ways by which candidates present themselves to voters is through television advertisements and campaign websites. As part of the data collection efforts for this project, these advertisements and websites were gathered for each of the candidates represented in the survey data. These campaign data offer a glimpse into the kinds of issue campaigns candidates present to the public and are the focus of the analysis presented here. In terms of television ads, some candidates for the House did not run ads, while all candidates for Senate and governor did. In all, there are 291 House candidates, 42 Senate candidates, and 36 candidates for governor reflected in the analysis of television ads. These House candidates presented a total of 1,012 campaign ads that mentioned at least one policy issue. Senate candidates produced 327 issue ads, and candidates for governor produced 357 ads. Each ad was coded for up to three issues mentioned. Because not all candidates created ads and those who did have them did not all have the same number of ads, the unit of analysis here is the ad. Ads were gathered from each candidate's campaign YouTube channel at multiple times during the general election and then after the election to ensure that all ads were captured. While the vast majority of ads produced by candidates included issues, ads that did not were excluded.

Fully 95 percent of the House candidates and all Senate and governor candidates maintained campaign websites. Candidate websites were downloaded in October 2010. Issue mentions were most often on an "issues" page or on the main page of the website. Each website was coded for the five most prominent issues mentioned. Surprisingly, issue representations on campaign websites are fairly static and generally do not evolve much over the course of the campaign season. Mention of an issue, but not the candidate's position on that issue, was coded. Since the intention was to examine the issue priorities that candidates chose to highlight, candidates who presented alphabetized lists of issues were eliminated from the analysis.[3]

House Races

The goal here is to determine whether women and men candidates for Congress and governor contribute to stereotyping by presenting different issue images to the public through their political advertising and campaigning. The analysis presented is conducted separately by office and by medium—television ads and websites.

We first turn to an examination of the ads that House candidates aired during the 2010 campaigns. As Table 6.7 demonstrates, comparing the issues women and men candidates highlighted in their ads offers only very limited support for the idea that candidate sex shapes issue campaigns. The

Table 6.7. HOUSE ADS BY CANDIDATE SEX

	Man Candidate (N = 815)	Woman Candidate (N = 197)	t-score (N = 1,012)
Economy/Jobs	54.72%	48.73%	1.51
Spending/Debt	39.39%	39.09%	0.08
Taxes	28.22%	30.97%	−0.76
Wall Street/Bailouts	17.42%	21.83%	−1.44
Health Care	15.71%	23.35%	**−2.56**
Government Reform	12.27%	15.74%	−1.30
Foreign Policy/Veterans	16.07%	11.17%	1.73
Social Security/Medicare	10.31%	7.61%	1.14
Energy/Environment	7.61%	10.15%	−1.17
Family/Children	7.61%	7.11%	0.24
Education	3.80%	7.11%	**−2.02**
Constituent Concerns	6.38%	4.06%	1.24
Smaller Government	5.89%	3.05%	1.59
Housing/Foreclosures	3.93%	4.06%	−0.09
Immigration	3.56%	3.56%	0.00
Agriculture	2.09%	2.03%	0.05
Women's Issues	1.60%	2.03%	−0.43
Abortion	1.23%	2.03%	−0.87
Guns	1.47%	1.52%	−0.06
Crime	1.23%	1.52%	−0.33
Terrorism	0.49%	1.02%	−0.86
Welfare	0.00%	1.52%	**−3.55**
Religion	0.86%	2.03%	−1.42
Race	0.12%	0.00%	0.49

Note: Significant differences are shown in boldface.

first thing to note is that the issues mentioned most often in candidate ads were the same for women and men and were the primary issues of focus in the 2010 elections—the economy and jobs, government spending and the federal debt, and taxes. Candidates for the House appeared to campaign similarly and on the issues of the day, which is what we would expect savvy candidates to do. And while most candidates mentioned a range of issues across all of their ads, many issues only received token representation in comparison to the main issues of the day. With regard to differences between women and men, there were significant differences on only three of the 24 issues included—health care, education, and welfare (shown in boldface). We can note that each of these three differences follows the stereotyped expectation in that women candidates aired more ads that mentioned these issues than did men. But, at the same time, we should note that two of these issues were minor foci for both sexes. Education issues only represented 7 percent of the ads of women candidates and 4 percent of men's ads. No men highlighted welfare in their ads, while just under 2 percent of women's ads included this issue. Even health care, which in 2010 was still a fairly visible political issue, only appeared in 23 percent of women's ads and 16 percent of men's.

A second step in examining whether candidates play strategically to stereotypes in their ads is to look at candidate matchups. When women run against men, either or both candidates may make decisions based on their own image calculations and also based on the sex of their opponent. Women running against men may feel particular pressure to burnish their credentials on male issues, while men running against women may be more attentive to issues of typical female strength (Dolan 2008; Fox 1997). This approach also allows us to examine whether political party is important to the ways that candidates shape their issue campaigns. Given that women who run for office in the United States are much more likely to be Democrats than Republicans, it is important to consider whether differences between women and men can be influenced more by party than by sex. Table 6.8 provides data on the mixed-sex House races and separates them by party of the woman candidate. The first two columns present issue representations for Republican women and their Democratic male opponents, while Columns 4–6 do the same for Democratic women and their Republican male opponents.

Again, the evidence here suggests that women and men do not present fundamentally different issues to the public in their campaigns or particularly stereotyped issues, even when they run against a candidate of the opposite sex. Out of 24 issues, Republican women and their Democratic male opponents were significantly different in their focus on six of those

Table 6.8. HOUSE ADS, MIXED-SEX RACES

	RW vs. DM (N = 53)	DM vs. RW (N = 59)	t-score (N = 112)	DW vs. RM (N = 82)	RM vs. DW (N = 120)	t-score (N = 202)
Economy/Jobs	60.38%	59.32%	0.11	50.00%	65.00%	**-2.14**
Spending/Debt	60.38%	11.86%	**6.19**	19.51%	71.67%	**-8.44**
Taxes	39.62%	22.03%	**2.04**	25.61%	31.67%	-0.93
Wall Street/Bailouts	13.21%	23.73%	-1.42	26.83%	17.50%	1.59
Health Care	37.74%	15.25%	**2.78**	8.54%	18.33%	**-1.96**
Government Reform	5.66%	10.17%	-0.87	21.95%	9.17%	**2.57**
Foreign Policy/ Veterans	9.43%	28.81%	**-2.63**	13.41%	9.17%	0.95
Social Security/ Medicare	5.66%	6.78%	-0.24	6.10%	2.50%	1.29
Energy/ Environment	9.43%	5.08%	0.89	12.20%	5.83%	1.60
Family/Children	5.66%	8.47%	-0.57	4.88%	5.83%	-0.29
Education	1.89%	11.86%	**-2.07**	12.20%	0.00%	**4.06**
Constituent Concerns	9.43%	6.78%	0.51	3.66%	0.83%	1.42
Smaller Government	3.77%	3.39%	0.11	2.44%	15.00%	**-2.99**

Housing/ Foreclosures	3.77%	6.78%	-0.73	2.44%	2.50%	-0.03
Immigration	1.89%	0.00%	1.06	4.88%	0.83%	1.82
Agriculture	0.00%	3.39%	-1.35	1.22%	0.00%	1.21
Women's Issues	0.00%	1.69%	-0.95	4.88%	0.83%	1.82
Abortion	0.00%	1.69%	-0.95	4.88%	0.83%	1.82
Guns	0.00%	8.47%	**-2.20**	2.44%	0.00%	1.72
Crime	0.00%	0.00%	–	2.44%	0.83%	0.92
Terrorism	1.89%	3.39%	-0.49	1.22%	0.00%	1.21
Welfare	0.00%	0.00%	–	3.66%	0.00%	**2.12**
Religion	1.89%	3.39%	-0.49	3.66%	0.00%	**2.12**
Race	0.00%	0.00%	–	0.00%	0.00%	–

Note: DM = Democratic man; DW = Democratic woman; RM = Republican man; RW = Republican woman. Significant differences are shown in boldface.

issues. Republican women focused more of their ad attention on spending/ debt, taxes, and health care than did their Democratic male opponents. Democratic men were more likely to include education, foreign policy, and guns in their ads than their female opponents. These differences reveal that women and men are driven more by party considerations than by a desire to engage in stereotyped issue construction—Republican women focusing on debt and taxes while male Democrats focus on education shows that candidates of both sexes try to capitalize on their party's ownership of issues. Even Republican women's focus on health care, which might be seen to conform to gender stereotypes, was probably driven more by party and the context of the 2010 elections, when health care reform as passed in the Affordable Care Act was quite controversial in Republican and conservative Tea Party circles.

The race in the 45th Congressional District in California provides a good illustration of these patterns. Incumbent Mary Bono Mack ran a classic Republican campaign in line with the partisan themes of 2010. She ran ads against her opponent, Democrat Steve Pougnet, in which she tied him visually and ideologically to Speaker Nancy Pelosi and President Barack Obama, hoping to capitalize on discontent with the president and Democrats in Congress. The main themes in her ads were attacking Pougnet and these national leaders for their support of the economic stimulus package passed in 2009, higher taxes, and "Obamacare," which Bono Mack argued would add to the national debt. Pougnet, the mayor of Palm Springs, California, focused his campaign ads on the classic Democratic issue of Social Security and economic security for all. He attacked Bono Mack's support for privatizing Social Security and questioned her close ties to Wall Street banks. There is little evidence here that either candidate was focused on conveying images based on gender stereotypes, as Bono Mack highlighted the traditionally male economic issues and Pougnet focused on a classic female issue in Social Security. Instead, each candidate was clearly running on partisan issues and the issues of primary importance in that election year.

Similar patterns of partisan difference in campaign ads are visible in matchups between Democratic women candidates and their Republican male opponents. There are eight issues on which there were significant differences. Three involved the top issues in the 2010 election—economy/ jobs, spending/debt, and health care—with Democratic women having spent less time in their ads on these issues than did the Republican men they opposed. This pattern may be explained by political party as much as by candidate sex. These are not traditional female issues, but they are also not issues that helped Democratic candidates in 2010. Republican men also were more likely to include calls for smaller government in their ads.

Democratic women talked more about government reform, education, welfare, and religion. While these appear to conform to gender-stereotyped expectations, they are such a minor focus for these women candidates that the differences are not of much substantive importance. In terms of the major issues of the day, any differences seen here among mixed-sex pairs appear to have been driven by party stereotypes and the demands of the issue agenda of 2010 and not by strategic calculations to appeal to voters based on gender-stereotyped expectations.

Because of the economy, Democratic candidates in 2010 had to find other issues on which to tout their strengths. Incumbent U.S. Representative Debbie Halvorson (IL-11) focused on Social Security in her ads. One ad had a series of elderly actors scolding her 32-year-old Republican opponent, Adam Kinzinger, for his support of an increase in the retirement age and a cap on benefits. A parade of elderly faces tell Kinzinger to "back off" on attacking Social Security, saying, "Don't you dare," and, "It's not right." The last actor says that "Adam" is "young" and "has a lot to learn." Kinzinger, on the other hand, hit Halvorson hard on the economic issues of the day, with ads that tied her to Speaker Pelosi and highlighted the national Republican themes on government spending, unemployment, and the size of the national debt. While in this race there is a more clear alignment between candidate sex and the issues in campaign ads (Halvorson and Social Security, Kinzinger and the economy), there is also the clear influence of political party. As the earlier analysis suggested, the overlap of party and gender considerations is most obvious in races between Democratic women and Republican men.

An additional way to look at whether women are making stereotyped issue campaign choices is to compare women with each other across party lines. If women candidates are crafting issue images with an eye to gender-stereotyped strengths, we would expect to see similarities among women candidates regardless of their political party. However, when we compare women candidates of different parties, this is not the case. In fact, as Table 6.9 shows, there are several issues on which women candidates campaigned differently. Republican women included spending/debt, taxes, and health care more often than did Democratic women, while Democratic women placed a greater emphasis on Wall Street bailouts, government reform, and foreign policy. These differences are clearly driven by the issues of the day and the relative importance of each issue to members of the political parties in 2010 and include a mix of both "female" and "male" issues. Interestingly, the areas of difference among women centered on the primary issues in the election. On the lower-visibility issues, many of which are stereotyped as "female" issues, such as education and

Table 6.9. HOUSE ADS, WOMEN CANDIDATES

	Republican Woman (N = 85)	Democratic Woman (N = 112)	t-score (N = 197)
Economy/Jobs	56.47%	42.85%	1.90
Spending/Debt	61.18%	22.32%	**5.99**
Taxes	40.00%	24.11%	**2.41**
Wall Street/Bailouts	12.94%	28.57%	**–2.66**
Government Reform	7.06%	22.32%	**–2.96**
Health Care	34.12%	15.18%	**3.18**
Foreign Policy/Veterans	5.88%	15.18%	**–2.06**
Social Security/Medicare	5.88%	8.93%	–0.80
Energy/Environment	5.88%	13.39%	–1.73
Family/Children	7.06%	7.14%	–0.02
Education	4.71%	8.93%	–1.14
Constituent Concerns	5.88%	2.68%	1.13
Smaller Government	4.71%	1.79%	1.18
Housing/Foreclosures	3.53%	4.46%	–0.33
Immigration	3.53%	3.57%	–0.02
Agriculture	0.00%	3.57%	–1.77
Women's Issues	0.00%	3.57%	–1.77
Abortion	0.00%	3.57%	–1.77
Guns	0.00%	2.68%	–1.52
Crime	1.18%	1.79%	–0.34
Terrorism	1.18%	0.89%	0.20
Welfare	0.00%	2.68%	–1.52
Religion	1.18%	2.68%	–0.74
Race	0.00%	0.00%	–

Note: Significant differences are shown in boldface.

elderly issues, women Republicans and Democrats exhibit no difference in focus.

Senate Races

In shifting attention to the campaign ads aired by U.S. Senate candidates, we see confirmation of the trends we saw in House ads: more similarity than difference among women and men candidates and evidence that differences are driven more by political party and the issues at play in the election. Table 6.10 presents the issue presentations for all women and men Senate candidates included in the data set. Out of the 24 issues coded, women and men are only significantly different in their presentation of

Table 6.10. SENATE ADS BY CANDIDATE SEX

	Man Candidate (N = 226)	Woman Candidate (N = 101)	t-score (N = 327)
Economy/Jobs	50.44%	57.43%	−1.17
Spending/Debt	34.96%	25.74%	1.65
Taxes	28.76%	34.65%	−1.07
Wall Street/Bailouts	17.70%	22.78%	−1.07
Health Care	19.91%	7.92%	**2.74**
Government Reform	8.40%	16.83%	−2.26
Foreign Policy/Veterans	7.08%	3.96%	1.09
Social Security/Medicare	13.27%	5.94%	**1.96**
Energy/Environment	10.18%	7.92%	0.64
Family/Children	3.98%	4.95%	−0.40
Education	5.75%	3.96%	0.67
Constituent Concerns	4.87%	5.94%	−0.40
Smaller Government	9.29%	2.97%	**2.03**
Housing/Foreclosures	3.54%	11.88%	−2.94
Immigration	2.21%	3.96%	−0.89
Agriculture	0.00%	0.00%	−
Women's Issues	2.65%	0.99%	0.96
Abortion	3.10%	0.99%	1.14
Guns	1.77%	0.99%	0.53
Crime	5.75%	2.97%	1.08
Terrorism	0.44%	0.00%	0.67
Welfare	1.33%	0.00%	1.16
Religion	0.44%	0.00%	0.67
Race	0.00%	0.00%	−

Note: Significant differences are shown in boldface.

five of these issues. On the vast majority, including the top issues in that election, women and men are giving similar amounts of attention to these issues and do not appear to be working to create gendered images around any particular issue. Even the issues on which there are differences do not necessarily conform to gender stereotypes. Men running for the Senate included more attention to health care, Social Security/Medicare, and calls for smaller government than did women candidates. Women candidates gave more attention to government reform and housing/foreclosure issues than did men. And all of these issues could be considered to be further down the agenda for both women and men, as treatment of these issues only occurred in three to 20 percent of total ads.

While these patterns in the ads run by women and men Senate candidates are clear, two examples offer good illustrations of the interplay of partisan and gender considerations in campaign ads in 2010. Republican John Boozman, a member of the U.S. House from Arkansas, defeated Democratic two-term incumbent U.S. Senator Blanche Lambert Lincoln in a campaign fought along several major national issues. In one prominent Boozman ad, the voice-over ties Lincoln to Obama, referring to "Obama and Blanche," who "gave us Obamacare, which cuts Medicare and threatens Social Security." The ad refers to these actions as "putting our seniors at risk and our kids in debt." It then promises that Boozman will "work to stop Obama's radical agenda, create jobs, and bring fiscal responsibility back to Congress." This ad accomplishes a number of different goals for the Boozman campaign. It takes on Senator Lincoln on a series of traditionally Democratic and female issues—health care, Medicare, and Social Security—suggesting that she has failed voters on each of these. In appearing to champion these issues, Boozman plays against party type. The ad then pivots to raising Republican themes of jobs, the economy, and the national debt. Given the kind of Republican ads run across the country, there is nothing in this ad that suggests Boozman was particularly mindful of the fact that his opponent was a woman.

In campaigning as a Democrat in a challenging election year for members of that party, U.S. Senator Kirsten Gillibrand of New York focused on strengths and played against stereotype, to her advantage. Gillibrand, who was a member of the U.S. House from New York, had been appointed in 2009 to fill the seat vacated because of Hillary Clinton's appointment as U.S. secretary of state. In 2010, she was facing her first statewide election to fill the remainder of Clinton's term. Instead of employing a voice-over actor, she appears in the ad herself. Addressing the anti-Washington and anti-incumbent themes at play in 2010, she begins the ad by stating, "I haven't made a career of serving in Washington," but continues on to say that one of the reasons she "came to Congress" was to "serve as a voice for military families." She goes on to talk about how "appalled" she has been at how "our troops and veterans have been shortchanged." Using the first person, Gillibrand catalogs her activities on behalf of military families, stating, "I fought to raise military pay; I cosponsored the new G.I. Bill and created incentives for veterans who start their own businesses." She ends the ad by reminding voters that the military fights for us and "we need to fight for them." As with the Boozman ad, Gillibrand is attempting to do several things simultaneously in the ad. First, she reminds voters that she is not a career politician, having only been in Congress two years at that point. She then raises an issue of importance to her, one that (1) allows her to play against stereotypes of women's lack of ability on military issues, (2) plays against the stereotype of Democrats as "soft" on military concerns, and (3) allows her to avoid having to talk about the economy and jobs, which was not an easy set of issues for Democrats that year. By personalizing her work and speaking directly to voters, Gillibrand hoped to inoculate herself against the coming Republican tide, something she was successful at doing.

Table 6.11 presents the issue campaigns for women Senate candidates and their male opponents broken down by party of the woman candidate. These data show that the races in which Republican women ran against Democratic men were quite similar with respect to the issues on which the candidates focused, with a couple of exceptions. The major one was the heavy focus that Republican women gave to spending/debt issues (40 percent of ads) compared with Democratic men (10 percent of ads). This clearly reflects the tenor of many Republican campaigns that carried the conservative and Tea Party message about the crisis of government spending, particularly the Republican women Senate candidates in this data set—Sharron Angle, Linda McMahon, Christine O'Donnell, and Kelly Ayotte. Other issues on which there were differences—energy/environment, housing/foreclosure, and constituent concerns—were lower priorities for both women and men. On the other hand, with the exception of the economy, issue presentation differences between Democratic women and Republican men all centered around the major issues at play in the election and clearly reflected party messaging. Democratic women gave more attention to taxes, Wall Street/bailouts, and government reform, while Republican men emphasized spending/debt and health care. There were no significant differences on any of the other issues, many of which are stereotyped as female.

Finally, in comparing women Senate candidates to each other, we see that women Senate candidates do not all craft similar issue campaigns (Table 6.12). Republican and Democratic women give different amounts of attention to seven of the 24 issues, although many of the areas of difference involve issues that did not receive large amounts of attention. The influence of election-year dynamics is evident on the primary issues in focus, in that Republican women focused five times as many of their ads on spending/debt issues than did Democratic women, while Democratic women spent twice as much time on Wall Street/bailout issues than did Republican women. Other issues on which there were differences—housing/foreclosure, immigration, foreign policy, education, constituency concerns—only appeared in a small number of ads run by these women candidates.

Table 6.11. SENATE ADS, MIXED-SEX RACES

	RW vs. DM (N = 42)	DM vs. RW (N = 50)	t-score (N = 92)	DW vs. RM (N = 44)	RM vs. DW (N = 49)	t-score (N = 93)
Economy/Jobs	57.14%	42.00%	1.45	47.73%	53.06%	-0.51
Spending/Debt	40.48%	10.00%	**3.61**	11.36%	57.14%	**-5.19**
Taxes	38.10%	30.00%	0.81	36.36%	18.37%	**1.97**
Wall Street/Bailouts	16.67%	18.00%	-0.17	36.36%	16.33%	**2.24**
Health Care	14.29%	14.00%	0.04	4.55%	30.61%	**-3.41**
Government Reform	7.14%	14.00%	-1.05	22.73%	8.16%	**1.98**
Foreign Policy/Veterans	0.00%	4.00%	-1.31	6.82%	4.08%	0.58
Social Security/Medicare	9.52%	14.00%	-0.65	4.55%	14.29%	-1.59
Energy/Environment	4.76%	18.00%	**-1.97**	6.82%	12.24%	-0.88
Family/Children	9.52%	2.00%	1.59	2.27%	10.20%	-1.56
Education	0.00%	6.00%	-1.62	6.82%	4.08%	0.58
Constituent Concerns	0.00%	12.00%	**-2.37**	6.82%	4.08%	0.58
Smaller Government	7.14%	8.00%	-0.15	0.00%	2.04%	-0.95
Housing/Foreclosures	21.43%	2.00%	**3.10**	6.82%	6.12%	0.13
Immigration	9.52%	2.00%	1.59	0.00%	6.12%	-1.68
Agriculture	0.00%	0.00%	–	0.00%	0.00%	–
Women's Issues	0.00%	6.00%	-1.62	2.27%	0.00%	1.06
Abortion	0.00%	4.00%	-1.31	2.27%	0.00%	1.06
Guns	0.00%	4.00%	-1.31	0.00%	0.00%	–
Crime	7.14%	16.00%	-1.30	0.00%	2.04%	-0.95
Terrorism	0.00%	0.00%	–	0.00%	0.00%	–
Welfare	0.00%	6.00%	-1.62	0.00%	0.00%	–
Religion	0.00%	0.00%	–	0.00%	0.00%	–
Race	0.00%	0.00%	–	0.00%	0.00%	–

Note: DM = Democratic man; DW = Democratic woman; RM = Republican man; RW = Republican woman. Significant differences are shown in boldface.

Table 6.12. SENATE ADS, WOMEN CANDIDATES

	Republican Woman (N – 49)	Democratic Woman (N = 52)	t-score (N – 101)
Economy/Jobs	59.18%	55.77%	0.34
Spending/Debt	42.86%	9.62%	**4.09**
Taxes	38.78%	30.77%	0.84
Wall Street/Bailouts	14.29%	30.77%	**−1.99**
Health Care	12.24%	3.85%	1.57
Government Reform	14.29%	19.23%	−0.66
Foreign Policy/Veterans	0.00%	7.69%	**−2.00**
Social Security/Medicare	8.16%	3.85%	0.91
Energy/Environment	4.08%	11.54%	−1.39
Family/Children	8.16%	1.92%	1.45
Education	0.00%	7.70%	**−2.00**
Constituent Concerns	0.00%	11.54%	**−2.50**
Smaller Government	6.12%	0.00%	1.82
Housing/Foreclosures	18.37%	5.77%	**1.97**
Immigration	8.16%	0.00%	**2.13**
Agriculture	0.00%	0.00%	–
Women's Issues	0.00%	1.92%	−0.97
Abortion	0.00%	1.92%	−0.97
Guns	0.00%	1.92%	−0.97
Crime	6.12%	0.00%	1.82
Terrorism	0.00%	0.00%	–
Welfare	0.00%	0.00%	–
Religion	0.00%	0.00%	–
Race	0.00%	0.00%	–

Note: Significant differences are shown in boldface.

Governor Races

Analysis of the ads run by candidates for governor continues to provide relatively little evidence that women candidates play to presumed stereotyped strengths in crafting their issue campaigns. Comparing women candidates with men (Table 6.13) identifies four issues on which we see a significant difference in focus and much commonality of focus. First, we see no differences between women and men running for governor on most of the major issues at stake in the 2010 elections—the economy/jobs, government spending/debt, health care—but instead see all candidates focusing on these important issues. Women candidates for governor are more likely than the men to include Social Security/Medicare, education, and immigration in their television ads, while men are more likely

Table 6.13. GOVERNOR ADS BY CANDIDATE SEX

	Man Candidate (N = 271)	Woman Candidate (N = 86)	t-score (N = 357)
Economy/Jobs	52.77%	48.84%	0.63
Spending/Debt	31.37%	24.42%	1.23
Taxes	35.79%	23.26%	**2.17**
Wall Street/Bailouts	6.27%	5.81%	0.15
Health Care	10.70%	8.13%	0.69
Government Reform	21.77%	24.42%	−0.51
Foreign Policy/Veterans	3.32%	1.16%	1.06
Social Security/Medicare	0.37%	6.98%	**−3.92**
Energy/Environment	5.17%	3.49%	0.64
Family/Children	9.59%	8.14%	0.41
Education	19.56%	30.23%	**−2.09**
Constituent Concerns	4.43%	2.33%	0.87
Smaller Government	8.12%	6.98%	0.34
Housing/Foreclosures	3.69%	3.49%	0.09
Immigration	4.43%	10.47%	**−2.08**
Agriculture	0.11%	0.00%	0.98
Women's Issues	2.21%	0.00%	1.39
Abortion	1.48%	0.00%	1.13
Guns	0.74%	0.00%	0.80
Crime	7.75%	13.95%	−1.73
Terrorism	0.74%	0.00%	0.80
Welfare	0.00%	0.00%	−
Religion	1.11%	2.33%	−0.84
Race	0.37%	0.00%	0.56

Note: Significant differences are shown in boldface.

to focus on taxes. Yet, even when these differences appear to be driven by gender stereotypes, a closer look reveals other influences. For example, what appears to be a greater focus on Social Security/Medicare by women candidates for governor is really an outsized focus on this issue by one woman candidate—Alex Sink (D-FL). Her Republican male opponent, Rick Scott, was chief executive of a large health care company that had been investigated for Medicare fraud, which Sink raised repeatedly in her ads. The greater focus that women candidates for governor give to immigration is largely driven by two candidates running in border states where these issues are very relevant—Jan Brewer (R-AZ) and Susana Martinez (R-NM). Given that Republicans tended to give immigration more attention than did Democrats, these women appear to be presenting an issue campaign crafted primarily around party and constituent issues.

The comparison of the television ads of women candidates and their male opponents (separated by party of the woman candidate) presented in Table 6.14 continues the patterns seen in Table 6.13. There are no significant differences in the issues presented by Republican women and their Democratic male opponents in these ads. One thing to note here is that these candidates campaigned over a more limited number of issues—only 12 out of the 24 coded—than did House or Senate candidates. Some of this is, of course, related to the difference in policies that are relevant to governors and also to the states in which these candidates were running. Democratic women candidates demonstrate a few areas of difference in focus from their Republican male opponents, but here we must acknowledge that only one governor's race is reflected here—that between Alex Sink (D) and Rick Scott (R) in Florida. Here we do not see any general patterns but, instead, the influences of their political parties and their personal backgrounds. Sink was chief financial officer of Florida when she ran, which stimulated her focus on the economy and jobs and her opponent's emphasis on levels of state spending and debt. In the end, there is little evidence that women and men running for governor attempted to create stereotyped issue campaigns in 2010. There was more similarity than difference among women and men, and differences were more consistent with partisan considerations than with gender.

The differences among women confirm that women candidates for governor are not attempting to place female issues and stereotypes at the center of their campaigns (Table 6.15). Republican women candidates placed significantly more emphasis on spending/debt, taxes, and the need for smaller government than did Democratic women, who focused on the economy/ jobs, Wall Street and corporate bailouts, Social Security/Medicare, and housing. Interestingly, no women candidates for governor of either party included in this analysis campaigned on the classically "female" issues of welfare, women's issues, or abortion.

ADS IN MALE-ONLY CAMPAIGNS

As a final check on whether candidate sex drives issue campaign choices, we can compare television ads from races with women candidates running and those in which both candidates are men. Such a comparison will allow us to see whether political party influences campaign issues more than candidate sex and gendered considerations. In general, the analysis suggests that this is the case. Table 6.16 presents male-only House races, where we see that the differences between Republican and Democratic

TABLE 6.14. GOVERNOR ADS, MIXED-SEX RACES

	RW vs. DM (N = 28)	DM vs. RW (N = 25)	t-score (N = 53)	DW vs. RM (N = 16)	RM vs. DW (N = 11)	t-score (N = 27)
Economy/Jobs	50.00%	32.00%	1.32	68.75%	18.18%	**2.87**
Spending/Debt	42.86%	36.00%	0.50	6.25%	36.36%	**-2.06**
Taxes	28.57%	40.00%	-0.87	18.75%	27.27%	-0.51
Wall Street/Bailouts	0.00%	12.00%	-1.92	0.00%	27.27%	-2.36
Health Care	7.14%	0.00%	1.36	6.25%	27.27%	-1.52
Government Reform	28.57%	24.00%	0.37	25.00%	36.36%	-0.62
Foreign Policy/Veterans	0.00%	0.00%	–	0.00%	0.00%	–
Social Security/Medicare	0.00%	0.00%	–	37.50%	0.00%	**2.47**
Energy/Environment	0.00%	0.00%	–	6.25%	9.09%	0.82
Family/Children	0.00%	4.00%	-1.06	6.25%	0.00%	-0.27
Education	28.57%	24.00%	0.37	18.75%	0.00%	1.53
Constituent Concerns	7.14%	0.00%	1.36	0.00%	0.00%	–
Smaller Government	7.14%	0.00%	1.36	0.00%	0.00%	–
Housing/Foreclosures	0.00%	4.00%	-1.06	0.00%	0.00%	–
Immigration	7.14%	20.00%	-1.38	0.00%	0.00%	–
Agriculture	0.00%	0.00%	–	0.00%	0.00%	–
Women's Issues	0.00%	0.00%	–	0.00%	0.00%	–
Abortion	0.00%	0.00%	–	0.00%	0.00%	–
Guns	0.00%	0.00%	–	0.00%	0.00%	–
Crime	10.71%	24.00%	-1.28	0.00%	0.00%	–
Terrorism	0.00%	0.00%	–	0.00%	9.09%	-1.22
Welfare	0.00%	0.00%	–	0.00%	0.00%	–
Religion	0.00%	4.00%	-1.06	0.00%	9.09%	-1.22
Race	0.00%	0.00%	–	0.00%	0.00%	–

Note: DM = Democratic man; DW = Democratic woman; RM = Republican man; RW = Republican woman. Significant differences are shown in boldface.

Table 6.15. GOVERNOR ADS, WOMEN CANDIDATES

	Republican Woman (N = 53)	Democratic Woman (N = 33)	t-score (N = 86)
Economy/Jobs	39.62%	63.64%	−2.20
Spending/Debt	37.74%	3.03%	**3.92**
Taxes	32.08%	9.09%	**2.51**
Wall Street/Bailouts	0.00%	15.15%	**−3.04**
Health Care	11.32%	3.03%	1.37
Government Reform	30.19%	15.15%	1.58
Foreign Policy/Veterans	1.89%	0.00%	0.79
Social Security/Medicare	0.00%	18.18%	**−3.39**
Energy/Environment	0.00%	9.09%	**−2.28**
Family/Children	7.55%	9.09%	−0.25
Education	24.53%	39.39%	−1.46
Constituent Concerns	3.77%	0.00%	1.12
Smaller Government	11.32%	0.00%	**2.03**
Housing/Foreclosures	0.00%	9.09%	**−2.28**
Immigration	15.09%	3.03%	1.79
Agriculture	0.00%	0.00%	–
Women's Issues	0.00%	0.00%	
Abortion	0.00%	0.00%	–
Guns	0.00%	0.00%	–
Crime	16.98%	9.09%	1.02
Terrorism	0.00%	0.00%	–
Welfare	0.00%	0.00%	–
Religion	3.77%	0.00%	1.12
Race	0.00%	0.00%	–

Note: Significant differences are shown in boldface.

men in their advertising focus—Republicans focusing more on spending/ debt, health care, and a desire for smaller government, while Democrats emphasized government reform, foreign policy, Social Security/Medicare, education, constituent services, and women's issues—just about exactly mirror the patterns revealed in the mixed-sex House races presented in Table 6.8. In that table, we saw that Democratic candidates focused on the same issues, regardless of their sex. The same was true for Republican candidates. Republican women and men ran very similar issue campaigns. The results demonstrate that candidates focus on the issues that are central to their political party and appear to give little attention to campaigning from a gendered perspective. This focus on a party message is reinforced in the analysis of the male-only races, where the candidates clearly align their television ads with partisan expectations.

Table 6.16. HOUSE ADS, MALE-ONLY RACES

	Republican Man (N = 307)	Democratic Man (N = 329)	t-score (N = 636)
Economy/Jobs	55.37%	49.54%	1.47
Spending/Debt	58.31%	14.89%	**12.77**
Taxes	31.27%	25.23%	1.69
Wall Street/Bailouts	14.01%	19.45%	−1.84
Health Care	24.76%	6.38%	**6.65**
Government Reform	8.79%	17.02%	**−3.10**
Foreign Policy/Veterans	7.17%	24.62%	**−6.14**
Social Security/Medicare	8.79%	15.20%	**−2.48**
Energy/Environment	8.47%	7.90%	0.26
Family/Children	5.54%	10.03%	**−2.11**
Education	0.33%	6.99%	**−4.47**
Constituent Concerns	3.26%	11.25%	**−3.89**
Smaller Government	8.79%	0.30%	**5.32**
Housing/Foreclosures	3.26%	4.56%	−0.84
Immigration	5.54%	3.34%	1.35
Agriculture	2.61%	2.13%	0.40
Women's Issues	0.65%	2.74%	**−2.02**
Abortion	0.65%	1.82%	−1.33
Guns	0.33%	1.82%	−1.81
Crime	1.95%	0.91%	1.11
Terrorism	0.33%	0.30%	0.05
Welfare	0.00%	0.00%	–
Religion	0.98%	0.61%	0.53
Race	0.00%	0.30%	−0.97

Note: Significant differences are shown in boldface.

Male-only Senate races demonstrate a continuation of the influence of political party on campaign issue choices (Table 6.17). The clear Republican focus in 2010 campaign ads was on the economy/jobs, smaller government, and health care, all of which are reflected in the campaigns of Republican men running for the Senate in male-only races. Democratic men followed other Democratic candidates in focusing on Wall Street/bailouts and foreign policy issues. These male-only races show the same patterns as the mixed-sex Senate races and confirm that the differences between women Senate candidates and their male opponents are driven by party, not attempts to play to voters' gender stereotypes.

As we have seen with the analysis of the male-only races for each chamber of Congress, male candidates for governor focus on their political party

Table 6.17. SENATE ADS, MALE-ONLY RACES

	Republican Man (N = 67)	Democratic Man (N = 60)	t-score (N = 127)
Economy/Jobs	61.19%	43.33%	**2.03**
Spending/Debt	62.69%	6.67%	**8.00**
Taxes	32.84%	31.67%	0.14
Wall Street/Bailouts	7.46%	30.00%	**−3.42**
Health Care	26.87%	8.33%	**2.77**
Government Reform	2.99%	10.00%	−1.63
Foreign Policy/Veterans	2.99%	16.67%	−2.69
Social Security/Medicare	7.46%	18.33%	−1.85
Energy/Environment	8.96%	3.33%	1.30
Family/Children	2.99%	1.67%	0.49
Education	2.99%	10.00%	−1.63
Constituent Concerns	1.49%	3.33%	−0.68
Smaller Government	22.39%	1.67%	**3.67**
Housing/Foreclosures	4.48%	1.67%	0.90
Immigration	1.49%	0.00%	0.95
Agriculture	0.00%	0.00%	–
Women's Issues	0.00%	5.00%	−1.86
Abortion	0.00%	8.33%	**−2.45**
Guns	0.00%	3.33%	−1.51
Crime	0.00%	6.67%	**−2.17**
Terrorism	1.49%	0.00%	0.95
Welfare	0.00%	0.00%	–
Religion	0.00%	1.67%	−1.06
Race	0.00%	0.00%	–

Note: Significant differences are shown in boldface.

when crafting television ads (Table 6.18). These candidates follow the same path as other sets of candidates—Republicans focused on spending/debt and smaller government, while Democratic men focused on Wall Street/ bailouts and foreign policy. These races played out in the same ways as did the mixed-sex races for governor. One additional difference in governor races was the fact that Democratic men included more mentions of women's issues and abortion than did their Republican male opponents, none of whom included either of these issues in a single ad.

This difference in representation of women's issues, including abortion, among male candidates for governor raises an interesting finding about campaigning on women's issues. As is not surprising, in races for all three offices, Democratic candidates, both women and men, were the most likely

Table 6.18. GOVERNOR ADS, MALE-ONLY RACES

	Republican Man (N = 117)	Democratic Man (N = 118)	t-score (N = 235)
Economy/Jobs	61.54%	51.69%	1.52
Spending/Debt	40.17%	21.19%	**3.21**
Taxes	38.46%	33.05%	0.86
Wall Street/Bailouts	0.85%	8.47%	**−2.80**
Health Care	7.69%	14.41%	−1.64
Government Reform	24.79%	16.95%	1.48
Foreign Policy/Veterans	0.85%	6.78%	**−2.38**
Social Security/Medicare	0.00%	0.85%	−1.00
Energy/Environment	3.42%	8.47%	−1.64
Family/Children	9.40%	11.02%	−0.41
Education	17.09%	22.88%	−1.11
Constituent Concerns	5.98%	4.24%	0.61
Smaller Government	13.68%	5.08%	**2.28**
Housing/Foreclosures	5.13%	2.54%	1.03
Immigration	3.42%	2.54%	0.39
Agriculture	2.56%	0.00%	1.75
Women's Issues	0.00%	5.08%	**−2.49**
Abortion	0.00%	3.39%	**−2.02**
Guns	0.00%	1.69%	−1.41
Crime	4.27%	8.47%	−1.32
Terrorism	0.85%	0.00%	1.00
Welfare	0.00%	0.00%	–
Religion	0.85%	0.00%	1.00
Race	0.85%	0.00%	1.00

Note: Significant differences are shown in boldface.

candidates to raise these issues. With the exception of a couple of male Republican House candidates, no Republican candidate, male or female, raised these issues. Of course, it should be noted that women's issues were not a top issue focus for any of the Democratic candidates and received only limited attention in television ads. But the almost complete silence of Republican candidates on these issues is worth noting. Also, women's issues got slightly more attention in male-only races at each level, with Democratic men running against Republican men being a bit more likely to raise these issues than were Democratic women when they ran against Republican men. While we might expect, based on gender stereotypes, that women would be more likely than men to raise women's issues, among Democrats, that does not appear to be the case. Among Republicans, no one raises these issues, regardless of sex. Among Democrats, men are as likely as, and sometimes more likely than, women to do so.

Ads from two Democratic men in 2010 provide excellent examples of this male advocacy of women's issues. In Colorado, appointed Democratic U.S. Senator Michael Bennet was in a tight race against Weld County District Attorney Ken Buck, a Tea Party favorite.[4] In a question-and-answer session at a campaign event in 2010, Buck talked about his position on abortion, stating, "I am pro-life. I don't believe in the exceptions for rape or incest." Bennet ran an ad using the video of Buck making that statement with a voice-over that called Buck "too extreme for Colorado." Bennet raised these concerns in the context of a campaign in which Buck had received criticism for his handling of a case of alleged rape in his capacity as district attorney, which probably increased attention to Buck's comments on abortion. Voters in Illinois saw a Democratic male candidate make an even broader attack on his Republican opponent's record on women's issues. Democratic Governor Pat Quinn launched an ad asking what "our daughters" could expect from Republican opponent Bill Brady's "17-year record of voting against working women." Employing a woman to provide the voice-over, the ad pointed out Brady's opposition to the Family and Medical Leave Act, increased coverage of mammograms, and abortion in cases of rape or incest. The ad concluded by reiterating that "our daughters" deserve better. Each of these ads highlights a partisan strategy on the part of Democratic men candidates in addressing women's issues, seeking to capitalize on their advocacy of these issues, presumably among women voters. The complete lack of attention that Buck and Brady gave to these issues in their own ads is perfectly in line with Republican candidates in 2010.

WEBSITES

Candidates spend a considerable amount of time and money crafting their images through their campaign advertisements. Yet almost all candidates also maintain campaign websites, which give us another view into their issue priorities. Websites offer candidates advantages that ads do not. They are relatively inexpensive, constantly available to the public, and able to communicate much more information than the average 30-second ad. Campaign websites have also become a widespread tool of campaigns. Analysis done on House candidate websites in 2000 found that approximately 65 percent of candidates maintained campaign sites (Dolan 2005). In this current project, that figure is 95 percent for House candidates and 100 percent for candidates for Senate and governor. As a result of their economy and ubiquity, campaign websites offer us a glimpse into the issue priorities of a more complete set of candidates for office.

Since campaign websites are a different medium than are ads, there are a couple of things to note. First, in the discussion of websites, the unit of analysis is the candidate. Unlike with ads, where there is variation across candidates in the number produced, each candidate had one campaign website. Second, since we want to examine the choices candidates make with regard to the issues they represent, any candidates who presented an alphabetized list of issues was excluded from the analysis. Finally, because the numbers of women candidates for Senate and governor were small, the analysis of the websites for these offices is more limited. While we have enough House candidates to make more extensive comparisons, the smaller number of women candidates whose websites included issues in a prioritized format (as opposed to alphabetical) limits our ability to make some comparisons.

House

As was noted earlier, most research on candidate websites does not find significant differences in the issue priorities presented by women and men candidates. The data for 2010 support those earlier studies and also confirm the findings of the analysis of the television ads. Table 6.19 presents issue presentation figures for women and men House candidates. There are a couple of things to note. First, we can still see the primacy of economic issues and health care in the issue images candidates present. Second, there are no differences in whether women and men include various of the top issues of the day on their campaign websites. There are only three issues on which there are differences, and two of them are issues that relatively few candidates included at all. Women are more likely to talk about housing/ foreclosure (8 percent) and women's issues (6 percent) on their websites, but only in very small numbers. Men are more likely to include immigration than are women (24 percent to 11 percent). These data seem to clearly indicate that women and men are much more concerned with addressing the important issues in the election than with crafting a stereotyped image to play to voters.

Table 6.20 reports the race matchup pairings based on candidate sex and party. The websites of Republican women running against Democratic men for the House are remarkably similar on 22 of the 25 issues, with Republican women showing the consistent greater focus on spending/debt, taxes, and smaller government. When Democratic women run again Republican men,

Table 6.19. HOUSE WEBSITES BY CANDIDATE SEX

	Man Candidate (N = 368)	Woman Candidate (N = 89)	t-score (N = 457)
Economy/Jobs	75.00%	71.91%	0.60
Spending/Debt	44.84%	40.45%	0.75
Taxes	21.74%	23.60%	−0.38
Wall Street/Bailouts	11.69%	14.61%	−0.75
Health Care	57.88%	57.30%	0.10
Government Reform	12.77%	13.48%	−0.18
Foreign Policy/Veterans	45.38%	43.82%	0.27
Social Security/Medicare	11.41%	11.24%	0.05
Energy/Environment	37.23%	35.96%	0.22
Family/Children	10.87%	10.11%	0.21
Education	27.72%	37.08%	−1.74
Constituent Concerns	11.69%	14.61%	−0.75
Smaller Government	6.25%	7.87%	−0.55
Housing/Foreclosures	3.26%	7.87%	**−1.96**
Immigration	23.91%	11.24%	**2.63**
Agriculture	7.88%	6.74%	0.36
Women's Issues	1.09%	5.62%	**−2.78**
Abortion	5.16%	4.49%	0.26
Guns	7.61%	3.37%	1.43
Crime	1.09%	1.12%	−0.03
Terrorism	4.08%	4.49%	−0.18
Welfare	0.54%	0.00%	0.70
Religion	0.00%	0.00%	–
Race	0.00%	0.00%	–
Values	9.78%	7.86%	0.56

Note: Significant differences are shown in boldface.

we see greater differences. Just like Democratic men, Democratic women are less likely than their opponents to highlight spending/debt and taxes. They also are less likely to campaign on smaller government and immigration and more likely to discuss education, women's issues, and housing/foreclosures than their Republican male opponents. In all of these race matchup differences, party is clearly at work. The primacy of party is reinforced by comparing women who belong to different parties. Women Democrats and Republicans display seven issues on which they differ, all of which fit party stereotypes (Table 6.21). Republican women were more likely to discuss spending/debt, taxes, a desire for smaller government, and immigration on their websites, while Democratic women were significantly

Table 6.20. HOUSE WEBSITES, MIXED-SEX RACES

	RW vs. DM (N = 22)	DM vs. RW (N = 26)	t-score (N = 48)	DW vs. RM (N = 55)	RM vs. DW (N = 58)	t-score (N = 113)
Economy/Jobs	72.73%	80.77%	-0.65	72.73%	74.14%	-0.17
Spending/Debt	72.73%	26.92%	**3.48**	23.64%	58.62%	**-4.00**
Taxes	50.00%	11.54%	**3.15**	9.09%	34.48%	**-3.38**
Wall Street/Bailouts	4.55%	23.08%	-1.84	21.82%	12.07%	1.38
Health Care	63.64%	61.54%	0.15	60.00%	50.00%	1.06
Government Reform	13.64%	19.23%	-0.51	12.73%	18.97%	-0.90
Foreign Policy/Veterans	40.91%	53.85%	-0.88	47.27%	39.66%	0.81
Social Security/Medicare	4.55%	15.38%	-1.22	12.73%	17.24%	-0.67
Energy/Environment	31.82%	34.62%	-0.20	38.18%	27.59%	1.20
Family/Children	0.00%	0.00%	–	14.55%	17.24%	-0.39
Education	13.64%	34.62%	-1.69	45.45%	24.14%	**2.42**
Constituent Concerns	9.09%	15.38%	-0.65	16.36%	10.34%	0.94
Smaller Government	22.73%	0.00%	**2.71**	0.00%	8.62%	**-2.26**
Housing/Foreclosures	4.55%	3.85%	0.12	10.91%	1.72%	**2.04**
Immigration	22.73%	19.23%	0.29	7.27%	31.03%	**-3.31**
Agriculture	4.55%	11.54%	-0.86	5.45%	1.72%	1.07
Women's Issues	0.00%	3.85%	-0.92	7.27%	0.00%	**2.11**
Abortion	4.55%	0.00%	1.09	3.64%	0.00%	1.47
Guns	9.09%	3.85%	0.74	0.00%	3.45%	-1.39
Crime	0.00%	0.00%	–	1.82%	0.00%	1.03
Terrorism	4.55%	0.00%	1.09	3.64%	1.72%	0.63
Welfare	0.00%	0.00%	–	0.00%	0.00%	–
Religion	0.00%	0.00%	–	0.00%	0.00%	–
Race	0.00%	0.00%	–	0.00%	0.00%	–
Values	13.64%	0.00%	**1.98**	5.45%	6.90%	-0.32

Note: DM = Democratic man; DW = Democratic woman; RM = Republican man; RW = Republican woman. Significant differences are shown in boldface.

Table 6.21. HOUSE WEBSITES, WOMEN CANDIDATES

	Republican Woman (N = 28)	Democratic Woman (N = 61)	t-score (N = 89)
Economy/Jobs	71.43%	72.13%	−0.07
Spending/Debt	71.43%	26.23%	**4.41**
Taxes	57.14%	8.20%	**5.91**
Wall Street/Bailouts	3.57%	19.67%	**−2.02**
Health Care	57.14%	57.38%	−0.02
Government Reform	14.29%	13.11%	0.15
Foreign Policy/Veterans	42.86%	44.26%	−0.12
Social Security/Medicare	10.71%	11.48%	−0.10
Energy/Environment	28.57%	39.34%	−0.98
Family/Children	0.00%	14.75%	**−2.18**
Education	14.29%	47.54%	**−3.15**
Constituent Concerns	7.14%	18.03%	−1.35
Smaller Government	25.00%	0.00%	**4.46**
Housing/Foreclosures	3.57%	9.84%	−1.01
Immigration	21.43%	6.56%	**2.09**
Agriculture	7.14%	6.56%	0.10
Women's Issues	0.00%	8.20%	−1.56
Abortion	3.57%	4.92%	−0.28
Guns	7.14%	1.64%	1.33
Crime	0.00%	1.64%	−0.68
Terrorism	3.57%	4.92%	−0.28
Welfare	0.00%	0.00%	–
Religion	0.00%	0.00%	–
Race	0.00%	0.00%	–
Values	10.71%	6.56%	0.67

Note: Significant differences are shown in boldface.

more likely to address education, family/children's issues, and Wall Street/bailouts. These choices clearly reflect the emphasis placed on these issues by the parties in 2010.

Senate and Governor

The smaller number of websites for women candidates for the Senate and governor limits our analysis to comparing all women and men candidates for each office. Tables 6.22–6.23 present both sets of findings. For Senate candidates, there are no differences between women and men on any of

Table 6.22. SENATE WEBSITES BY CANDIDATE SEX

	Man Candidate (N = 22)	Woman Candidate (N = 9)	t-score (N = 31)
Economy/Jobs	81.82%	88.89%	−0.47
Spending/Debt	45.46%	66.67%	−1.06
Taxes	40.91%	22.22%	0.97
Wall Street/Bailouts	18.18%	11.11%	0.47
Health Care	63.63%	77.78%	−0.75
Government Reform	18.18%	22.22%	−0.25
Foreign Policy/Veterans	45.46%	33.33%	0.60
Social Security/Medicare	13.64%	22.22%	−0.57
Energy/Environment	40.91%	22.22%	0.97
Family/Children	0.00%	44.44%	**−4.06**
Education	45.46%	33.33%	0.60
Constituent Concerns	4.55%	11.11%	−0.66
Smaller Government	0.00%	0.00%	–
Housing/Foreclosures	4.55%	0.00%	0.63
Immigration	9.09%	0.00%	0.92
Agriculture	0.00%	0.00%	–
Women's Issues	4.55%	0.00%	0.63
Abortion	4.55%	11.11%	−0.66
Guns	9.09%	0.00%	0.92
Crime	4.55%	0.00%	0.63
Terrorism	4.55%	11.11%	−0.66
Welfare	0.00%	0.00%	–
Religion	0.00%	0.00%	–
Race	0.00%	0.00%	–
Values	4.55%	11.11%	−0.66

Note: Significant difference is shown in boldface.

the top 10 issues that candidates represented on their websites or on the vast majority of more "minor" issues. Indeed, the only difference here is women's greater likelihood over men of discussing family and children's issues. Interestingly, while almost half of the women Senate candidates gave some attention to this issue, not one of the 22 men running for the Senate did so. Finally, with regard to governors, men were more likely to highlight taxes, but women were more likely to discuss immigration, crime, and values. Beyond this, there were no differences in the websites on 21 of the 25 issues coded.

Table 6.23. GOVERNOR WEBSITES BY CANDIDATE SEX

	Man Candidate (N = 29)	Woman Candidate (N = 8)	t-score (N = 37)
Economy/Jobs	96.55%	100.00%	−0.52
Spending/Debt	41.38%	25.00%	0.83
Taxes	37.93%	0.00%	**2.15**
Wall Street/Bailouts	0.00%	0.00%	–
Health Care	27.59%	25.00%	0.14
Government Reform	51.72%	37.50%	0.70
Foreign Policy/Veterans	17.24%	12.50%	0.32
Social Security/Medicare	0.00%	0.00%	–
Energy/Environment	37.93%	25.00%	0.66
Family/Children	13.79%	12.50%	0.09
Education	58.62%	75.00%	−0.83
Constituent Concerns	17.24%	0.00%	1.26
Smaller Government	6.90%	0.00%	0.75
Housing/Foreclosures	0.00%	0.00%	–
Immigration	6.90%	37.50%	**−2.35**
Agriculture	6.89%	12.50%	−0.50
Women's Issues	10.34%	0.00%	0.93
Abortion	3.45%	0.00%	0.52
Guns	3.45%	0.00%	0.52
Crime	3.45%	25.00%	**−2.03**
Terrorism	0.00%	0.00%	–
Welfare	3.45%	0.00%	0.52
Religion	0.00%	0.00%	–
Race	0.00%	0.00%	–
Values	3.45%	25.00%	**−2.03**

Note: Significant differences are shown in boldface.

WEBSITES IN MALE-ONLY RACES

Websites for candidates in male-only House races confirm the pattern of a party-based narrative in the 2010 elections (Table 6.24). Almost all candidates talked about the economy and jobs on their websites. After that, Republicans were significantly more likely to talk about spending/debt, taxes, health care, smaller government, and immigration, while Democrats focused on Wall Street/bailouts, foreign policy and veterans' issues, government reform, education, Social Security/Medicare, and housing. These are the same differences that play out in the mixed-sex races: plainly partisan themes that have been clear and consistent across all races and each media.

Table 6.24. HOUSE WEBSITES, MALE-ONLY RACES

	Republican Man (N = 152)	Democratic Man (N = 132)	t-score (N = 284)
Economy/Jobs	72.37%	77.23%	−0.95
Spending/Debt	61.18%	23.48%	**6.88**
Taxes	32.24%	6.06%	**5.79**
Wall Street/Bailouts	4.61%	17.42%	**−3.57**
Health Care	67.11%	50.00%	**2.96**
Government Reform	8.55%	13.64%	−1.37
Foreign Policy/Veterans	40.13%	52.27%	**−2.06**
Social Security/Medicare	6.58%	13.64%	**−2.00**
Energy/Environment	34.87%	44.70%	−1.69
Family/Children	12.50%	8.33%	1.14
Education	15.13%	42.42%	**−5.35**
Constituent Concerns	7.89%	15.91%	**−2.11**
Smaller Government	11.84%	0.00%	**4.20**
Housing/Foreclosures	0.66%	6.82%	**−2.84**
Immigration	32.89%	11.36%	**4.44**
Agriculture	6.58%	11.36%	−1.42
Women's Issues	0.66%	1.52%	−0.70
Abortion	7.89%	5.30%	0.87
Guns	9.21%	8.33%	0.26
Crime	1.97%	0.76%	0.87
Terrorism	5.92%	3.79%	0.83
Welfare	0.66%	0.76%	−0.10
Religion	0.00%	0.00%	−
Race	0.00%	0.00%	−
Values	13.82%	8.33%	1.46

Note: Significant differences are shown in boldface.

As with the websites for women Senate and governor candidates, there are smaller numbers of men in male-only races for these offices. However, these campaigns look remarkably similar to all of the others, with issue differences between candidates clearly being driven by partisan priorities (Tables 6.25–6.26). The one remarkable thing about the races for governor is that these candidates exhibited no differences at all in the issues they presented. There is a clear focus in these campaigns on economic issues and a lack of attention to some of the issues that are more national in scope, such as the government bailout of Wall Street banks and Social Security.

Table 6.25. SENATE WEBSITES, MALE-ONLY RACES

	Republican Man (N = 6)	Democratic Man (N = 7)	t-score (N = 13)
Economy/Jobs	66.67%	85.71%	−0.77
Spending/Debt	83.33%	28.57%	2.17
Taxes	83.33%	14.29%	3.17
Wall Street/Bailouts	33.33%	28.57%	0.17
Health Care	50.00%	57.14%	−0.24
Government Reform	16.67%	14.29%	0.11
Foreign Policy/Veterans	50.00%	42.86%	0.24
Social Security/Medicare	16.67%	14.29%	0.11
Energy/Environment	33.33%	42.86%	−0.33
Family/Children	0.00%	0.00%	–
Education	16.67%	71.43%	−2.17
Constituent Concerns	0.00%	14.29%	−0.92
Smaller Government	0.00%	0.00%	–
Housing/Foreclosures	0.00%	14.29%	−0.92
Immigration	0.00%	0.00%	–
Agriculture	0.00%	0.00%	–
Women's Issues	0.00%	0.00%	–
Abortion	0.00%	0.00%	–
Guns	16.67%	14.29%	0.11
Crime	16.67%	0.00%	1.09
Terrorism	16.67%	0.00%	1.09
Welfare	0.00%	0.00%	–
Religion	0.00%	0.00%	–
Race	0.00%	0.00%	–
Values	0.00%	14.29%	−0.92

Note: Significant differences are shown in boldface.

CONCLUSION

Taken together, these campaign media data describe candidates, male and female, who frame their issue campaigns around the "issues of the day," the topics that voters are concerned about in a particular electoral context. The bulk of ads and the majority of websites focused on a set of economic issues important in 2010—the economy, jobs, government spending, taxes, and the impact of health care reform. Other issues received attention, but in much lower concentrations than the economic. Candidates, particularly through websites, can touch on a wide range of issues in an attempt to present a balanced image of their issue concerns. But, in all, these candidates are paying attention to the issues of concern to voters.

Table 6.26. GOVERNOR WEBSITES, MALE-ONLY RACES

	Republican Man (N = 12)	Democratic Man (N = 13)	t-score (N = 25)
Economy/Jobs	100.00%	92.31%	0.96
Spending/Debt	50.00%	38.46%	0.56
Taxes	50.00%	30.77%	0.96
Wall Street/Bailouts	0.00%	0.00%	–
Health Care	33.33%	23.08%	0.55
Government Reform	58.33%	53.85%	0.22
Foreign Policy/Veterans	8.33%	23.08%	–0.98
Social Security/Medicare	0.00%	0.00%	–
Energy/Environment	16.67%	46.15%	–1.60
Family/Children	16.67%	7.69%	0.67
Education	41.67%	69.23%	–1.38
Constituent Concerns	25.00%	7.69%	1.16
Smaller Government	0.00%	15.38%	–1.42
Housing/Foreclosures	0.00%	0.00%	–
Immigration	8.33%	0.00%	1.04
Agriculture	8.33%	7.69%	0.06
Women's Issues	8.33%	15.38%	–0.52
Abortion	8.33%	0.00%	1.04
Guns	8.33%	0.00%	1.04
Crime	0.00%	7.69%	–0.96
Terrorism	0.00%	0.00%	–
Welfare	8.33%	0.00%	1.04
Religion	0.00%	0.00%	–
Race	0.00%	0.00%	–
Values	0.00%	7.69%	–0.96

These issue campaigns also reflect the centrality of political party in shaping the issues on which candidates spend their time and money. Candidates of both parties spent the bulk of their time and attention on the economy and jobs. But beyond that, party differences are clear. In fact, one of the most striking aspects of the media data is the clear partisan orientation to the issue campaign run by candidates for all three offices and regardless of sex. Republican campaigns looked alike regardless of the candidate or the office the candidate sought, and the same was largely true for Democrats.

In almost every case and for each of the three offices considered, any divergence between women and men candidates in the issue campaigns they ran was along political party lines, not gender. There is no real evidence that women or men positioned themselves on particular issues in the hopes of capitalizing on the public's gender-stereotyped expectations. Indeed, to do so would be foolish for most candidates much of the time. The election of 2010 was overwhelmingly focused on economic issues, and candidates focused their time and attention there. In the context of this, candidates do give attention to other issues, whether to respond to a particular constituency or to present a balanced set of issues to voters. But even here, with the issues to which candidates give less attention, there are no clear gendered patterns of effort or concentration.

The findings of this analysis do not mean to suggest that gender differences in issue focus never exist, but they do suggest that they occur less often than we might think. The data also clearly show that women candidates do not appear to be playing to stereotyped strengths in creating their issue images. Because of this, we can say with some confidence that candidates are not contributing to any stereotyped impressions voters might hold. This analysis fits nicely with the analysis of voter attitudes and behaviors to strongly suggest that gender stereotypes have less impact and less of a presence in election campaigns than the conventional wisdom would suggest.

CHAPTER 7

The Landscape for Women Candidates

What not to do. . . getting locked out of the Governor's mansion in your robe while sending the kids off to school. Sigh. . . #adayinthelife

Nikki Haley, Governor (R-SC)

I think my experience is one of the things that sets me apart as a candidate for governor. First of all, being a mother, having children, raising a family.

Mary Fallon, U.S. Representative (R-OK)

When Nikki Haley locked herself out of the governor's mansion one school-day morning in September 2013 wearing just a robe, she waved to the security camera at the front door until someone noticed her and let her in. Then she took to Twitter, sharing her amusing moment of exasperation with the world. Parents all across the country probably smiled in recognition at the crazy moments having children can bring to life. As a mother, what Haley did that morning was not remarkable. But what she did as a woman politician certainly was. It is not an exaggeration to say that most women candidates or officeholders would not have shared that story with the world 30, 20, or even 10 years ago. Counseled for so long that issues of children and family could work against them in the minds of voters, most political women in this situation might have chosen not to share this story and run the risk of being perceived as "mom" instead of "Madam Governor." But in 2013, Haley was not inhibited by a traditional sense of how she should present herself to the public. That she shared this human moment with the world suggests that she did not fear a sexist backlash. Mary Fallon, in running for governor of Oklahoma in 2010, emphasized her experience as a mother as a strength of her candidacy instead of something to downplay or avoid discussing. That she was running against another woman, who happened to be single and childless, only highlighted the sense that Fallon was trying to identify something she thought made her a superior candidate by comparison. Haley and Fallon each offered a view of herself as a woman and mother as well as a leader and likely did so because she calculated that this view would be seen in a positive light. Their decisions say a great deal about how we think about women in politics today.

For more than 40 years, political scientists, campaign professionals, and women candidates themselves have struggled to understand how the American public evaluates women who run for office. What these attempts at understanding have revealed is a country that has experienced significant evolution in its thinking about the appropriate place for women in our political life. In 1958, U.S. Representative Coya Knutson (DFL-MN) was defeated for re-election, in part, because of the public backlash she endured after her husband's public call, "Coya, come home" to "make a home for your husband and son." Her Republican opponent, Odin Langen, ran on the slogan "A big man for a man-sized job" (Palmer and Simon 2012). In 1973, newly elected to the U.S. House from Colorado, Pat Schroeder, a Harvard-educated lawyer, was asked by a male House colleague how she could handle being both a mother and a member of Congress. Her famous reply was, "I have a brain and a uterus and I use both" (Lowy 2003). In 2014, things are a bit different. In the past seven years, five sitting members of Congress have given birth to seven children, all while campaigning for, and serving in, office (Kim 2013). Clearly these women have not suffered a political consequence from being mothers and officeholders simultaneously.

These anecdotes illustrate a progression in public thinking about women candidates. However, we also have data to support these anecdotes, revealing that voters in the United States take a more egalitarian and less gendered perspective on women in elected office than has been the case in years past. This project, which is an attempt to expand our understanding of whether and how gendered attitudes and stereotypes shape the fortunes of women candidates, has demonstrated that these gendered considerations appear to influence voters much less often than conventional wisdom and scholarly research would suggest. The central findings of this work point to

- positive attitudes toward the idea of women in elected office
- a lessening of gender stereotypes of women and men
- evaluations of candidates that are relatively unaffected by gender stereotyping
- vote choice decisions that are driven by traditional political influences

In all, the results of this analysis demonstrate that gender stereotypes are not a significant impediment to the success of women candidates. While stereotypes and less supportive attitudes do still exist among some voters, the majority of people appear to evaluate women candidates in less gendered terms and with a greater focus on their political characteristics. Women candidates are as successful as men in running for Congress and governor and largely experience the same sorts of campaign dynamics as men do.

MAJOR FINDINGS

This project began as an attempt to examine one of the implicit, and sometimes explicit, assumptions about the experience of women candidates—that the public's gender stereotypes about the capacities of women and men could damage women's credibility and chances for electoral success. A long history of anecdotal evidence about sexist reactions to women candidates has served to confirm concerns about the way the public might evaluate these women. However, the evidence offered here suggests that these assumptions are less well supported than scholars might have thought. High-visibility anecdotes are still a part of our election environment, but there is little evidence that women are significantly or consistently affected by negative gender stereotypes. In fact, the recent political and media coverage of women candidates may actually suggest a period of ascendancy for women in American political life.

Voter Attitudes about Women in Politics

The results of the 2010 survey suggest that the public largely holds supportive attitudes about women in political life. Majorities of respondents believe that there should be more women in elected office than is currently the case, that women are as emotionally well suited for politics as are men, and that more women in office would be a positive for our system. About half of respondents articulate a baseline gender preference for women candidates, a finding that is in line with other work (Sanbonmatsu 2002a). It should not be surprising that women are more likely than men to hold the most positive attitudes toward women in politics, being more likely than men to want more women in office, to prefer women candidates, and to see same-sex representation to be an important consideration. One interesting exception is that women are no more likely than men to see women as emotionally well suited for politics. In terms of abstract gender stereotypes, the findings here are in line with other recent works that suggest an easing of stereotyped reactions to women and men in politics (Pew Research Center 2008). Respondents think that there are fewer differences than more in the policy abilities and traits of "women and men who run for office." Among those who do stereotype, attitudes continue to skew in expected directions, although more so on policies than on traits. One interesting finding with regard to stereotypes is what I call the "sex superiority" position. Women respondents identified "women" as likely to be better at all policy areas—female and male—and more likely to possess both female and male traits than men. Men in the sample were more likely to say that they thought of "men" as more superior on every dimension. This might suggest that there is some measure of gender identity at work in the articulation of abstract gender stereotypes, something that has received relatively little attention from scholars.

One of the other assumptions about the importance of gender stereotypes advanced by earlier works is the idea that gender stereotypes could hurt women candidates because voters would employ these stereotypes in their political evaluations and vote decisions. Again, there is less evidence that this is the case in the real world. This raises issues of research design, since the vast majority of examinations of gender stereotypes involve experiments and surveys with hypothetical election matchups between fictitious candidates. It is easy to imagine that abstract stereotype attitudes about "women and men" could be related to considering hypothetical election situations. Indeed, the analysis in chapter 3 demonstrated that abstract gender stereotypes are significantly and consistently related to abstract measures of support for women, such as baseline gender preference, support for gender parity, and support for more women in elected office. However, the true test of the utility of gender stereotypes is whether or not they are related to voting for real candidates in actual elections. And here we see that they are not. Using real candidates from the 2010 House elections, we saw that abstract gender stereotypes are not related to voting in races in which women ran against men. An additional key here is, of course, that these two analyses are conducted with the same respondents. The abstract gender stereotypes that respondents hold are related to their abstract gender attitudes but not to their vote choice decisions about real women candidates. This is clear evidence that we need to examine gender stereotypes in the real world to get a true sense of their power in elections.

Candidate Evaluations

A related goal of this project was to examine the gap between abstract gender stereotypes of "women and men" and the evaluations that voters make of specific women and men candidates in real elections. This analysis reveals two important patterns. First, stereotypes are different from evaluations. While large majorities of respondents saw no difference between abstract "women and men" with regard to policies and traits, they were able to make more detailed evaluations of the specific candidates in their elections for Congress and governor. Much smaller numbers of people saw no difference between the woman and man they evaluated, and most were able to identify the woman or man as better than her or his opponent on these dimensions. Second, a more complete analysis of the factors that shape specific candidate evaluations reveals that abstract gender stereotypes had relatively limited influence. Instead, what matters most to people's evaluations of candidates, women or men, are traditional political considerations such as political party, incumbency, and campaign spending. The importance of political and contextual influences is apparent throughout the analysis. Abstract gender stereotypes are not relevant to candidate evaluations in all circumstances but, instead, vary in their influence, depending on the political party of the woman candidate and the office she seeks. Stereotypes were related to evaluations of Democratic women candidates but not Republican women and were more important to evaluations of women Senate candidates than for women candidates for House or governor.

Vote Choice

While candidate evaluations are an important part of relating to candidates, it is vote choice decisions that hold the key to success. The ultimate concern that scholars and campaign professionals have about gender stereotypes is that they will result in people not being willing to vote for women candidates. While this may have been a legitimate concern in years past, there is little evidence that stereotypes matter to vote choice in contemporary times. When we consider abstract stereotypes alongside the host of important political and contextual variables, we see that they are not directly related to vote choice for women, regardless of political party or level of office. Instead, we see the expected influence of traditional variables. Primary here is political party and, specifically, whether a voter shares the party of the woman candidate. In every circumstance, a shared party correspondence is the strongest predictor of choosing a woman candidate over her male opponent. People vote for women candidates of their party. There is no evidence that voters cross party lines to avoid voting for a woman. This dynamic works in the same way to shape voting for men. Beyond political party, we see that other political influences matter, depending on the party of the candidate and the office being considered. Some incumbent candidates receive the advantage of their position, but Democratic incumbents had a harder time in the Republican tide of 2010.

The Experiences of Men

While the primary focus of this work is on the experiences of women candidates in mixed-sex races, a complete consideration of the importance of candidate sex and abstract gender stereotypes requires an awareness of the experiences of men candidates. To that end, this project also examines the dynamics of candidate evaluation and vote choice in races between two men. These male-only races offer a comparison to the mixed-sex elections. In general, the findings on the male races suggest that gender stereotypes can be active in races without women and might signal an important interaction between gender and political party. For example, candidate evaluations of Democratic men running for the House and for governor were influenced by abstract gender stereotypes about male and female policy competence, with those who held traditional stereotypes about female policies evaluating the Democratic men highly and those who held traditional stereotypes about male policies evaluating them lower than their Republican opponents. Abstract female policy stereotypes also had a positive impact on vote choice for Democratic men running for the House. These findings suggest that an interaction between gender and partisan stereotypes may be driving things here, which means that these attitudes might be relevant more widely than scholars had thought.

Candidate Quality and Issue Campaigns

The final aspect of this project looked at whether other points in the campaign process were influenced by candidate sex and gender stereotypes. In taking up the question of whether women candidates were of comparable quality to men, the analysis here indicates that the women and men candidates in this sample had similar education levels and political experiences. Women candidates raised as much money as did men and won at the same rates. With regard to the kinds of campaigns candidates run, some scholars have asked whether women contribute to the stereotypes voters hold by running campaigns that play to women's perceived strengths. In a comprehensive examination of the television ads and campaign websites of all of the candidates in this sample, I find no evidence that women or men engage in creating issue campaigns that play to gender stereotypes. Instead, both women and men focused their attention on the dominant issues of the day and campaigned in a way that was consistent with the agenda of their political party.

In the end, the findings on the impact of abstract gender stereotypes on candidate evaluations and vote choice provide several new insights. First, gender stereotypes are clearly not powerful or important enough to be an influence on election outcomes. Stereotypes are only related to attitudes and behaviors toward women candidates in a few circumstances. They are not a significant or consistent influence on evaluations or vote choice. They do not affect all women in the same way but, rather, depend on important aspects of political and electoral context. And, interestingly, abstract stereotypes are related to evaluations and vote choice in male-only races exactly as often as they are to women in mixed-sex races. This clearly signals the importance of partisan stereotypes. Finally, the analysis reinforces the primacy of political party and other traditional influences such as incumbency, campaign spending, and competitiveness in shaping political decisions in the United States. When we compare the impact of stereotypes to that of these political forces, we see that stereotypes clearly play a minor role. We also see that the determinants of vote choice are the same regardless of the sex of the candidates in an election. Indeed, there is no evidence that the presence of a woman candidate disrupts expected patterns of voter decision making. There is also no evidence that candidates engage in the intentional creation of gendered images by campaigning on issues from a gendered perspective. Instead, both women and men behaved like partisans and strategic politicians.

Political Party

The centrality of political party to the dynamics of American elections comes through in this analysis in several ways. First, in every analysis of candidate evaluation and vote choice, in mixed-sex and male-only races, sharing the political party of a candidate is the most significant influence on those evaluation and vote choice decisions. Voters who share the party of a woman candidate are overwhelmingly likely to vote for her. There is no evidence that people cross party lines to avoid or seek out a woman candidate. There is no evidence that abstract gender stereotypes override the more central influence of partisan ties. Most important, the presence of a woman candidate does not alter the traditional dynamics of elections.

Party is also clearly relevant to the ways in which voters see candidates. Voters who hold a baseline preference for women candidates and who support the idea of more women in office are more likely to vote for Democratic candidates and less likely to vote for Republican women. These voters do not simply want more women in office; they want a particular kind of woman in office. While gender stereotypes are not often related to candidate evaluations and vote choice in this analysis, when they are, they influence reaction to Democratic candidates much more often than to Republican candidates. This is true for mixed-sex and male-only races. This pattern of relationship would suggest that partisan stereotypes are at work alongside gender stereotypes to shape how voters approach politics. Finally, women and men clearly shape issue campaigns along partisan, not gender, lines. The media data demonstrated that Democrats and Republicans staked out consistent and distinct issue campaigns regardless of the sex of the candidates, the level of office, or the candidate pairs involved. In all, the analysis presented here demonstrates time and again that political party shapes the political decisions of both voters and candidates.

REMAINING QUESTIONS

Despite the contributions that this project makes to our understanding of whether and how gender stereotypes affect the success of women candidates, there are still many avenues of exploration left to those interested in these issues. The first of these is to continue to examine questions of voter gender stereotypes in real-world elections in as many settings as possible. This project demonstrates the utility of moving away from a reliance on experimental hypotheticals and fictitious candidates and joins a small, but growing, set of projects that have had success in studying voter reactions to real candidates (Fridkin and Kenney 2009 Lawless and Hayes 2013). To the extent possible, scholars should endeavor to study subsequent election years and different levels of office to increase the number and diversity of elections and candidates available for examination. Key here might be attempts to determine whether and how candidate sex matters in elections that receive little scholarly attention, such as those for state legislative office and statewide office other than governor. While studying state- and local-level races presents a myriad of logistical challenges, our knowledge will remain incomplete until we can examine women's opportunities at all levels of government and in all types of offices. At the other end of the political spectrum, scholars also need to be poised to respond to the candidacy of the first major-party woman candidate for president, whenever she appears. This will require careful thinking about appropriate research designs and ways of studying what will certainly be a momentous period in American politics.

Related to the need to continue these investigations is the need for scholars to "spread the word" on the findings we currently have about women candidates and inform campaign professionals, members of the media, and the general public about the realities facing women candidates. It is clear that the conventional wisdom about women candidates includes beliefs that women face a sexist political environment, will be affected by voter stereotypes, and have a harder time raising money than do men. This wisdom exists in the face of scholarly research that would dispute these ideas (Brooks 2013; Burrell 1988; Dolan 2004; Lawless and Fox 2010). If, as Lawless and Fox find, women are less likely to consider a candidacy because of concerns like these, women's opportunities for integration into elected office are harmed as long as these inaccurate impressions exist. Convincing people that the challenges facing women may be changing will be difficult, but we can employ the evidence from a growing body of research that paints a more positive picture of current reality.

I argue here that political context matters in thinking about women candidates. While I investigate both mixed-sex and male-only races and examine elections for different offices, there are other situations about which we still know less. One obvious example is elections in which two women candidates run. As the number of woman-only races increases over time, efforts to gather data on these elections would give us an opportunity to examine whether and how gender plays out in these races. Mary Fallon's invocation of her motherhood status as a qualification for seeking the governor's office in Oklahoma was launched in the context of her race against a single, childless woman. In playing the "gender card," or perhaps more accurately, the "mom card," Fallon appeared to make distinctions among women and their experiences. We need to know more about whether this sort of strategy is common in these races and whether political party stereotypes become more important in races where candidate sex is held constant. At the same time, we need to continue to examine whether gender stereotypes are at work in male-only races. The findings here would suggest that this would be fruitful. Studying single-sex candidate pairings of both types would also provide unique opportunities to examine how partisan considerations interact with candidate sex.

We would also benefit from continued investigation into the links between party and gender stereotypes. Nicholas Winter (2010) and Danny Hayes (2011) provide convincing evidence that the political parties in the United States have become gendered in the minds of voters. Given the findings here that gender stereotypes are only significant in relationship to Democratic candidates (both women and men), we should investigate how much of this dynamic is related to candidate sex and how much is related to changes in the way we perceive parties. If it is more the latter, then we need to consider whether what we think of as gender stereotypes are, in part, the articulation of attitudes about parties.

The campaign data in this project strongly suggest that women and men candidates campaign as strategic politicians concerned about the issues of the day. But we know little about how candidates make campaign decisions. Is the apparent lack of a gendered issue campaign the result of women's success in controlling and creating campaigns that neutralize stereotypes and gender issues? Recent work by Kelly Dittmar (2010) on how campaign professionals think about candidate sex in creating strategies clearly shows that these staffers believe voters see women through the lens of gender stereotypes. If campaigns are working to manage reactions to women candidates, then we need to understand the effect that these efforts have on voters, their reactions, and their decisions.

One other area that requires attention involves the possibility that stereotypes of women have swung in the other direction, away from the negative evaluations of the past to a present in which women candidates and officeholders are increasingly lionized for their perceived superiority on several dimensions. The attention to women candidates during the last six months of 2013 serves as a good example of this new dynamic. In July of that year, the *National Journal* ran a story entitled "Do Women Make Better Senators than Men?" in which the author reported on the close relationships, both personal and legislative, among the 20 women senators. Time and again the article focuses on women's supposed ability to get along well with others and their possession of a style for doing business that is "more collaboration, less confrontation; more problem-solving, less ego; more consensus-building, less partisanship" (Lawrence 2013). While some of this description of the style differences between women and men in the chamber comes from the women senators themselves, it is important to note that these beliefs are echoed by commentators and reporters. The groundswell of media attention to women officeholders hit its peak during the government shutdown in the fall of 2013. When a bipartisan group of senators began work on a legislative compromise that served to reopen the government, the involvement of Senator Susan Collins (R-ME) and several of her women colleagues, particularly Kelly Ayotte (R-NH), Lisa Murkowski (R-AK), Patty Murray (D-WA), Heidi Heitkamp (D-ND), Barbara Mikulski (D-MD), and Jeanne Shaheen (D-NH), garnered attention. Once the government was functioning again, there was a 10-day period during which a flurry of articles that gave a significant amount of the credit for that functioning to the women senators appeared in a variety of media. "Senate Women Lead in Effort to Find Accord," declared an article in the *New York Times* (Weisman and Steinhauer 2013). *Time* magazine ran a story entitled "Women Are the Only Adults Left in Washington" (Newton-Small 2013), while MSNBC determined that "Republican Women Lead the Way" (Khimm and Taylor 2013). Opinion pieces from newspapers around the country declared "A Woman's Place Is Making Washington Work" (Milligan 2013), "Thank Women for Ending Government Shutdown" (McFeatters 2013), and "When the U.S. Needed Leaders, Women Saved the Day" (Bennett 2013). Each of these stories focused on what was perceived as women's greater ability to compromise, reach across the aisle, and work for the good of the country. The coverage of these women was uniformly glowing, referring to them as pragmatic, unselfish, hard working, sensible, and determined. While it may well be the case that these women senators are indeed hard-working individuals who are superb at their jobs, it is somewhat dangerous to ascribe their success and superiority to their being women, which is exactly what these stories did. The reporters and commentators did not refer to their collective 83 years of Senate experience, or to their placement on key legislative committees, or even to the particular skills and abilities of the seven individual women who worked on the bipartisan compromise but, instead, to an essentialist assumption about the character and abilities of "women" as a group. This is stereotyping just as clearly as is believing that women are especially well suited to handle education policy or are more shrill than men. That these current stereotypes are uniformly positive should not make them any less concerning to scholars who study women candidates. Women's integration into political life will be most successful when women are perceived as individuals and not primarily through group associations, whether negative or positive. As such, scholars should continue to monitor the ways in which women candidates and officeholders are covered by the media and perceived by the public.

CONCLUSION

In finding that abstract gender stereotypes do not appear to be a significant influence on, or impediment to, the success of women candidates, I do not mean to suggest that candidate sex and gender never work to shape reactions to women. Scholars have identified various aspects of our political system in which women and men still have different experiences, such as in self-evaluation as candidates and recruitment by political elites. We should continue to be attentive to the ways in which candidate sex can interact with various aspects of political life. But this work does suggest that the relationship between women candidates and the public is relatively free of gender bias and that the steady integration of women into political life has resulted in their sex being a less central, and less burdensome, aspect of their experiences. Although it is still the case that women do not run for office nearly as often as do men, the available evidence suggests that, when they do, they can have every expectation of being perceived fairly by voters.

Candidate Lists

HOUSE

Congressional Districts

Two men candidates: 173 races

AL-3, 5; AZ-2, 3, 5; AR-1, 3; CA-1, 2, 3, 4, 7, 10, 11, 13, 15, 17, 18, 20, 24, 26, 27, 28, 29, 30, 31, 41, 42, 43, 44, 46, 49, 51, 52; CO-2, 3, 5, 6, 7; CT-4, 5; DE-AL; FL-2, 5, 8, 10, 13, 14, 16, 19, 22, 23, 25; GA-1, 2, 3, 5, 7, 8, 10, 12, 13; IL-1, 2, 3, 4, 5, 6, 7, 10, 14, 15, 16, 17, 19; IA-1, 3, 4, 5; KS-1, 4; KY-1, 2, 3, 4, 5, 6; ME-2; MN-1, 3, 5, 7, 8; MO-2, 3, 5, 6, 7; NM-1, 2, 3; NY-1, 2, 3, 5, 6, 7, 9, 13, 15, 16, 20, 21, 22, 23, 24, 26, 27, 29; NC-1, 3, 4, 6, 7, 8, 10, 11, 12, 13; OH-1, 3, 4, 5, 6, 7, 8, 10, 14, 16, 17, 18; OK-2, 3, 5; PA-2, 4, 5, 6, 7, 8, 9, 10, 11, 12, 15, 17, 18, 19; SC-1, 2, 4, 5, 6; WA-1, 2, 4, 6, 9; WI-1, 3, 5, 6, 8

Democratic woman candidate running against a Republican man: 64 races

AL-7; AZ-1, 6, 8; AR-2; CA-5, 6, 8, 9, 12, 14, 16, 19, 23, 25, 32, 33, 34, 35, 38, 39, 40, 47, 48, 50, 53; CO-1, 4; CT-3; FL-3, 7, 9, 11, 12, 15; IL-8, 9, 11, 18; KS-3; ME-1; MN-2; NV-1, 2, 3; NH-1, 2; NY-4, 11, 14, 18; OH-9, 11, 12, 13, 15; PA-3, 13, 16; SC-3; WA-8; WI-2, 4, 7

Republican woman candidate running against a Democratic man: 27 races

AL-2; AZ-4, 7; AR-4; CA-45, CT-1, 2; FL-18; GA-4; IL-12, 13; IA-2; MO-1, 4, 8; NY-8, 10, 19, 25; NC-2; 5, 9; OH-2; PA-14; WA-3, 5; WY-AL

Democratic woman candidate running against a Republican woman: 9 races

CA-36, 37; FL-20, 24; KS-2; MN-4, 6; NY-28; SD-AL

SENATE

State	Democratic Candidate	Republican Candidate
AL	William Barnes	Richard Shelby
AZ	Rodney Glassman	John McCain
AR	Blanche Lincoln	John Boozman
CA	Barbara Boxer	Carly Fiorina
CO	Michael Bennet	Ken Buck
CT	Richard Blumenthal	Linda McMahon
DE	Chris Coons	Christine O'Donnell
GA	Mike Thurmond	Johnny Isakson
IL	Alexi Giannoulias	Mark Kirk
IA	Roxanne Conlin	Chuck Grassley
KS	Lisa Johnston	Jerry Moran
KY	Jack Conway	Rand Paul
MO	Robin Carnahan	Roy Blunt
NC	Elaine Marshall	Richard Burr
NH	Paul Hodes	Kelly Ayotte
NV	Harry Reid	Sharron Angle
NY	Kirsten Gillibrand	Joe DioGuardi
PA	Joe Sestak	Pat Toomey
OH	Lee Fisher	Rob Portman
SC	Alvin Greene	Jim DeMint
WA	Patty Murray	Dino Rossi

GOVERNORS

State	Democratic Candidate	Republican Candidate
AL	Ron Sparks	Robert Bentley
AZ	Terry Goddard	Jan Brewer
AR	Mike Beebe	Jim Keet
CA	Jerry Brown	Meg Whitman
CT	Dan Malloy	Tom Foley
GA	Roy Barnes	Nathan Deal
FL	Alex Sink	Rick Scott
IL	Pat Quinn	Bill Brady
IA	Chet Culver	Terry Branstad
KS	Tom Holland	Sam Brownback
NH	John Lynch	John Stephen
NM	Diane Denish	Susana Martinez
NY	Andrew Cuomo	Carl Paladino
PA	Dan Onorato	Tom Corbett
OH	Ted Strickland	John Kasich
OK	Jari Askins	Mary Fallin
SC	Vincent Sheheen	Nikki Haley
SD	Scott Heidepriem	Dennis Daugaard
WI	Tom Barrett	Scott Walker
WY	Leslie Petersen	Matt Mead

APPENDIX B

Variable Construction

DEPENDENT VARIABLES

Chapter 3

Baseline Preference: 0 = man, 1 = woman

Number of Women in Office: 0 = fewer women/number about right, 1 = more women

Gender Parity: 0 = majority men, 1 = parity/majority women

Emotional Suitability: 0 = strongly disagree/disagree, 1 = agree/strongly agree

Same-Sex Representation: 0 = not at all important, 1 = somewhat/very important

Percent Women in Government: 0–100 percent

Education Policy: 0 = men better/no difference, 1 = women better

Health Care Policy: 0 = men better/no difference, 1 = women better

Child Care Policy: 0 = men better/no difference, 1 = women better

Abortion Policy: 0 = men better/no difference, 1 = women better

Crime Policy: 0 = women better/no difference, 1 = men better

Economic Policy: 0 = women better/no difference, 1 = men better

National Security Policy: 0 = women better/no difference, 1 = men better

Immigration Policy: 0 = women better/no difference, 1 = men better

Deficit Policy: 0 = women better/no difference, 1 = men better

Honest: 0 = men better/no difference, 1 = women better

Consensus Building: 0 = men better/no difference, 1 = women better

Compassion: 0 = men better/no difference, 1 = women better

Change Government: 0 = men better/no difference, 1 = women better

Intelligence: 0 = women better/no difference, 1 = men better

Decisiveness: 0 = women better/no difference, 1 = men better

Leadership: 0 = women better/no difference, 1 = men better

Experience: 0 = women better/no difference, 1 = men better

House Vote Choice (Democratic Women versus Republican Men): 0 = vote for Republican man, 1 = vote for Democratic woman

House Vote Choice (Republican Women versus Democratic Men): 0 = vote for Democratic man, 1 = vote for Republican woman

Chapter 4

(All policy and trait evaluations for mixed-sex races coded 1 = man candidate, 2 = no difference, 3 = woman candidate; all male-only races coded 1 = Republican candidate, 2 = no difference, 3 = Democratic candidate)

Female Policy Evaluations: education + health care + child care + abortion

Male Policy Evaluations: crime + economy + national security + immigration + deficit (note male policy evaluations for gubernatorial races: crime + economy + deficit)

Female Trait Evaluations: honest + consensus building + compassion + change government

Male Trait Evaluations: intelligent + decisive + leadership + experience

Chapter 5

Vote for Democratic candidate: 0 = vote for Republican candidate, 1 = vote for Democratic candidate

INDEPENDENT VARIABLES

Education: 1 = no formal, 2 = 1st–4th grade, 3 = 5th or 6th grade, 4 = 7th or 8th grade, 5 = 9th grade, 6 = 10th grade, 7 = 11th grade, 8 = 12th grade no diploma, 9 = high school graduate/GED, 10 = some college, 11 = associate's degree, 12 = bachelor's degree, 13 = master's degree, 14 = doctorate/professional degree

Age: respondent age in years (ranges from 18 to 94)

Woman: 0 = respondent not a woman, 1 = respondent is a woman

Party ID: 1 = strong Republican, 2 = not strong Republican, 3 = leans Republican, 4 = independent, 5 = leans Democrat, 6 = not strong Democrat, 7 = strong Democrat

Ideology: 1 = extremely liberal, 2 = liberal, 3 = slightly liberal, 4 = moderate, 5 = slightly conservative, 6 = conservative, 7 = extremely conservative

White: 0 = respondent not white, 1 = respondent is white

(Female policy and trait stereotypes coded 1 = man, 2 = no difference, 3 = woman)

Female Policy Stereotypes: education + health care + child care + abortion

Female Trait Stereotypes: honest + consensus building + compassion + change government

(Male policy and trait stereotypes coded 1 = woman, 2 = no difference, 3 = man)

Male Policy Stereotypes: crime + economy + national security + immigration + deficit (note male policy stereotypes for gubernatorial races: crime + economy + deficit)

Male Trait Stereotypes: intelligent + decisive + leadership + experience

Share Party: 0 = respondent does not identify with the party of the woman candidate, 1 = respondent shares the partisan affiliation of the woman candidate

Independent: 0 = respondent not an Independent, 1 = respondent is an Independent

Baseline Gender Preference: 0 = man, 1 = woman

Number of Women in Office: 1 = should be fewer women, 2 = current number of women is about right, 3 = should be more women

Gender Parity in Government: 0 = majority men, 1 = gender parity, 2 = majority women

Percent Women in Government: 0–100 percent

Emotional Suitability: 1 = strongly agree men better suited emotionally, 2 = agree, 3 = disagree, 4 = strongly disagree

Importance of Same-Sex Representation: 1 = not at all important, 2 = only somewhat important, 3 = very important

Woman Incumbent: 0 = woman candidate not an incumbent, 1 = woman candidate is incumbent

Open Seat: 0 = not an open seat, 1 = open seat

Percent of Spending by Woman: amount spent by woman candidate/ (amount spent by woman candidate + amount spent by male candidate)

Competitive Race: 0 = noncompetitive, 1 = competitive (a race is coded as competitive if the winner received 55% of the two-party vote or less)

Interest in House Race: 1 = not following closely at all, 2 = not following too closely, 3 = following fairly closely, 4 = following very closely

Interest in Senate Race: 1 = not following closely at all, 2 = not following too closely, 3 = following fairly closely, 4 = following very closely

Interest in Governor Race: 1 = not following closely at all, 2 = not following too closely, 3 = following fairly closely, 4 = following very closely

Democrat: 0 = respondent not a Democrat, 1 = respondent is a Democrat

Democrat Incumbent: 0 = Democratic candidate not an incumbent, 1 = Democratic candidate is incumbent

Percent of Spending by Democrat: amount spent by Democratic candidate/ (amount spent by Democratic candidate + amount spent by Republican candidate)

Democratic Woman versus Republican Man: 0 = other, 1 = race between a
Democratic woman candidate and a Republican man candidate
Republican Woman versus Democratic Man: 0 = other, 1 = race between a
Republican woman candidate and a Democratic man candidate

APPENDIX C

Campaign Ads and Websites

ADVERTISEMENTS

House

28 states (Wyoming only state in survey without any), 178 races, 291 candidates

1,080 total ads, 1,012 that reference at least one policy issue

Senate

20 states, 40 candidates

369 total ads, 327 that reference at least one policy issue

Governors

20 states, 40 candidates

390 total ads, 357 that reference at least one policy issue

WEBSITES

House

Have website = 94.67% (515)

Do not have website = 5.33% (29)

Have website, list issues = 96.90% (499)

Have website, do not list issues = 3.11% (16)

List issues, alphabetical order = 8.42% (42)

List issues, not alphabetical order = 91.58% (457)

Senate

Have website = 100% (42)

Do not have website = 0% (0)

Have website, list issues = 100% (42)
Have website, do not list issues = 0% (0)
List issues, alphabetical order = 26.19% (11)
List issues, not alphabetical order = 73.81% (31)

Governors
Have website = 100% (40)
Do not have website = 0% (0)
Have website, list issues = 100% (40)
Have website, do not list issues = 0% (0)
List issues, alphabetical order = 7.50% (3)
List issues, not alphabetical order = 92.50% (37)

ISSUE CODES FOR TELEVISION ADS/WEBSITES

1. Social Security/Medicare (Social Security and Medicare)
2. Health Care (health reform, drug coverage, "repeal and replace," "Obamacare," single-payer plan)
3. Foreign Policy (defense, national security, military, veterans, wars [Afghanistan, Iraq], foreign trade, China, Israel, Iran)
4. Family (parent, parent/child, family, seniors)
5. Economy (economy, jobs, support small businesses, unemployment)
6. Taxes (taxes, tax cuts, tax code reform)
7. Education (teachers, testing, teacher training, vouchers, school choice, making college affordable/accessible)
8. Crime (fighting crime, tougher laws, punishment, addressing root causes)
9. Environment/Energy (general mentions, protecting natural resources, global warming/climate change, cap and trade, BP oil spill, "green jobs," energy independence, clean energy, energy exploration)
10. Agriculture/Rural Development (general agriculture mentions, farm subsidies, helping family farms, new farming technology)
11. District Concerns (specific constituent interests, issues that pertain narrowly to the district/state, transportation, water)
12. Fiscal Policy (balanced budget, deficit, spending, national debt, Federal Reserve, stimulus)
13. Abortion (general mentions, specific pro-choice/pro-life positions)
14. Guns (general mentions, gun control, pro-gun positions, 2nd Amendment)
15. Smaller Government (general mentions, cutting the size of government, regulations, services)

16. Government Reform (general mentions, campaign finance reform, restoring honest and integrity to government, corruption, ethics, partisanship, bipartisanship, leadership, fraud)
17. Women's Issues (general mentions, women's health)
18. Homeland Security (general mentions, terrorism, war on terrorism)
19. Immigration (illegal immigration, path to citizenship, 14th Amendment, amnesty, border, "build the dang fence," John McCain)
20. Wall Street (bailouts, corporate malfeasance and corruption, bank bonuses, Wall Street regulations, Troubled Asset Relief Program)
21. Values (general mention of conservative/liberal values, philosophy, freedom, liberty, civil rights, civil liberties)
22. Housing (homeownership, Housing and Urban Development, homelessness, foreclosures)
23. President (Obama, administration)
24. The Other Side (Republicans, Democrats, Tea Party, Pelosi, Reid)
25. Welfare (lack of self-sufficiency, relying on the government, handouts)
26. Religion (turning away from God, fear of Islam, too much religion in public life)
27. Race/Discrimination (racism, racial inequality)
28. Media

APPENDIX D

Survey Instrument

2010 CONGRESSIONAL AND STATEWIDE ELECTIONS SURVEY—
WAVE 1, SEPTEMBER 2010

This survey is being conducted by researchers at the University of Wisconsin–Milwaukee to learn about people's attitudes about political issues in the elections this fall.

First, we have some general questions about politics.

1. What do you think is the **most** important problem facing this country today?
2. What do you think is the **second** most important problem?
3. Listed below are characteristics that some people say are important in a political leader and others say are not important. For each, please say whether you think it is very important, important, only somewhat important, or not at all important that a political leader be: (RANDOMIZE LIST OF TRAITS)

Very Important   Important   Only Somewhat Important   Not At All Important

　　Honest
　　Intelligent
　　Can build consensus
　　Decisive
　　Compassionate
　　Has political experience
　　Provides strong leadership
　　Can change the way government works

Next are a few questions about the government in Washington, D.C.

4. Do you happen to know what job or political office is now held by Joe Biden?
5. Do you happen to know how many women currently serve on the U.S. Supreme Court?
6. Do you happen to know which political party has the most members in the House of Representatives in Washington right now?
7. Taking your best guess, what percentage of the seats in the U.S. Congress do you think are held by women?
8. Would you say that one of the political parties is more conservative than the other at the national level? Which party is more conservative?
9. Do you happen to know whether women in the U.S. Congress are more likely to be Democrats or Republicans? Next are some questions about women and men as elected officials.
10. Which of the following statements comes closest to your opinion about men and women as local elected officials, such as city council members or mayors? (Rotate responses 1 and 2)
    ___Men generally make better local political leaders than women
    ___Women generally make better local political leaders than men
    ___In general, women and men make equally good local elected officials
11. Which of the following statements comes closest to your opinion about men and women as state-level elected officials, such as state legislators or governors? (Rotate responses 1 and 2)
    ___Men generally make better state-level political leaders than women
    ___Women generally make better state-level political leaders than men
    ___In general, women and men make equally good state-level elected officials
12. Which of the following statements comes closest to your opinion about men and women as national elected officials, such as members of Congress? (Rotate responses 1 and 2)
    ___Men generally make better national political leaders than women
    ___Women generally make better national political leaders than men
    ___In general, women and men make equally good national elected officials

Now we have some questions about different political issues in the news.
13. In general, how would you say things are going with the U.S. military effort in Afghanistan: very well, somewhat well, somewhat badly, or very badly?
    ___Very well

__Somewhat well

__Somewhat badly

__Very badly

14. Would you say that over the past year, economic conditions in the country as a whole have gotten better, stayed about the same, or gotten worse?

__Gotten better

__Stayed about the same

__Gotten worse

15. If two equally qualified candidates of your party were running for office, one a man and the other a woman, do you think you would be more inclined to vote for the man or the woman?

16. Do you think abortion should be legal under any circumstances, legal only under certain circumstances, or illegal in all circumstances?

__Legal under any circumstances

__Legal only under certain circumstances

__Illegal in all circumstances

17. As you may know, a new health reform bill was signed into law earlier this year. Given what you know about the new health reform law, do you have a generally favorable or generally unfavorable opinion of it, or don't you know enough about it to have an opinion?

__Generally favorable

__Don't know enough

__Generally unfavorable

18. In your opinion, in the best government the United States could have, what percent of elected officials would be men and what percent would be women?

__Percent men

__Percent women

19. Which of the following comes closest to your views on the issues of same-sex marriage? Gay couples should be allowed to legally marry. Or gay couples should be allowed to form civil unions but not legally marry. Or there should be no legal recognition of a gay couple's relationship.

__Gay couples should be allowed to legally marry.

__Gay couples should be allowed to form civil unions but not legally marry.

__There should be no legal recognition of a gay couple's relationship.

20. As you may know, the Constitution says that all children born in the United States are automatically U.S. citizens regardless of their parents' status. Would you favor or oppose a Constitutional amendment to prevent children born here from becoming U.S. citizens unless their

parents are also U.S. citizens, or don't you know enough about it to have an opinion?

__Favor

__Don't know enough

__Oppose

The next section asks some questions about people who serve as candidates and officeholders in the United States.

21. When it comes to governing, some people think different types of officeholders are better able to handle certain issues than others, although others don't. For each of the issues listed below, indicate whether you think that women or men (randomize) in elected office are better able to handle them or whether you don't think there is a difference. (Randomize order of issues)

Men   Women   No Difference

Education
Crime and Public Safety
Health Care
Economy and Jobs
Child Care
National Security
Immigration
Abortion
The Deficit

The next series of questions asks about some specific characteristics of women and men who run for political office.

22. Some people think that women and men display different characteristics, although others don't feel this way. For each, please say whether you think that it generally best describes women candidates or best describes men candidates or whether you don't think there is a difference. (Randomize order of traits)

Best describes women   Best describes men   No difference

Intelligent
Honest
Decisive
Can build consensus
Provides strong leadership

Compassionate
Can change the way government works
Has political experience

23. Thinking about the number of women in important political office such as governors and members of Congress, would you say that there should be more women in these positions or fewer women, or is the number about right?
___Should be more women in those positions
___Should be fewer women in those positions
___Number is just about right

24. We hear a lot of talk these days about liberals and conservatives. Below is a scale that runs from extremely liberal to extremely conservative. Thinking about members of Congress, where would you place a typical woman member of Congress on this scale?
___Extremely liberal
___Liberal
___Slightly liberal
___Moderate, middle of the road
___Slightly conservative
___Conservative
___Extremely conservative

25. Where would you place the typical man member of Congress on this scale?
___Extremely liberal
___Liberal
___Slightly liberal
___Moderate, middle of the road
___Slightly conservative
___Conservative
___Extremely conservative

26. Do you agree or disagree with the following statement: Most men are better suited emotionally for politics than are most women. Strongly agree, agree, disagree, strongly disagree (Rotate women and men)
___Strongly agree
___Agree
___Disagree
___Strongly disagree

Now we have a couple of questions about the media.

27. How closely have you been following news stories about the (insert office) election campaign this fall? Very closely, fairly closely, not too closely, not at all closely
__Very closely
__Fairly closely
__Not too closely
__Not at all closely
28. People are using a wide variety of resources to keep up with political news about the fall elections. From the list below, thinking just about political news, indicate how often you have used the following outlets to get political news and information about the upcoming elections—daily, at least once a week, occasionally, rarely, never.

Daily   Once a Week   Occasionally   Rarely   Never

    Local television
    National television
    Radio
    Newspapers
    Candidate websites
    Facebook/Twitter
    Political blogs
    Newspaper websites

Next are some questions about what you think about the government and various leaders.

29. People can prefer political candidates for a variety of different reasons. How important is it for you that people elected to represent your interests are women/men—not at all important, only somewhat important, very important?
__Not at all important
__Only somewhat important
__Very important
30. Thinking now about **members of the U.S. Congress**, indicate who you think would do a better job at handling each of the following issues.

A Democratic man   A Democratic woman

    Ending the wars in Iraq and Afghanistan
    Implementing health care reform
    Improving our public schools
    Fighting crime and ensuring public safety

Addressing the budget deficit
Dealing with the issue of abortion
Reforming government

31. Thinking again about **members of the U.S. Congress**, indicate who you think would do a better job at handling each of the following issues.

A Republican man   A Republican woman

> Ending the wars in Iraq and Afghanistan
> Implementing health care reform
> Improving our public schools
> Fighting crime and ensuring public safety
> Addressing the budget deficit
> Dealing with the issue of abortion
> Reforming government

32. In general, are you satisfied or dissatisfied with the way things are going in the United States at this time?
    __Satisfied
    __Dissatisfied

(Randomize order of Q33–Q36)

33. What is your impression of Barack Obama? As of today, is it very favorable, somewhat favorable, somewhat unfavorable, or very unfavorable, or haven't you heard enough about him to say?
    __Very favorable
    __Somewhat favorable
    __Somewhat unfavorable
    __Very unfavorable

34. What is your impression of Sarah Palin? As of today, is it very favorable, somewhat favorable, somewhat unfavorable, or very unfavorable, or haven't you heard enough about her to say?
    __Very favorable
    __Somewhat favorable
    __Somewhat unfavorable
    __Very unfavorable

35. What is your impression of Newt Gingrich? As of today, is it very favorable, somewhat favorable, somewhat unfavorable, or very unfavorable, or haven't you heard enough about him to say?
    __Very favorable
    __Somewhat favorable

__Somewhat unfavorable

__Very unfavorable

36. What is your impression of Nancy Pelosi? As of today, is it very favorable, somewhat favorable, somewhat unfavorable, or very unfavorable, or haven't you heard enough about her to say?

__Very favorable

__Somewhat favorable

__Somewhat unfavorable

__Very unfavorable

37. Do you approve or disapprove of the way Congress is handling its job?

__Approve

__Disapprove

38. Would you say that you think that most members of Congress deserved to be reelected this fall or not?

__Yes

__No

Please say whether you agree or disagree with the following statements.

39. Discrimination against women is no longer a problem in the United States.

__Strongly agree

__Agree somewhat

__Disagree somewhat

__Strongly disagree

40. When women demand equality, they are actually seeking special favors.

__Strongly agree

__Agree somewhat

__Disagree somewhat

__Strongly disagree

41. Women who complain about harassment cause more problems than they solve.

__Strongly agree

__Agree somewhat

__Disagree somewhat

__Strongly disagree

42. Although women can achieve the highest levels of professional success, they often have to overcome more obstacles to get there.

__Strongly agree

__Agree somewhat

__Disagree somewhat

__Strongly disagree

Finally, we have a few questions about participating in elections.

43. Some people participate in politics regularly, while others are often too busy to participate. How about you? Were you able to participate in any of the following activities in the past two years?

Yes   No

    Voted in a presidential or congressional election
    Contacted a public official (by phone, letter, e-mail, etc.)
    Contributed money to a political party or a candidate's campaign
    Attended a political rally, meeting, or speech

44. Did you get a chance to vote in the 2008 presidential election? If so, for which candidate did you vote?
    __Obama
    __McCain
    __Other candidate
45. Are you registered to vote in the upcoming election this November?
    __Yes
    __No
    __I am not sure
46. If the election for (office) were being held today, would you vote for (Candidate 1) or (Candidate 2), or wouldn't you vote?

2010 CONGRESSIONAL AND STATEWIDE ELECTIONS SURVEY—WAVE 2, OCTOBER 2010

This is the second part of a survey being conducted by researchers at the University of Wisconsin–Milwaukee to learn about people's attitudes about political issues in the elections this fall.

The first section asks some questions about the candidates for governor in your state this fall. These candidates are the Democrat (Candidate Name) and the Republican (Candidate Name). (Rotate order of names; only asked of respondents with governor races in their state)

1. In thinking about issues, which of the candidates do you see as better able to handle each of the issues listed below, or don't you think there is a difference between them? **(Randomize order of issues)**

Candidate 1 Name Better   Candidate 2 Name Better   No Difference

Education
Crime and Public Safety
Health Care
Economy and Jobs
Child Care
Abortion
Budget Deficits

2. In thinking about the characteristics of each candidate, do you see each of the terms below as better at describing **(Candidate 1 Name)** or **(Candidate 2 Name)**, or don't you think there is a difference between them? **(Randomize order of traits)**

Best describes (Candidate 1 Name)　　Best describes (Candidate 2 Name)　　No difference

Intelligent
Honest
Decisive
Can build consensus
Provides strong leadership
Compassionate
Can change the way government works
Has political experience
Better suited emotionally for politics

3. We hear a lot of talk these days about liberals and conservatives. Below is a scale that runs from extremely liberal to extremely conservative. Where would you place **(Candidate 1 Name)** on this scale?
    __Extremely liberal
    __Liberal
    __Slightly liberal
    __Moderate, middle of the road
    __Slightly conservative
    __Conservative
    __Extremely conservative
4. Where would you place **(Candidate 2 Name)** on this scale?
    __Extremely liberal
    __Liberal
    __Slightly liberal
    __Moderate, middle of the road

__Slightly conservative

__Conservative

__Extremely conservative

The next section asks some questions about the candidates for U.S. senator from your state this fall. These candidates are the Democrat (Candidate Name) and the Republican (Candidate Name). (Rotate order of names; only asked of respondents with U.S. Senate races in their state)

5. In thinking about issues, which of the candidates do you see as better able to handle each of the issues listed below, or don't you think there is a difference between them? **(Randomize order of issues)**

Candidate 1 Name Better   Candidate 2 Name Better   No Difference

Education

Crime and Public Safety

Health Care

Economy and Jobs

Child Care

National Security

Immigration

Abortion

The Deficit

6. In thinking about the characteristics of each candidate, do you see each of the terms below as better at describing **(Candidate 1 Name)** or **(Candidate 2 Name)**, or don't you think there is a difference between them? **(Randomize order of traits)**

Best describes (Candidate 1 Name)   Best describes (Candidate 2 Name)   No difference

Intelligent

Honest

Decisive

Can build consensus

Provides strong leadership

Compassionate

Can change the way government works

Has political experience

Better suited emotionally for politics

7. Below is a scale that runs from extremely liberal to extremely conservative. Where would you place **(Candidate 1 Name)** on this scale?
   __Extremely liberal
   __Liberal
   __Slightly liberal
   __Moderate, middle of the road
   __Slightly conservative
   __Conservative
   __Extremely conservative
8. Where would you place **(Candidate 2 Name)** on this scale?
   __Extremely liberal
   __Liberal
   __Slightly liberal
   __Moderate, middle of the road
   __Slightly conservative
   __Conservative
   __Extremely conservative

The next section asks some questions about the candidates for U.S. House of Representatives from your congressional district this fall. These candidates are the Democrat (Candidate Name) and the Republican (Candidate Name). (Rotate order of names)

9. In thinking about issues, which of the candidates do you see as better able to handle each of the issues listed below, or don't you think there is a difference between them? **(Randomize order of issues)**

Candidate 1 Name Better	Candidate 2 Name Better	No Difference
Education		
Crime and Public Safety		
Health Care		
Economy and Jobs		
Child Care		
National Security		
Immigration		
Abortion		
The Deficit		

10. In thinking about the characteristics of each candidate, do you see each of the terms below as better at describing **(Candidate 1 Name)** or **(Candidate 2 Name)**, or don't you think there is a difference between them? **(Randomize order of traits)**

Best describes (Candidate 1 Name)   Best describes (Candidate 2 Name)   No difference

    Intelligent
    Honest
    Decisive
    Can build consensus
    Provides strong leadership
    Compassionate
    Can change the way government works
    Has political experience
    Better suited emotionally for politics

11. Below is a scale that runs from extremely liberal to extremely conservative. Where would you place **(Candidate 1 Name)** on this scale?
    __Extremely liberal
    __Liberal
    __Slightly liberal
    __Moderate, middle of the road
    __Slightly conservative
    __Conservative
    __Extremely conservative

12. Where would you place **(Candidate 2 Name)** on this scale?
    __Extremely liberal
    __Liberal
    __Slightly liberal
    __Moderate, middle of the road
    __Slightly conservative
    __Conservative
    __Extremely conservative

Next, we have a couple of questions about your interest in this fall's congressional and statewide elections.

13. How interested have you been in information about what's going on in government and politics this fall?
    __Extremely interested
    __Very interested
    __Moderately interested
    __Slightly interested
    __Not interested at all

14. How closely have you been following news stories about the election campaigns this fall? Very closely, fairly closely, not too closely, not at all closely
    __Very closely
    __Fairly closely
    __Not too closely
    __Not at all closely
15. Which particular election in your state would you say that you have been following most closely? (Response choices offered to respondent will depend on whether this office was being contested in respondent's state)
    __U.S. Senate
    __U.S. House
    __Governor
    __Attorney general
    __State education official
    __None of the above

Finally, here are a few questions about voting in this fall's election.

16. In some states, people are able to vote before Election Day, either by absentee ballot or in person at a polling place. Did you happen to vote before Election Day (November 2)?
    __Yes, in person
    __Yes, by absentee ballot
    __No, I did not vote early
17. In your state's election for governor, did you/do you plan to vote for (Candidate Name 1) or (Candidate Name 2)?
    __(Candidate Name 1)
    __(Candidate Name 2)
18. In the election for the U.S. senator from your race, **did you/do you plan to** vote for **(Candidate Name 1)** or **(Candidate Name 2)**?
    __(Candidate Name 1)
    __(Candidate Name 2)
19. In the election for the member of the U.S. House of Representatives from your congressional district, **did you/do you plan to** vote for **(Candidate Name 1)** or **(Candidate Name 2)**?
    __(Candidate Name 1)
    __(Candidate Name 2)

Thank you for your participation in this study.

APPENDIX E

Additional Vote Choice Analysis

Table E.1. SENATE VOTE CHOICE, REPUBLICAN WOMEN VERSUS DEMOCRATIC MEN

	Vote for Woman	Vote for Woman
Stereotypes		
Female policy	−0.260	0.648
	(0.20)	(0.48)
Male policy	0.375*	0.141
	(0.18)	(0.64)
Female trait	0.714*	−2.834*
	(0.31)	(1.21)
Male trait	0.083	−1.665
	(0.25)	(0.86)
Evaluations		
Female policy	–	−0.486
	–	(0.91)
Male policy	–	2.836*
	–	(1.39)
Female trait	–	4.990
	–	(4.33)
Male trait	–	−1.880
	–	(0.97)
Same party	3.507***	−2.498
	(0.64)	(3.64)
Open seat	1.961*	1.057
	(0.97)	(3.49)
Percent of spending by woman	−5.586	−17.973*
	(2.99)	(8.11)
Interest in Senate race	0.050	3.675

(Continued)

Table E.1. (*Continued*)

	Vote for Woman	Vote for Woman
	(0.35)	(3.28)
Constant	−8.083*	−13.617
	(3.65)	(24.30)
Pseudo R^2	.45	.92
N	134	124

* p <.05, *** p <.001, two-tailed test of significance.
Note: This table contains logistic regression for candidate vote choice. Independent respondents are excluded due to the small number of Independent identifiers. Additionally, women incumbent and competitive race are excluded because none of the Republican women were incumbents and the only race that was competitive (Nevada) is also the only race where that was not an open seat. Standard errors are in parentheses.

Table E.2. GOVERNOR VOTE CHOICE, DEMOCRATIC WOMEN VERSUS REPUBLICAN MEN

	Vote for Woman	Vote for Woman
Stereotypes		
Female policy	0.428*	0.971**
	(0.17)	(0.36)
Male policy	−0.182	−0.125
	(0.22)	(0.43)
Female trait	−0.435	−1.084*
	(0.25)	(0.45)
Male trait	−0.112	−0.967*
	(0.24)	(0.42)
Evaluations		
Female policy	−	0.486
	−	(0.31)
Male policy	−	1.344*
	−	(0.59)
Female trait	−	0.948*
	−	(0.46)
Male trait	−	−0.900
	−	(0.62)
Same party	3.474***	3.210***
	(0.47)	(0.86)
Interest in governor race	−0.101	0.034
	(0.23)	(0.36)
Constant	0.574	−4.935
	(3.16)	(3.95)
Pseudo R^2	.39	.77
N	219	207

* p < .05, ** p < .01, *** p < .001, two-tailed test of significance.
Note: This table contains logistic regression for candidate vote choice. Independent respondents are excluded due to the small number of Independent identifiers. The contextual variables are excluded for Democratic women candidates because of the small number of races. Standard errors are in parentheses.

NOTES

CHAPTER 1

1. After the 2012 elections, all four members of New Hampshire's congressional delegation and its governor are women—Governor Maggie Hassan, U.S. Senator Kelly Ayotte, U.S. Senator Jeanne Shaheen, U.S. Representative Carol Shea-Porter, and U.S. Representative Ann Kuster. Shaheen was first elected in 2008; Ayotte, in 2010; and Hassan, Shea-Porter, and Kuster, in 2012.

CHAPTER 2

1. Given that the current question asks people whether they would vote for a woman candidate of their own party and the lack of evidence that people desert their party to avoid voting for a woman (Dolan 2004), why these levels of support are assumed to be inflated by socially desirable responses is unclear.

CHAPTER 3

1. I should note that this first analysis of vote choice employs a simple model and serves to provide an illustration of the difference between hypotheticals and real election decisions. I turn to a more complete analysis of the relationship of abstract stereotypes to vote choice in Cchapter 5.
2. Male policy = economy/jobs, crime, national security, immigration, and the deficit;. Ffemale policy = education, health care, child care, abortion;. Mmale traits = intelligent, decisive, experienced, strong leader; Ffemale traits = honest, consensus builder, compassionate, can change the way government works.
3. There were many fewer incumbent Republican women in these races, which may explain why incumbency is not an important influence on their success.

CHAPTER 4

1. Male traits = intelligent, decisive, provides strong leadership, has political experience; female traits = honest, can build consensus, compassionate, can change the way government works; male policies = crime and public safety, economy and jobs, national security, immigration, the deficit; female policies = education, health care, abortion, child care.
2. For example, for the variable measuring beliefs about the competence of women and men to handle traditional male policy areas, higher values indicate that respondents see men as better at these issues than women.

3. Readers should note that the male policy stereotype and evaluation variables used in this analysis exclude the national security and immigration variables.

CHAPTER 5

1. While national public opinion polls show generally high levels of support for the idea of a woman president, some research suggests that these responses are hampered by social desirability effects. Streb et al. (2008) argue that support for a woman president is overstated in polls and that as many as 25 percent of Americans would be opposed.
2. There is no evidence in this analysis that stereotypes are having an indirect impact on vote choice through candidate evaluations. This is confirmed by the lack of impact for stereotypes on candidate evaluations (chapter 4) and also through the tests of mediation conducted on the results of the analysis in Table 5.1. For mediation to be present, a stereotype would demonstrate an effect on vote choice in Column 1 and then a diminished impact in the model in Column 2. Since stereotypes are not related to vote choice in either model of voting for a Democratic woman candidate, no tests for mediation were necessary.
3. The only instance where a test of mediation was necessary involved the female policy stereotypes and evaluations in Columns 3 and 4 (Table 5.1). Sobel tests (stat = $-.67$, $p < .51$) indicate that mediation was not taking place.
4. Analysis of the races with Republican women Senate candidates running against Democratic men is available in appendix E.
5. Sobel test stat for male policy = -2.75, $p < .05$; female trait = 2.05, $p < .05$.
6. Analysis of the races in which Democratic women ran for governor against Republican men is available in appendix E.
7. Sobel test statistic = 2.01, $p < .05$.

CHAPTER 6

1. Since there was only one Republican woman who ran as an open-seat candidate, it is difficult to make comparisons.
2. There were no incumbent Republican women Senate candidates to compare with the incumbent Republican men.
3. This had a larger impact on the pool of Senate candidates, where fully a quarter of the candidates alphabetized the issues they discussed.
4. Bennet had been appointed on January 3, 2009, to the seat of Ken Salazar, who had been named secretary of the interior in the Obama administration.

BIBLIOGRAPHY

Adams, William. 1975. "Candidate Characteristics, Office of Election, and Voter Responses." *Experimental Study of Politics* 4: 76–88.

Alexander, Deborah, and Kristi Andersen. 1993. "Gender as a Factor in the Attribution of Leadership Traits." *Political Research Quarterly* 46: 527–545.

Anzia, Sarah, and Christopher Berry. 2011. "The Jackie (and Jill) Robinson Effect: Why Do Congresswomen Outperform Congressmen?" *American Journal of Political Science* 55: 478–493.

Atkeson, Lonna Rae, and Nancy Carrillo. 2007. "More Is Better: The Impact of Female Representation on Citizen Attitudes toward Government Responsiveness." *Politics & Gender* 3: 79–101.

Atkeson, Lonna Rae, and Timothy Krebs. 2008. "Press Coverage of Mayoral Candidates: The Role of Gender in News Reporting and Campaign Issue Speech." *Political Research Quarterly* 61: 239–252.

Banducci, Susan, Joanna Everitt, and Elisabeth Gidengil. 2002. "Gender Stereotypes of Political Candidates: A Meta-analysis." Paper presented at the meeting of the International Society of Political Psychology, Berlin, July 16–19.

Banwart, Mary Christine, Dianne Bystrom, and Terry Robertson. 2003. "From the Primary to the General Election: A Comparative Analysis of Media Coverage of Candidates in Mixed-Gender Races for Governor and U.S. Senate in 2000." *American Behavioral Scientist* 46: 658–676.

Bargh, John. 1994. "The Four Horsemen of Automaticity." In *Handbook of Social Cognition*, ed. R. Wyer and T. Sroll. Hillsdale, NJ: Erlbaum.

Bartels, Larry. 2000. "Partisanship and Voting Behavior, 1956–1996." *American Journal of Political Science* 44: 35–50.

Bauer, Nichole. 2013. "Rethinking Stereotype Reliance: Understanding the Connection between Female Candidates and Gender Stereotypes." *Politics and the Life Sciences* 32: 22–42.

Bennett, Siobhan. 2013. "When the U.S. Needed Leaders, Women Saved the Day." *Women's E-News*, October 23. http://womensenews.org/story/leadership/131023/when-the-us-needed-leaders-women-saved-the-day#.Utic_WRDvMo.

Blair, Irene. 2002. "The Malleability of Automatic Stereotypes and Prejudice." *Personality and Social Psychology Review* 6: 242–261.

Braden, Maria. 1996. *Women Politicians and the Media*. Lexington: University of Kentucky Press.

Brady-Myerov, Monica. 2012. "Warren's Slow and Steady Strategy Is to Tell Her Story." WBUR Radio, April 4. http://www.wbur.org/2012/04/04/warren-strategy.

Brooks, Deborah Jordan. 2011. "Testing the Double Standard for Candidate Emotionality: Voter Reaction to the Tears and Anger of Male and Female Politicians." *Journal of Politics* 73: 597–615.

Brooks, Deborah Jordan. 2013. *He Runs, She Runs: Why Gender Stereotypes Do Not Harm Women Candidates*. Princeton: Princeton University Press.

Brown, Clyde, Neil Heighberger, and Peter Shocket. 1993. "Gender-Based Differences in Perceptions of Male and Female City Council Candidates." *Women and Politics* 13: 1–17.

Bureau of Labor Statistics. 2013. *BLS Reports. Women in the Labor Force: A Databook*. U.S. Bureau of Labor Statistics, Department of Labor. http://www.bls.gov/cps/wlf-databook-2012.pdf.

Burns, Nancy, Kay Scholzman, and Sidney Verba. 2001. *The Private Roots of Public Action*. Cambridge: Harvard University Press.

Burrell, Barbara. 1988. "The Political Opportunity of Women Candidates for the U.S. House of Representatives in 1984." *Women and Politics* 8: 51–68.

Burrell, Barbara. 1994. *A Woman's Place Is in the House: Campaigning for Congress in the Feminist Era*. Ann Arbor: University of Michigan Press.

Burrell, Barbara. 2008. "Likeable? Effective Commander in Chief? Polling on Candidate Traits in the 'Year of the Presidential Woman.'" *PS: Political Science and Politics* 61: 747–752.

Bystrom, Dianne, Terry Robertson, and Mary Christine Banwart. 2001. "Framing the Fight: An Analysis of Coverage of Female and Male Candidates in Primary Races for Governor and U.S. Senate in 2000." *American Behavioral Scientist* 44: 1999–2013.

Bystrom, Dianne, Mary Christine Banwart, Lynda Lee Kaid, and Terry Robertson. 2004. *Gender and Candidate Communication*. New York: Routledge.

Caliper Corporation. 2013. *The Qualities that Distinguish Women Leaders*. https://www.calipercorp.com/portfolio/the-qualities-that-distinguish-women-leaders/.

Campbell, Angus, Philip Converse, Warren Miller, and Donald Stokes. 1960. *The American Voter*. Chicago: University of Chicago Press.

Campbell, David, and Christina Wolbrecht. 2006. "See Jane Run: Women Politicians as Role Models for Adolescents." *Journal of Politics* 68: 233–247.

Carroll, Sue, and Ronnee Schreiber. 1997. "Media Coverage of Women in the 103rd Congress." In *Women, Media, and Politics*, ed. Pippa Norris. New York: Oxford, 131–148.

Center for American Women and Politics. 2010. *Year of the Republican Woman? Yes and No: Women Candidates in the 2010 General Elections*. Center for American Women and Politics, Eagleton Institute, Rutgers University, New Brunswick, NJ.

Center for American Women and Politics. 2012a. *Summary of Women Candidates for Selected Offices 1970–2012*. Center for American Women and Politics, Eagleton Institute, Rutgers University, New Brunswick, NJ.

Center for American Women and Politics. 2012b. *Women Candidates in 1992–2012: A Summary of Major Party Candidates for U.S. Senate, U.S. House*. Center for American Women and Politics, Eagleton Institute, Rutgers University, New Brunswick, NJ.

Center for American Women and Politics. 2013. *Women in Elective Office 2013*. Center for American Women and Politics, Eagleton Institute, Rutgers University, New Brunswick, NJ.

Chang, Chingching, and Jacqueline Hitchon. 2004. "When Does Gender Count? Further Insights into Gender Schematic Processing of Female Candidates' Political Advertising." *Sex Roles* 51: 197–208.

Citrin, Jack, Donald Philip Green, and David O. Sears. 1990. "White Reactions to Black Candidates: When Does Race Matter?" *Public Opinion Quarterly* 54: 74–96.

Conover, Pamela, and Stanley Feldman. 1989. "Candidate Perception in an Ambiguous World." *American Journal of Political Science* 33: 912–939.

Cook, Charlie. 2010. "Hurricane GOP on the Way." *National Journal.* July 3, 2010. http://www.nationaljournal.com/columns/cook-report/hurricane-gop-on-the-way-20100703.

Darcy, Robert, and Sarah Slavin Schramm. 1977. "When Women Run against Men." *Public Opinion Quarterly* 41: 1–12.

Darcy, Robert, Susan Welch, and Janet Clark. 1987. *Women, Elections, and Representation.* New York: Longman.

Deaux, Kay, and Marianne LaFrance. 1998. "Gender." In *The Handbook of Social Psychology,* vol. 1, 4th ed., ed. Daniel Gilbert, Susan Fiske, and Gardner Lindzey. Boston: McGraw-Hill, 788–828.

Deaux, Kay, and Laurie Lewis. 1984. "Structure of Gender Stereotypes: Interrelationships among Components and Gender Label." *Journal of Personality and Social Psychology* 46: 991–1004.

Decker, Cathleen. 2011. "A New-Old Mission for Feinstein." *Los Angeles Times,* January 16. http://articles.latimes.com/2011/jan/16/local/la-me-0116-theweek-20110116.

Delli Carpini, Michael, and Scott Keeter. 1996. *What Americans Know about Politics and Why It Matters.* New Haven: Yale University Press.

Delli Carpini, Michael, and Scott Keeter. 2000. "Gender and Political Knowledge." In *Gender and American Politics: Women, Men, and the Political Process,* ed. Sue Tolleson Rinehart and Jyl Josephson. Armonk, NY: M. E. Sharpe, 21–47.

Dennis, J. Michael, and Rick Li. 2007. "More Honest Answers to Web Surveys? A Study of Data Collection Mode Effects." *Journal of Online Research,* October.

Devitt, James. 1999. "Framing Gender on the Campaign Trail: Women's Executive Leadership and the Press." Report for the Women's Leadership Fund, New York.

Ditonto, Tess, Allison Hamilton, and David Redlawsk. 2013. "Gender Stereotypes, Information Search, and Voting Behavior in Political Campaigns." *Political Behavior,* Online First, May. http://link.springer.com/article/10.1007%2Fs11109-013-9232-6.

Dittmar, Kelly. 2010. "Inside the Campaign Mind: Gender, Strategy, and Decision-Making in Statewide Races." Paper presented at the annual meeting of the Midwest Political Science Association, Chicago, April 22–25.

Dodson, Debra. 1998. "Representing Women's Interests in the U.S. House of Representatives. In *Women in Elective Office: Past, Present, and Future,* ed. Sue Thomas and Clyde Wilcox. New York: Oxford University Press.

Dodson, Debra. 2006. *The Impact of Women in Congress.* New York: Oxford University Press.

Dolan, Kathleen. 1997. "Gender Differences in Support for Women Candidates: Is There a Glass Ceiling in American Politics?" *Women and Politics* 17: 27–41.

Dolan, Kathleen. 2004. *Voting for Women: How the Public Evaluates Women Candidates.* Boulder: Westview Press.

Dolan, Kathleen. 2005. "Do Women Candidates Play to Gender Stereotypes? Do Men Candidates Play to Women? Candidate Sex and Issue Priorities on Campaign Websites." *Political Research Quarterly* 58: 31–44.

Dolan, Kathleen. 2008. "Running against a Woman: Do Female Opponents Shape Male Candidate Behaviors?" *Social Science Quarterly* 89: 765–779.

Dolan, Kathleen. 2010. "The Impact of Gender Stereotyped Evaluations on Support for Women Candidates." *Political Behavior* 32: 69–88.

Dolan, Kathleen. 2014. "Gender Stereotypes, Candidate Evaluations, and Voting for Women Candidates: What Really Matters?" *Political Research Quarterly* 67: 96–107.

Dolan, Kathleen, and Lynne E. Ford. 1997. "Change and Continuity among Women State Legislators: Evidence from Three Decades." *Political Research Quarterly* 50: 137–151.

Dolan, Kathleen, and Kira Sanbonmatsu. 2009. "Gender Stereotypes and Attitudes Toward Gender Balance in Government." *American Politics Research* 37: 409–428.

Downs, Anthony. 1957. *An Economic Theory of Democracy*. New York: Harper.

Duverger, Maurice. 1955. *The Political Role of Women*. Paris: UNESCO.

Dwyer, Caitlin, Daniel Stevens, and Barbara Allen. 2009. "Racism, Sexism, and Candidate Evaluations in the 2008 U.S. Presidential Elections." *Analyses of Social Issues and Public Policy* 9: 223–240.

Dwyer, Devin. 2010. "Oklahoma Governor Candidates Debate Marital Status, Parenting Experience." *ABCNews.com*, October 26. http://abcnews.go.com/Politics/vote-2010-oklahoma-governors-debate-motherhood-prerequisite-office/story?id=11971580.

Eagly, Alice. 1987. *Sex Differences in Social Behavior: A Social Role Interpretation*. Hillsdale, NJ: Erlbaum.

Eagly, Alice, and Linda Carli. 2007. *Through the Labyrinth: The Truth about How Women Become Leaders*. Cambridge: Harvard Business Press.

Eagly, Alice, and Wendy Wood. 1982. "Inferred Sex Differences in Status as a Determinant of Gender Stereotypes about Social Influence." *Journal of Personality and Social Psychology* 43: 915–928.

Eckstrand, Laurie, and William Eckert. 1981. "The Impact of Candidate's Sex on Vote Choice." *Western Political Quarterly* 34: 78–87.

Emily's List. 2013. "Findings from the Madam President Battleground Poll." https://emilyslist.org/sites/default/files/Madam_President_Poll_Release.pdf.

Fiorina, Morris, Samuel Abrams, and Jeremy Pope. 2006. *Culture War? The Myth of a Polarized America*. New York: Pearson Education, Inc.

Fiske, Susan. 1998. "Stereotyping, Prejudice, and Discrimination." In *The Handbook of Social Psychology*, vol. 2, ed. Daniel Gilbert, Susan Fiske, and Gardner Lindzey. Boston: McGraw-Hill, 357–414.

Fiske, Susan, and Steven Neuberg. 1990. "A Continuum of Impression Formation, from Category-Based to Individuating Processes: Influences of Information and Motivation on Attention and Interpretation." In *Advances in Experimental Social Psychology*, ed. Mark Zanna. New York: Academic Press, 1–74.

Fiske, Susan, and Shelley Taylor. 1991. *Social Cognition*. 2nd ed. New York: McGraw-Hill.

Fowler, Linda, and Jennifer Lawless. 2009. "Looking for Sex in All the Wrong Places: Press Coverage and the Electoral Fortunes of Gubernatorial Candidates." *Perspectives on Politics* 7: 519–536.

Fox, Richard. 1997. *Gender Dynamics in Congressional Elections*. Thousand Oaks: Sage Publications.

Fox, Richard. 2006. "Congressional Elections: Where Are We on the Road to Gender Parity?" In *Gender and Elections*, ed. Susan Carroll and Richard Fox. New York: Cambridge University Press, 97–116.

Fox, Richard. 2010. "Congressional Elections: Women's Candidacies and the Road to Gender Parity." In *Gender and Elections: Shaping the Future of American Politics*, 2nd ed., ed. Susan Carroll and Richard Fox. New York: Cambridge University Press, 187–209.

Fox, Richard, and Zoe Oxley. 2003. "Gender Stereotyping in State Executive Elections: Candidate Selection and Success." *Journal of Politics* 65: 833–850.

Fox, Richard, and Eric R. A. N. Smith. 1998. "The Role of Candidate Sex in Voter Decision-Making." *Political Psychology* 19: 405–419.

Fridkin, Kim, and Patrick Kenney. 2009. "The Role of Gender Stereotypes in U.S. Senate Campaigns." *Politics & Gender* 5: 301–324.

Fridkin, Kim, Patrick Kenney, and Gina Serignese Woodall. 2009. "Bad for Men, Better for Women: The Impact of Stereotypes during Negative Campaigns." *Political Behavior* 31: 53–78.

Fulton, Sarah. 2012. "Running Backwards and in High Heels: The Gendered Quality Gap and Incumbent Electoral Success." *Political Research Quarterly* 65: 303–314.

Fulton, Sarah, Cherie Maestas, L. Sandy Maisel, and Walter Stone. 2006. "The Sense of a Woman: Gender, Ambition, and the Decision to Run for Office." *Political Research Quarterly* 59: 235–248.

Gordon, Ann, and Jerry Miller. 2005. *When Stereotypes Collide: Race/Ethnicity, Gender, and Videostyle in Congressional Campaigns*. New York: Peter Lang.

Gordon, Ann, David Shafie, and Ann Crigler. 2003. "Is Negative Advertising Effective for Female Candidates? An Experiment in Voters' Use of Stereotypes." *Press/Politics* 8: 35–53.

Hajnal, Zoltan. 2001. "White Residents, Black Incumbents, and a Declining Racial Divide." *American Political Science Review* 95: 603–617.

Hayes, Danny. 2005. "Candidate Qualities through a Partisan Lens." *American Journal of Political Science* 49: 908–923.

Hayes, Danny. 2010. "Trait Voting in U.S. Senate Elections." *American Politics Research* 38: 1102–1129.

Hayes, Danny. 2011. "When Gender and Party Collide: Stereotyping in Candidate Trait Attribution." *Politics and Gender* 7: 133–165.

Heerwegh, Dirk. 2009. "Mode Differences between Face-to-Face and Web Surveys: An Experimental Investigation of Data Quality and Social Desirability Effects." *International Journal of Public Opinion Research* 21: 111–121.

Heldman, Caroline, Susan Carroll, and Stephanie Olson. 2005. "She Brought Only a Skirt: Print Media Coverage of Elizabeth Dole's Bid for the Republican Presidential Nomination." *Political Communication* 22: 315–335.

Herrnson, Paul, Celeste Lay, and Atiya Stokes. 2003. "Women Running 'as Women': Candidate Gender, Campaign Issues, and Voter-Targeting Strategies." *Journal of Politics* 65: 244–255.

Highton, Benjamin. 2004. "White Voters and African American Candidates for Congress." *Political Behavior* 26: 1–25.

Hillygus, D. Sunshine, and Todd Shields. 2008. *The Persuadable Voter: Wedge Issues in Presidential Campaigns*. Princeton: Princeton University Press.

Hitchon, Jacqueline, Chingching Chang, and Rhonda Harris. 1997. "Should Women Emote? Perceptual Bias and Opinion Change in Response to Political Ads for Candidates of Different Genders." *Political Communication* 14: 49–69.

Hopkins, Daniel. 2009. "No More Wilder Effect. Never a Whitman Effect: When and Why Polls Mislead about Black and Female Candidates." *Journal of Politics* 71: 769–781.

Huddy, Leonie. 1994. "The Political Significance of Voters' Gender Stereotypes." In *Research in Micropolitics: New Directions in Political Psychology*, vol. 4, ed. Michael Delli-Carpini, Leonie Huddy, and Robert Shapiro. Greenwich: JAI Press, 169–187.

Huddy, Leonie, Joshua Billig, John Bracciodieta, Lois Hoeffler, Patrick Moynihan, and Patricia Pugliani. 1997. "The Effect of Interviewer Gender on the Survey Response." *Political Behavior* 19: 197–220.

Huddy, Leonie, and Theresa Capelos. 2002. "Gender Stereotyping and Candidate Evaluation: Good News and Bad News for Women Politicians." In *The Social Psychology of Politics: Research, Policy, Theory, Practice*, ed. Victor Ottati, R. Tindale, J. Edwards, F. Bryant, L. Heath, D. O'Connell, Y. Suarez-Balcazar, and E. Posavac. New York: Kluwer Academic/Plenum Publishers, 29–54.

Huddy, Leonie, and Nayda Terkildsen. 1993a. "The Consequences of Gender Stereotypes for Women Candidates at Different Levels and Types of Offices." *Political Research Quarterly* 46: 503–525.

Huddy, Leonie, and Nayda Terkildsen. 1993b. "Gender Stereotypes and the Perception of Male and Female Candidates." *American Journal of Political Science* 37: 119–147.

Iyengar, Shanto, Nicholas Valentino, Stephen Ansolabehere, and Adam Simon. 1997. "Running as a Woman: Gender Stereotyping in Women's Campaigns." In *Women, Media, and Politics*, ed. Pippa Norris. New York: Oxford University Press, 77–98.

Jacobson, Gary. 2012. *The Politics of Congressional Elections*. 8th ed. Upper Saddle River, NJ: Pearson.

Jones, Jeffrey. 2012. "Atheists, Muslims See Most Bias as Presidential Candidates." Gallup.com June 21, 2012. http://www.gallup.com/poll/155285/Atheists-Muslims-Bias-Presidential-Candidates.aspx.

Kahn, Kim. 1992. "Does Being Male Help? An Investigation of the Effects of Candidate Gender and Campaign Coverage on Evaluations of U.S. Senate Candidates." *Journal of Politics* 54: 497–517.

Kahn, Kim. 1994. "Does Gender Make a Difference? An Experimental Examination of Sex Stereotypes and Press Patterns in Statewide Campaigns." *American Journal of Political Science* 38: 162–195.

Kahn, Kim. 1996. *The Political Consequences of Being a Woman*. New York: Columbia University Press.

Kahn, Kim, and Edie Goldenberg. 1991. "Women Candidates in the News: An Examination of Gender Differences in U.S. Senate Campaign Coverage." *Public Opinion Quarterly* 55: 180–199.

Kantor, Jodi, and Kate Taylor. 2013. "In Quinn's Loss, Questions about the Role of Gender and Sexuality." *New York Times*, November 18.

Karnig, Albert, and B. Oliver Walter. 1976. "Election of Women to City Councils." *Social Science Quarterly* 56: 605–613.

Khimm, Suzy, and Jessica Taylor. 2013. "Republican Women Lead the Way." *MSNBC*, October 22. http://www.msnbc.com/msnbc/gop-women.

Kim, Eun Kyung. 2013. "Representative Sets Congressional Record: Most Babies in Office." *Today News*, July 19. http://www.today.com/news/rep-s ets-congressional-record-most-babies-office-6C10680009.

Kinder, Donald, and David Sears. 1981. "Prejudice and Politics: Symbolic Racism versus Racial Threats to the Good Life." *Journal of Personality and Social Psychology* 40: 414–431.

King, David, and Richard Matland. 2003. "Sex and the Grand Old Party: An Experimental Investigation of the Effect of Candidate Sex on Support for a Republican Candidate." *American Politics Research* 31: 595–612.

Kittilson, Miki Caul, and Kim Fridkin. 2008. "Gender, Candidate Portrayals and Election Campaigns: A Comparative Perspective." *Politics and Gender* 4: 371–392.

Koch, Jeffrey. 1997. "Candidate Gender and Assessments of Women Candidates." *Social Science Quarterly* 80: 84–96.

Koch, Jeffrey. 2000. "Do Citizens Apply Gender Stereotypes to Infer Candidates' Ideological Orientations?" *Journal of Politics* 62: 414–429.

Koch, Jeffrey. 2002. "Gender Stereotypes and Citizens' Impression of House Candidates' Ideological Orientations." *American Journal of Political Science* 46: 453–462.

Kornblut, Anne. 2009. *Notes from the Cracked Ceiling. Hillary Clinton, Sarah Palin, and What It Will Take for a Woman to Win.* New York: Crown Publishers.

Kreuter, Frauke, Stanley Presser, and Roger Tourangeau. 2008. "Social Desirability Bias in CATI, IVR, and Web Surveys." *Public Opinion Quarterly* 72: 847–865.

Kunda, Ziva, and Lisa Sinclair. 1999. "Motivated Reasoning with Stereotypes: Activation, Application, and Inhibition." *Psychological Inquiry* 10: 12–22.

Kunda, Ziva, and Steven Spencer. 2003. "When Do Stereotypes Come to Mind and When Do They Color Judgment? A Goal-Based Theoretical Framework for Stereotype Activation and Application." *Psychological Bulletin* 129: 522–544.

Lansing, Jewel. 1991. *101 Campaign Tips for Women Candidates and Their Staff.* Saratoga, CA: R+E Publishing.

Lau, Richard, and David Redlawsk. 2001. "Advantages and Disadvantages of Cognitive Heuristics in Political Decision Making." *American Journal of Political Science* 45: 951–971.

Lawless, Jennifer. 2004. "Women, War, and Winning Elections: Gender Stereotyping in the Post–September 11th Era." *Political Research Quarterly* 57: 479–490.

Lawless, Jennifer, and Richard Fox. 2010. *It Still Takes a Candidate: Why Women Don't Run for Office.* New York: Cambridge University Press.

Lawless, Jennifer, and Danny Hayes. 2013. "A Non-gendered Lens: The Absence of Stereotyping in Contemporary Congressional Elections." Paper presented at the annual meeting of the Southern Political Science Association, Orlando.

Lawless, Jennifer, and Kathryn Pearson. 2008. "The Primary Reason for Women's Underrepresentation? Reevaluating the Conventional Wisdom." *Journal of Politics* 70: 67–82.

Lawrence, Jill. 2013. "Do Women Make Better Senators than Men?" *National Journal*, July 11. http://www.nationaljournal.com/women-of-washington/do-women-make-better-senators-than-men-20130711.

Layman, Geoffrey, Thomas Carsey, and Juliana Horowitz. 2006. "Party Polarization in American Politics: Characteristics, Causes, and Consequences." *Annual Review of Political Science* 9: 83–110.

Leeper, Mark. 1991. "The Impact of Prejudice on Female Candidates: An Experimental Look at Voter Inference." *American Politics Quarterly* 19: 248–261.

Locksley, Anne, Eugene Borgida, Nancy Brekke, and Christine Hepburn. 1980. "Sex Stereotypes and Social Judgment." *Journal of Personality and Social Psychology* 39: 821–831.

Lowy, Joan. 2003. *Pat Schroeder: A Woman of the House.* Albuquerque: University of New Mexico Press.

Macrae, C. Neil, Charles Stangor, and Miles Hewstone. 1996. *Stereotypes and Stereotyping.* New York: Guilford Press.

Malhotra, Neil, and Jon Krosnick. 2007. "Retrospective and Prospective Performance Assessments during the 2004 Election Campaign: Tests of Mediation and News Media Priming." *Political Behavior* 29: 249–278.

Mansbridge, Jane. 1999. "Should Blacks Represent Blacks and Women Represent Women? A Contingent 'Yes.'" *Journal of Politics* 61: 628–657.

McDermott, Monika. 1997. "Voting Cues in Low-Information Elections: Gender as a Social Information Variable in Contemporary United States Elections." *American Journal of Political Science* 41: 270–283.

McDermott, Monika. 1998. "Race and Gender Cues in Low Information Elections." *Political Research Quarterly* 51: 895–918.

McDermott, Monika. 2009. "Religious Stereotyping and Voter Support for Evangelical Candidates." *Political Research Quarterly* 62: 340–354.

McFeatters, Ann. 2013. "Thank Women for Ending Government Shutdown." *Scripps Howard News Service*, October 24. http://www.newsday.com/opinion/oped/ann-mcfeatters-thank-women-for-ending-the-government-shutdown-1.6278148.

Meeks, Lindsey. 2012. "Is She 'Man Enough'? Women Candidates, Executive Political Offices, and News Coverage." *Journal of Communication* 62: 175–193.

Mehta, Seema, and Maeve Reston. 2011. "Jerry Brown Nearly Matched Meg Whitman's Campaign Spending on TV in Final Weeks of Race." *Los Angeles Times*, February 1. http://articles.latimes.com/2011/feb/01/local/la-me-governor-money-20110201.

Milbank, Dana. 2008. "A Thank-You for the 18 Million Cracks in the Glass Ceiling." *Washington Post*, June 8. http://articles.washingtonpost.com/2008-06-08/opinions/36846272_1_hillary-clinton-bill-clinton-50th-woman.

Milligan, Susan. 2013. "A Woman's Place Is Making Washington Work." *US News*, October 18. http://www.usnews.com/opinion/blogs/susanmilligan/2013/10/18/women-solved-the-government-shutdown-maybe-they-can-fix-the-rest-of-washington.

Mondak, Jeffrey, and Belinda Creel Davis. 2001. "Asked and Answered: Knowledge Levels When We Won't Take 'Don't Know' for an Answer." *Political Behavior* 23: 199–224.

Murakami, Michael. 2008. The Power of Identity: The Consequences of Party Polarization for the Attitudes and Behaviors of the Mass Public. Unpublished dissertation, Berkeley, CA: University of California.

Newman, Jody. 1994. *Perception and Reality: A Study Comparing the Success of Men and Women Candidates*. Washington, DC: National Women's Political Caucus.

Newton-Small, Jay. 2013. "Women Are the Only Adults Left in Washington." *Time*, October 16. http://swampland.time.com/2013/10/16/women-are-the-only-adults-left-in-washington/.

Niven, David. 1998. *The Missing Majority: The Recruitment of Women as State Legislative Candidates*. Westport: Praeger.

Ondercin, Heather and Susan Welch. 2009. "Comparing Predictors of Women's Congressional Election Success: Candidates, Primaries, and the General Election." *American Politics Research* 37: 593–613.

Page, Susan. 2013. "For S.C. Governor Nikki Haley, 'It's Been a Long Year.'" *USA Today*, November 4. http://www.usatoday.com/story/news/politics/2013/11/04/sc-governor-its-been-a-long-year/3422841/.

Palmer, Barbara, and Dennis Simon. 2012. *Women and Congressional Elections: A Century of Change*. Boulder: Lynne Rienner Publishers.

Paolino, Philip. 1995. "Group-Salient Issues and Group Representation: Support for Women Candidates in the 1992 Senate Elections." *American Journal of Political Science* 39: 294–313.

Paul, David, and Jessi Smith. 2008. "Subtle Sexism? Examining Vote Preferences When Women Run against Men for the Presidency." *Journal of Women, Politics, and Policy* 29: 451–476.

Pearson, Kathryn and Logan Dancey. 2011. "Elevating Women's Voices in Congress: Speech Participation in the House of Representatives." *Political Research Quarterly* 64: 910–923.

Pearson, Kathryn, and Eric McGhee. 2013. "Should Women Win More Often than Men? The Roots of Electoral Success and Gender Bias in U.S. House Elections." Unpublished manuscript, Minneapolis, MN: University of Minnesota.

Petrocik, John. 1996. "Issue Ownership in Presidential Elections, with a 1980 Case Study." *American Journal of Political Science* 40: 825–850.

Pew Research Center. 2008. *Men or Women: Who's the Better Leader? A Paradox in Public Attitudes.* http://www.pewsocialtrends.org/2008/08/25/men-or-women-who s-the-better-leader/.

Pew Research Center. 2011. *Women in the U.S. Military: Growing Share, Distinctive Profile.* http://www.pewsocialtrends.org/2011/12/22/women-in-the-u-s-milita ry-growing-share-distinctive-profile/.

Philpot, Tasha, and Hanes Walton Jr. 2007. "One of Our Own: Black Female Candidates and the Voters Who Support Them." *American Journal of Political Science* 51: 49–62.

Popkin, Samuel. 1995. "Information Shortcuts and the Reasoning Voter." In *Information, Participation, and Choice: An Economic Theory of Democracy in Perspective*, ed. Bernard Grofman. Ann Arbor: University of Michigan Press, 17–35

Pringle, Paul. 2006. "Feinstein Focusing on Global Warming." *Los Angeles Times*, October 26. http://articles.latimes.com/2006/oct/26/local/me-senate26.

Rahn, Wendy. 1993. "The Role of Partisan Stereotypes in Information Processing about Political Candidates." *American Journal of Political Science* 37: 472–496.

Riggle, Ellen, Victor Ottati, Robert Wyer, James Kuklinski, and Norbert Schwarz. 1992. "Bases of Political Judgment: The Role of Stereotypic and Nonstereotypic Information." *Political Behavior* 14: 67–87.

Rosenthal, Cindy Simon. 1995. "The Role of Gender in Descriptive Representation." *Political Research Quarterly* 48: 599–611.

Rosenwasser, Shirley, and Norma Dean. 1989. "Gender Role and Political Office: Effects of Perceived Masculinity/Femininity of Candidate and Political Office." *Psychology of Women Quarterly* 13: 77–85.

Sanbonmatsu, Kira. 2002a. *Democrats/Republicans and the Politics of Women's Place.* Ann Arbor: University of Michigan Press.

Sanbonmatsu, Kira. 2002b. "Gender Stereotypes and Vote Choice." *American Journal of Political Science* 46: 20–34.

Sanbonmatsu, Kira. 2003. "Gender-Related Political Knowledge and the Descriptive Representation of Women." *Political Behavior* 25: 367–388.

Sanbonmatsu, Kira. 2006. *Where Women Run: Gender and Party in the American States.* Ann Arbor: University of Michigan Press.

Sanbonmatsu, Kira, and Kathleen Dolan. 2009. "Do Gender Stereotypes Transcend Party?" *Political Research Quarterly* 62: 485–494.

Sapiro, Virginia. 1981/1982. "If U.S. Senator Baker Were a Woman: An Experimental Study of Candidate Images." *Political Psychology* 2: 61–83.

Sapiro, Virginia, Katherine Cramer Walsh, Patricia Strach, and Valerie Hennings. 2011. "Gender, Context, and Television Advertising: A Comprehensive Analysis of 2000 and 2002 House Races." *Political Research Quarterly* 64: 107–119.

Schaeffer, Nora Cate, and Stanley Presser. 2003. "The Science of Asking Questions." *Annual Review of Sociology* 29: 65–88.

Schneider, Monica, and Angela Bos. 2014. "Measuring Stereotypes of Female Politicians." *Political Psychology*, 35: 245–266.

Schoof, Renee. 2013. "Sen. Patty Murray Calls for Support for New Preschool Legislation, Tells Her 'Mom in Tennis Shoes' Story." *McClatchy DC*, November 13. http://www.mcclatchydc.com/2013/11/13/208458/sen-patty-murray-tells-her-mom.html.

Seltzer, Richard, Jody Newman, and Melissa Leighton. 1997. *Sex as a Political Variable: Women as Candidates and Voters in U.S. Elections*. Boulder: Lynne Rienner.

Sigelman, Lee, and Susan Welch. 1993. "The Contact Hypothesis Revisited: Black–White Interaction and Positive Racial Attitudes." *Social Forces* 71: 781–795.

Simmons, Wendy. 2001. "Majority of Americans Say More Women in Political Office Would Be Positive for Country." *Gallup Poll Monthly*, January: 7–8.

Smith, Eric R. A. N., and Richard Fox. 2001. "The Electoral Fortunes of Women Candidates for Congress." *Political Research Quarterly* 54: 205–221.

Smith, Jessi, David Paul, and Rachel Paul. 2007. "No Place for a Woman: Evidence for Gender Bias in Evaluations of Presidential Candidates." *Basic and Applied Social Psychology* 29: 225–233.

Smith, Kevin. 1997. "When All's Fair: Signs of Parity in Media Coverage of Female Candidates." *Political Communication* 14: 71–81.

Smith, Tom. 1979. "A Study of Trends in the Political Role of Women, 1936–1974." In *Studies of Social Change Since 1948*, ed. James A. Davis. NORC Report 127B. Chicago: NORC.

Stout, Christopher and Reuben Kline. 2011. "I'm Not Voting for Her: Polling Discrepancies and Female Candidates." *Political Behavior* 33: 479–503.

Strach, Patricia, and Virginia Sapiro. 2011. "Campaigning for Congress in the '9/11' Era: Considerations of Gender and Party in Response to an Exogenous Shock." *American Politics Research* 39: 264–290.

Streb, Matthew, Barbara Burrell, Brian Frederick, and Michael Genovese. 2008. "Social Desirability Effects and Support for a Female American President." *Public Opinion Quarterly* 72: 76–89.

Sweet, Lynn. 2008. "House Speaker Nancy Pelosi Says 'I'm a Victim of Sexism Myself All the Time.'" *Chicago Sun-Times*, June 24. http://blogs.suntimes.com/sweet/2008/06/house_speaker_nancy_pelosi_say.html.

Swers, Michele. 2013. *Women in the Club: Gender and Policy Making in the Senate*. Chicago: University of Chicago Press.

Swim, Janet, Kathryn Aikin, Wayne Hall, and Barbara Hunter. 1995. "Sexism and Racism: Old-Fashioned and Modern Prejudice." *Journal of Personality and Social Psychology* 68: 199–214.

Tourangeau, Roger, and Tom W. Smith. 1996. "Asking Sensitive Questions: The Impact of Data Collection Mode, Question Format, and Question Context." *Public Opinion Quarterly* 60: 275–304.

Traister, Rebecca. 2010. *Big Girls Don't Cry. The Election that Changes Everything for American Women*. New York: Free Press.

Trent, Judith and Robert Friedenberg. 1995. *Political Campaign Communications: Principles and Practices*. 3rd ed. Westport, CT: Praeger.

Weisman, Jonathan, and Jennifer Steinhauer. 2013. "Senate Women Lead in Effort to Find Accord." *New York Times*, October 14. http://www.nytimes.com/2013/10/15/us/senate-women-lead-in-effort-to-find-accord.html?_r=0.

Williams, Leonard. 1998. "Political Advertising in the Year of the Woman: Did X Mark the Spot?" In *The Year of the Woman: Myths and Realities*, ed. Elizabeth Adell Cook, Sue Thomas, and Clyde Wilcox. Boulder, CO: Westview.

Winter, Nicholas J. G. 2010. "Masculine Republicans and Feminine Democrats: Gender and Americans' Explicit and Implicit Images of the Political Parties." *Political Behavior* 32: 587–618.

Witt, Linda, Karen Paget, and Glenna Matthews. 1994. *Running as a Woman: Gender and Power in American Politics*. New York: Free Press.

Wolbrecht, Christina. 2000. *The Politics of Women's Rights: Parties, Positions, and Change*. Princeton: Princeton University Press.

Wood, Wendy, and Stephen Karten. 1986. "Sex Differences in Interaction Style as a Product of Inferred Sex Differences in Competence." *Journal of Personality and Social Psychology* 50: 341–347.

Zipp, John, and Eric Plutzer. 1985. "Gender Differences in Voting for Female Candidates: Evidence from the 1982 Election." *Public Opinion Quarterly* 49: 179–197.

INDEX

Ability to change government, 45, 62, 73
Abortion, 45, 62, 66
Abstract gender stereotypes, 45, 94–101,
    189. *See also* Gender stereotypes
Advertising, 16, 156–169. *See also*
    Negative advertising
  campaign issues in, 153–154
  gender stereotypes and, 34, 47
  gubernatorial electoral races, 167–169
  House electoral races, 156–162
  male-only races, 169–175
  research methodology, 205–207
  Senate electoral races, 162–167
  women candidates appearing in own
    ads, 28
Age as predictor of gendered attitudes,
    46, 71, 73
Allen, Barbara, 93
Ambition, 32
American National Election Studies, 39
Angle, Sharron, 40, 110, 165
Askins, Jari, 2, 41
Assertiveness, 63
Atkeson, Lonna Rae, 10
Attack ads, 10. *See also* Negative
    advertising
Ayotte, Kelly, 2, 12, 165, 196

Bachmann, Michele, 2
Baseline gender preference
  defined, 20
  gendered attitudes and, 46, 69, 90
  same-sex representation and, 57–58
  vote choice and, 76, 77, 82–89,
    188–189, 193
Bauer, Nichole, 23

Bennet, Michael, 175
Bias, 43–44, 152
Biden, Joe, 59
Bono Mack, Mary, 160
Boozman, John, 164
Bos, Angela, 32
Boxer, Barbara, 40, 148
Brady, Bill, 175
Brewer, Jan, 113, 114, 168
Brooks, Deborah Jordan, 32, 63, 65
Brown, Jerry, 114, 134
Buck, Ken, 175
Burrell, Barbara, 148
Bush, George H. W., 30
Bystrom, Dianne, 10, 154

Campaign advertising. *See* Advertising
Campaign issues, 9–11, 153–155,
    191–192
Campaign spending
  Democrats, 119
  gender stereotypes and, 47
  gubernatorial campaigns, 114
  influence on elections, 14, 33–35, 47
  specific candidate evaluation and, 100,
    114, 115
  vote choice analysis and, 127
  women candidates, 148
Candidate evaluations. *See* Specific
    candidate evaluations
Candidate quality, 27, 47, 144–155,
    191–192
Candidate selection process, 7–9
Candidate websites. *See* Websites of
    candidates
Castle, Mike, 40

Chang, Chingching, 153
Child care as campaign issue, 20, 45, 62, 66
Childrearing. *See* Family and childrearing responsibilities
Clinton, Hillary, 1–2, 28, 40, 123–124, 126
Collins, Susan, 12, 49–50, 195–196
Compassion, 19, 45, 62, 73, 81
Competitiveness of election
    influence on elections, 33–35, 47
    specific candidate evaluation and, 100
    vote choice analysis and, 127, 133, 141
Consensus-building, 45, 62, 64, 73
Cooperative Congressional Election Study, 39
Crime issues, 45, 62
Cross-sectional surveys, 39
Cultural attitudes, 19, 50

Darcy, Robert, 125
Dean, Norma, 111
Decisiveness, 45, 62
Defense issues, 45, 62, 109
Deficit as campaign issue, 45, 62, 157
Democrats
    advertising by, 160–161, 165, 171, 173
    campaign spending, 119
    female policy stereotypes and, 136–138
    feminized Democrats, 100
    fundraising by women vs. men, 8
    gender stereotypes as advantage to, 42
    male-only races, 116, 119
    partisan stereotypes, 34
    predictors of gendered attitudes, 70, 71
    specific candidate evaluations, 97–98, 101–103, 105–107
    vote choice analysis for, 79, 81, 133, 134, 141
    women candidates, 9, 40, 59
Denish, Diane, 41
Dittmar, Kelly, 195
Division of labor, 22–23
Dolan, Kathleen, 125
Dole, Elizabeth, 126
Duverger, Maurice, 19
Dwyer, Caitlin, 93

Eagly, Alice, 22, 32
Economic issues
    campaign emphasis on, 155, 157, 181
    issue competencies, 20, 45, 62

partisan stereotypes and, 109
specific candidate evaluation and, 95
Education
    campaign emphasis on, 157, 160, 165, 167, 179
    of candidate, 47, 145, 146, 149, 191–192
    issue competencies, 20, 45, 62
    partisan stereotypes and, 109
    as predictor of gendered attitudes, 70, 71, 73
    of respondent, 46
    specific candidate evaluation and, 95
Edwards, John, 126
Egalitarianism, 43, 74, 84
Electoral competitiveness. *See* Competitiveness of election
Elites, 8–9, 197
Emily's List, 125
Emotional suitability for office, 52, 61–62, 76, 77
Evaluations. *See* Specific candidate evaluations
Executive offices, 41, 133. *See also* Gubernatorial electoral races
Experience, 45, 63

Fallon, Mary, 41, 186–187, 194
Family and childrearing responsibilities, 7, 61, 179, 180
Family and Medical Leave Act, 30, 175
Feinstein, Diane, 28
Female policy
    abstract gender stereotypes vs. specific candidate evaluation, 94–99
    gendered attitudes and, 77
    vote choice analysis and, 127, 131, 136–138, 140–141
Feminine traits, 20, 30
Feminized Democrats, 100
Fiorina, Carly, 40, 146, 148
Foreclosure crisis, 163, 165
Foreign policy, 95, 160, 165, 171, 173
Fox, Richard, 7, 8, 9, 111, 125–126, 134, 144, 147, 194
Fridkin, Kim, 31, 32, 75, 92, 153
Fulton, Sarah, 7, 144
Fundraising, 8, 145, 148. *See also* Campaign spending
Future research directions, 193–196

Gallup Organization, 51, 124
Gendered attitudes, 45–46, 68–73. *See also* Gender stereotypes
Gendered psyche, 7
Gender stereotypes, 14–15, 18–48. *See also* Abstract gender stereotypes; Specific candidate evaluations
  campaign issues and, 47, 153–154
  candidate image and, 152–153
  candidate quality and, 47, 144–153
  data limitations, 35–37
  elections of 2010 and, 39–41
  electoral influences and, 33–35
  gendered attitudes and, 45–46
  level of office and, 41–43
  limitations on influence of, 23–25, 30–33
  partisan stereotypes interacting with, 42
  political impact of, 12–14, 33–35
  political party and, 41–43
  research methodology, 35–39
  role of, 22–23
  traditional influences on politics and, 46–47
  women candidates and campaigns, 25–30
Gillibrand, Kirsten, 3, 164–165
Ginsburg, Ruth Bader, 60
Giuliani, Rudy, 126
Gordon, Ann, 29
Government shut-down (2013), 49–50, 195–196
Government spending as campaign issue, 155, 157
Greenberg, Anna, 143
Gubernatorial electoral races
  campaign advertising, 167–169
  campaign spending, 114
  candidate lists, 200
  education level of candidates, 146
  gender stereotypes and, 13
  male-only races, 115, 119–120, 138–141
  specific candidate evaluations in, 111–115, 121
  vote choice analysis, 133–135, 138–141
  websites, 179–180
  women candidates in, 40–41
  women's issues in campaigns, 173–175

Haley, Nikki, 41, 113, 114, 186–187
Halvorson, Debbie, 161
Hayes, Danny, 11, 32, 93, 109, 195
Health care
  campaign emphasis on, 155, 157, 160, 161, 163, 171
  gender stereotypes and, 20
  issue competencies, 45, 62
  partisan stereotypes and, 109
  specific candidate evaluation and, 95
Heitkamp, Heidi, 49, 196
Higher-status women, 32
Highton, Ben, 75
Hill, Anita, 31
Hitchon, Jacqueline, 153
Honesty, 19, 32, 45, 62, 81, 92
"House Bank" scandal, 30
House of Representatives electoral races
  campaign advertising, 156–162
  candidate lists, 199
  education level of candidates, 146
  gender stereotypes and, 13
  male-only races, 115, 116–118, 136–138
  media coverage of candidates, 152
  specific candidate evaluations in, 99, 101–105, 121
  vote choice analysis, 76, 128–130, 136–138
  websites, 175, 176–179
  women candidates in, 7–8, 40
Housing issues, 163, 165, 176
Huddy, Leonie, 32, 43, 107, 111, 130
Hypothetical candidates research method, 35, 43, 75

Ideology. *See also* Political parties
  gender stereotypes and, 20
  as predictor of gendered attitudes, 70
  specific candidate evaluation and, 93
  vote choice and, 81
  of women candidates, 66–68
Immigration as campaign issue, 45, 62, 165, 167–168, 176
Incumbency
  advantages of, 9, 149–151
  specific candidate evaluation and, 93, 99, 104, 115
  vote choice analysis and, 13–14, 34, 46–47, 79, 81, 83, 87–88, 125, 127, 131, 141

Independent voters, 105, 117, 127, 141
Intelligence, 32, 45, 62, 64
Interpersonal skills, 63–64
Issue competencies, 20, 44–45. *See also* specific issues

"Jackie and Jill Robinson effect," 27

Kagan, Elena, 60
Kahn, Kim, 28
Kenney, Pat, 31, 32, 75, 92, 153
King, David, 67
Kinzinger, Adam, 161
Klobuchar, Amy, 49
Knowledge about women in politics, 46, 59–61
Knutson, Coya, 187
Koch, Jeffrey, 42, 67, 92
Krebs, Timothy, 10
Kunda, Ziva, 24

Labor market participation, 31
Langen, Odin, 187
Lawless, Jennifer, 7, 8, 9, 11, 20, 32, 93, 126, 144, 147, 194
Leadership ability, 19, 45, 62, 73, 92
Level of office, 41–43, 99
Lincoln, Blanche Lambert, 164
Locksley, Anne, 29

Madigan, Lisa, 2, 11
Male-only races
    campaign advertising, 169–175
    governor races, 115, 119–120, 138–141
    House races, 96, 115, 116–118, 136–138
    Senate races, 115, 118–119, 138
    specific candidate evaluations in, 96, 98, 115–120
    vote choice analysis, 135–141, 191
    websites, 181–183
Male policy
    abstract gender stereotypes vs. specific candidate evaluation, 94–99, 107
    vote choice analysis and, 77, 127, 131, 140–141
Mansbridge, Jane, 5
Martinez, Susana, 41, 168
Masculine traits, 19–20, 30

Masculinized Republicans, 100
Matland, Richard, 67
McCain, John, 1, 49, 50, 126
McDermott, Monika, 20
McGhee, Eric, 8, 144
McMahon, Linda, 40, 110, 146, 148, 165
Media
    candidate image and, 152–153
    coverage of women candidates, 29
    women candidates and, 9–11
Medicare, 163, 167, 171, 181
Methodology, 35–39, 201–223
Mikulski, Barbara, 49, 196
Military
    issue competencies, 20
    partisan stereotypes and, 109
MSNBC on women senators, 196
Murkowski, Lisa, 12, 49, 196
Murray, Patty, 18, 196

National Journal on women senators, 50, 195
National security issues, 45, 62, 109
Negative advertising, 10, 153
Newman, Jody, 125
New York Times
    on Quinn, 6
    on women senators, 196
Niven, David, 8
Noem, Kristi, 12

Obama, Barack, 93, 123, 160, 164
O'Donnell, Christine, 40, 110, 146, 165
Opinion polls. *See* Public opinion
Oxley, Zoe, 9, 111, 134

Palin, Sarah, 1–2, 40, 93, 124
Panel studies, 38–39
Paolino, Phil, 53
Partisan stereotypes
    gender stereotypes interacting with, 33–34, 42, 109
    gubernatorial races, 119
    influence on vote choice, 143
    male-only races, 116
    specific candidate evaluation and, 114, 119
Party identification, 46. *See also* Political parties
Passivity, 29

Paul, David, 126
Pearson, Kathryn, 8, 9, 144
Pelosi, Nancy, 1, 160
Personality traits, 19. *See also* Trait
    stereotypes
Persuasiveness, 63
Petersen, Leslie, 112
Pew Research Center, 31, 64
Philpot, Tasha, 36, 75
Policy competence, 62–66, 77. *See also*
    Female policy; Male policy
Political experience, 47, 145, 191–192
Political knowledge, 59–61
Political parties. *See also* Democrats;
    Republicans
  advertising influence of, 171–173
  campaign issues and, 157
  candidate selection process of, 8–9
  gender stereotypes and, 41–43
  male-only races and, 191
  role of stereotypes in, 22
  specific candidate evaluation and, 92,
      93, 99
  vote choice analysis and, 13–14, 33–
      35, 79, 85–88, 90, 125, 128, 141,
      143, 190–193
  website treatment of policy issues and,
      177, 179, 181
Pougnet, Steve, 160
Poverty issues, 20
Power differentials, 23
Predictors of gendered attitudes, 68–73
Public opinion
  as data source, 39
  on gendered attitudes, 45, 51–52
  vote choice and, 126
  on women candidates, 19, 54–61,
      76–78

Quality threshold, 7–8
Quinn, Christine, 6, 12, 28, 91
Quinn, Pat, 175

Rahn, Wendy, 33
Reid, Harry, 40
Republicans
  advertising by, 160–161, 165, 171, 173
  fundraising by women vs. men, 8
  gender stereotypes as disadvantage
      to, 42

male-only races, 116, 119
masculinized Republicans, 100
partisan stereotypes, 34
predictors of gendered attitudes, 71,
    73
specific candidate evaluations, 97–98,
    103, 104–105, 107–110
vote choice analysis for, 79, 81, 84,
    131, 134
women candidates, 9, 40
Research methodology, 35–39, 201–223
Respondent characteristics, 46–47
Rodgers, Cathy McMorris, 3
Rosenthal, Cindy Simon, 20, 57–58
Rosenwasser, Shirley, 111

Same-sex representation preferences,
    57–59, 83
Same-sex superiority, 73, 189
Sanbonmatsu, Kira, 8, 20, 46, 53, 57
Sandlin, Stephanie Herseth, 3
Sapiro, Virginia, 154
Schneider, Monica, 32
Schramm, Sarah Slavin, 125
Schroeder, Pat, 187
Scott, Rick, 112, 134, 168, 169
Self-governance, 5
Senate electoral races
  campaign advertising, 162–167
  candidate lists, 200
  education level of candidates, 146
  gender stereotypes and, 13
  male-only races, 115, 118–119, 138
  specific candidate evaluations in, 99,
      105–111, 121
  vote choice analysis, 130–133, 138
  websites, 179–180
  women candidates in, 7–8, 40
Sex superiority position, 73, 189
Shaheen, Jeanne, 196
Sink, Alex, 41, 112, 134, 168, 169
Smith, Eric R. A. N., 125, 126
Smith, Jessi, 126
Smith, Kevin, 10
Smith, Scott, 91
Social attitudes, 19, 50
Social desirability, 44
Social psychology approach, 22, 24
Social Security, 161, 163, 167, 171, 181
Social status, 23

Sotomayor, Sonia, 60
Specific candidate evaluations, 91–122
  abstract stereotypes vs., 94–99
  in context, 99–101
  gender stereotypes and, 15–16, 24, 190
  in gubernatorial electoral races, 111–115
  in House electoral races, 101–105
  in male-only races, 115–120
  measures of, 44–45
  research methodology, 45
  in Senate electoral races, 105–111
Spencer, Steven, 24
Steinem, Gloria, 91
Stereotypes. See Abstract gender
    stereotypes; Gender stereotypes;
    Trait stereotypes
Stevens, Daniel, 93
Strach, Patricia, 154
Streb, Matthew, 43
Study methodology, 35–39, 201–223
Supreme Court, 60
Survey-based research, 35–36, 37, 43

Taxes as campaign issue, 20, 155, 157,
    160, 161
Tea Party, 40, 110
Television ads. See Advertising
Terkildsen, Nayda, 32, 111, 130
Thomas, Clarence, 30–31
Time magazine
  on Bachmann, 2
  on women senators, 196
Trade issues, 20
Traditional influences on elections, 13–
    14, 46–47, 92. See also Incumbency;
    Political parties
Trait stereotypes
  gender stereotypes and, 19–20
  limits of, 30
  measures of, 44–45
  specific candidate evaluation and, 92,
    94–99, 107, 111–112
  vote choice analysis and, 77, 127, 128, 130

Underrepresentation of women, 4–5, 27,
    53, 54

Varilek, Matt, 12
Vote choice analysis, 123–142
  baseline gender preference and, 82–89

  in election of 2010, 126–135
  gender stereotypes and, 16, 74–89,
    190–191
  gubernatorial electoral races,
    133–135, 138–141
  House electoral races, 128–130, 136–138
  incumbency as factor for, 34
  male-only races, 135–141
  political party as factor for, 34
  research methodology, 222–223
  Senate electoral races, 130–133, 138
  women candidates and, 124–126
Voters, 11–12. See also Vote choice
    analysis; Specific candidate
    evaluations

Wall Street bailouts, 161, 165, 173, 179
Walton, Hanes, 36, 75
Warren, Elizabeth, 18
Websites of candidates, 175–181
  campaign issues presented on, 155
  gender stereotypes and, 16, 47, 154
  gubernatorial electoral races, 179–180
  House electoral races, 176–179
  male-only races, 181–183
  research methodology, 205–207
  Senate electoral races, 179–180
Welfare issues, 157
Whitman, Meg, 41, 113, 114, 134, 148
Winter, Nicholas, 100, 195
Wisconsin Ads Project, 154
Women candidates
  campaign environment and, 9–11
  campaign issues and, 9–11, 153–155,
    191–192
  consideration of candidacy by, 7–8
  devaluation of own skills and abilities
    by, 7, 144, 197
  emotional suitability for office, 61–62
  gender stereotypes, 18–48. See also
    Gender stereotypes
  historical trends in, 25–26
  ideology, 66–68
  knowledge about women in politics,
    59–61
  media environment and, 9–11
  policy competence, 62–66, 77. See also
    Female policy
  political effects of, 6–12
  predictors of gendered attitudes, 68–73